BLOODSONG!

American freelance journalist Jim Hooper has covered Third World conflict in Africa and the Balkans for almost 20 years. During the 1980s he reported on both South African and Unita forces in Angola, then later was given unique access to Executive Outcomes in Sierra Leone and the Congo. He has contributed to a wide range of international publications as well as the BBC and ABC. Wounded twice while reporting from the world's hot spots, he is the author of *Koevoet, Beneath the Visiting Moon*, and [with Ken Guest and Anthony Rogers] *Flashpoint! At the Frontline of Today's Wars*. He lives in England.

BLOODSONG!

An account of
Executive Outcomes
in Angola

Jim Hooper

In the UK for information please contact:
HarperCollins *Publishers*
77–85 Fulham Palace Road
Hammersmith
London W6 8JB
Great Britain

everything clicks at:
www.collins.co.uk

First published by HarperCollins*Publishers* 2002
This edition published by HarperCollins*Publishers* 2003

ISBN 0 00 711916 X

Printed and bound in England by Clays Press Ltd, St Ives plc

Photos not credited to Pine Pienaar or the author have been provided
courtesy of C. Alberts, Col H. Blaauw, 'Carlos', J. Joubert and 'Ricardo'.

A catalogue record for this book is available from the British Library.

Contents

Foreword

From Frederick Forsyth's *The Dogs of War* to Richard Burton and Roger Moore in *The Wild Geese,* soldiers of fortune have enjoyed a romantic image in fiction and film in the last decades – yet suffered scathing criticism from a pacifist and too often politically correct press. Were the media's only terms of reference *les affreaux* of the 1960s or the psychopathic "Colonel Callan" a decade later, their perceptions might carry weight. Such is not the case, however.

It is conveniently forgotten, for example, that the new Continental Army was bolstered by citizens of France during America's War of Independence; that Scottish-born John Paul Jones, the American hero of the War of 1812, became an admiral in the Imperial Russian navy; or that, as in Earnest Hemingway's *For Whom the Bell Tolls,* American and British idealists, civilians all, fought Fascism during the Spanish Civil War of the 1930s. Almost as forgotten are the Flying Tigers, American pilots hired by China to fight the Japanese, and more in the RAF's Eagle Squadron long before the United States joined the war against Hitler. Perhaps better remembered are the French Foreign Legion, British Army Ghurkhas and Swiss Vatican Guards.

The definition into which they all fall – "**mer cen ary** *n* : one that serves merely for wages; *esp* : *a soldier hired into foreign service*" – may be clear to Mr Webster, but can blur in the application.

Though Executive Outcomes certainly fell within the broader definition, it fitted no previous mould. Founded as a "military advisory company ... to work all over the world training armies and getting involved in conflict resolution, but more related to the battlefield, not in the political sense,"[1] it succeeded beyond anyone's expectations.

---

[1] Eeben Barlow in a taped interview with the author in 1997.

The reasons for EO's success were varied. It was in the right place – southern Africa – at the right time, when a desperate Angolan government (and, ironically enough, former enemy) needed help. More practically, its staff of professional warriors had learned their trade in the South African Defence Force[2] and shared a corporate philosophy of aggressive, unconventional warfare against numerically and materially superior opponents. Africans who understood Africa, they had been the architects and hands-on practitioners of an immensely successful military doctrine throughout their SADF careers.

Their detractors were legion. Former colleagues, some retired, others still serving, actively sought to sabotage the company for "switching sides," ignoring the fact that South Africa's war in Angola had finished almost five years earlier. The campaign was joined by Pretoria's Department of Foreign Affairs and both organizations are alleged to have passed intelligence about the company to Jonas Savimbi's Unita rebel movement. Whether this was due to a misplaced historical allegiance or more sinister and cynical reasons, as some of EO's senior officers still believe, has never been answered.

More predictable were strident shrieks from the white Left, though the reasons were muddled: the Angolan government, after all, enjoyed good Marxist-Leninist credentials, while Unita had been supported by the capitalist-imperialist West and apartheid South Africa. They were also stymied in the use of the pejorative "white mercenary," given that EO was predominantly black. Unable to play a straightforward ideological or race card, they had to settle for the immorality of the mercenary *métier* in general, refusing to acknowledge the Angolan government buying the services of thousands of Cuban troops before signing a contract with Executive Outcomes. Interestingly, while white liberals fulminated against the company, there was not a whisper of condemnation from any black African country

Nonetheless, it was this white minority view that forced the withdrawal of EO from Angola and, later, Sierra Leone. In both instances a few score South Africans were replaced by thousands of United Nations troops who stood by and watched impotently as the wars and killing resumed.

---

[2] Now the South African National Defence Force (SANDF) including former members of Umkhonto weSizwe, the armed wing of the African National Congress, as well as troops from the former Homeland states of Transkei and Ciskei, it is a poor imitation of the old SADF.

A philosophy that sees the butchering of innocents as preferable to the stability brought by a private military company is the same to insist that terrorists – to include the perpetrators of the September 11 atrocity – should be engaged in meaningful discussion. God save the innocent from the sanctimonious.

My own path to writing *Bloodsong!* began over 1986-89. Six months covering the war in northern Namibia with the South West Africa Police Counter-insurgency Unit – "Koevoet" – which later made up a large part of EO, was followed by three extended trips into Angola with Unita. Extensive exposure to these inter-connected conflicts resulted in two books and dozens of articles. That the allied groups I came to know well would later become bitter enemies seemed beyond the realm of possibility.

I was first offered a story on Executive Outcomes in June 1994, when Unita's representative in London invited me to lunch, declaring that some 6,000 South Africans were fighting in Angola. Despite a photograph of three dead mercenaries under the caption "Not a pretty picture," the claim seemed oddly out of sync: recruiting that many men would have been problematic, and even more so the logistics of the alleged operation. As a result, I forbore writing anything without direct access to the war, which the rebel movement refused to grant. As later emerged, Unita had exaggerated the number of actual EO combatants on the order of two-thousand percent, in retrospect a clear indication of the threat they posed.

Assignments in the Balkans and elsewhere kept me occupied until 1996, when Executive Outcomes agreed to my requests to report on its operations in Sierra Leone. By good fortune, I became the only journalist taken on active operations and articles about the company appeared in a wide range of publications from *Jane's Intelligence Review* to the best-selling *World's Most Dangerous Places.* Later, a trip to Lubumbashi in the Democratic Republic of Congo with EO's advance element provided more background, and at the beginning of 2001 I was asked by those you will meet here to write their story.

Bloodsong! was originally intended to document all of the company's operations, which would have meant reducing each campaign to a husk of dry facts and figures. Ian Tandy, HarperCollins' Military Reference editor, agreed that the wealth of information and recollections of combat in Angola and Sierra Leone deserved a book of its own. Based on personal war diaries and interviews, all ruthlessly vetted by the co-contributors themselves to ensure their experiences were neither sensationalised nor exaggerated, it is as true an account as was possible to compile. My constant badgering and nitpicking regarding names, dates, places and "details, give me more details" – not to mention a barrage of successively less rough drafts emailed for critique – must surely have tested their patience. But the story that emerged – never before told outside EO ranks – must take its place among the most dramatic and enthralling of post-WWII Africa. A second volume covering Irian Jaya, Papua New Guinea and the Democratic Republic of Congo is already in progress.

If the reader is expecting a Hollywood tale of perfect prescience and planning at every level, then I must disabuse you from the outset. Unita were a determined and competent foe. The fighting was vicious and in some cases the outcome a close-run thing. Twenty-one Executive Outcomes employees died or remain missing in action in Angola. It was, as you will see, no walk in the park.

For personal and professional reasons, some of the principal contributors to this volume have preferred *noms de guerre*. I trust the reader will understand. In order to explain how they came to play central rôles in the Angola and subsequent contracts, I have asked that they introduce themselves with previously classified accounts from their days in the South African Reconnaissance Commandos and Air Force. Their later experiences with Executive Outcomes were equally and, in some cases, even more gripping. Of that, however, you must be the judge.

Jim Hooper

Far better it is to dare mighty things, to win glorious triumphs, even though chequered by failure, than to take rank with those poor spirits who neither enjoy much nor suffer much, because they live in the grey twilight that knows not victory nor defeat.

Theodore Roosevelt

Colonel Hennie Blaauw

In late 1975 the Portuguese communist junta handed power to the Marxist MPLA[3] liberation movement in Angola and welcomed thousands of Cuban soldiers to its former colony. Faced with the nightmare of a powerful enemy on its doorstep, the South African Defence Force, encouraged by the United States, launched Operation Savannah to support the Unita[4] and FNLA[5] guerrilla movements. The South Africans had advanced to within sight of Luanda, when Washington did a volte face and Pretoria was obliged to withdraw. With the South West Africa Peoples Organization (Swapo) given free reign by the MPLA to attack Namibia, the SADF extended covert military support to Unita's leader, Dr Jonas Malheiro Savimbi, who was determined to continue his struggle for a democratic nation.

Following their destruction of the FNLA in December 1976, the Cubans and Fapla,[6] the new Angolan army, turned their attention to Savimbi, and by August the following year were closing in on him in the remote south-eastern province of Cuando Cubango. He needed help desperately, and a Special Forces team was selected from 1 Reconnaissance Commando to find and, if necessary, rescue the rebel leader.

★

---

[3] MPLA – Movimiento Popular de Libertação de Angola – People's Movement for the Liberation of Angola

[4] Unita – União Nacional para a Independencia Total de Angola – National Union for the Total Independence of Angola

[5] FNLA – Frente Nacional de Libertação de Angola – National Front for the Liberation of Angola.

[6] Forças Armadas de Popular de Libertação de Angola – People's Armed Forces for the Liberation of Angola.

"Sergeant Gerald, Amilcar and I were briefed in Pretoria by military intelligence," said then-Major Hendrik 'Hennie' Blaauw, "and flown to Rundu near the Namibian-Angolan border. Colonel Phillips of MI gave us the latest intelligence, before we were taken to the nearby town of Katuitui to meet Unita's secretary-general, N'Zau Puna.[7] The situation was critical, Puna told us, and we set off on a two-day drive along a bush track to Unita's base at Chimpolo on the Cavango River. Brigadier Samuel Chiwale, the six-foot-three Unita chief of the armed forces, said that Savimbi was en route from the Benguela Railway line but no one knew when he would arrive. A young captain by the name of Tito Chingunji[8] was assigned as my personal liaison officer, and each of us given a bodyguard, mine a very tough guy called Abel.

"At about 1100 on Sunday morning excitement rippled through the base as the exhausted column entered. Savimbi, a pearl-handled .357 magnum revolver strapped to his waist, was at its head, having obviously stopped to change into a neat set of camouflages and red paratrooper's beret before entering.

"I was surprised to see a white man with him. Tito told me he was a French journalist who had been with Savimbi for the last two months. That afternoon everyone gathered and Savimbi made a dramatic speech about continuing the struggle against overwhelming Cuban forces. He was a powerful and incredibly charismatic speaker. At the end he turned to me. His voice was loud and forceful, but buried within it was a plea. 'Major, do you have a message for my people?'

"Having no mandate from MI and none whatsoever from my government to make any commitments, I was caught off guard. But with Tito translating, I nonetheless offered my respects to His Excellency the President of Unita and his followers for their courage, devotion and sacrifice. 'We are here to observe your struggle,' I said. 'We will discuss with your cabinet your immediate requirements and your determination to continue. I will present this to my superiors in South Africa. I am convinced that my country will come to your assistance as we have a mutual interest in the struggle against communism.'

---

[7] After the failed elections in 1992 Puna would defect to the MPLA.

[8] Chingunji, an exceptionally gifted and popular officer, eventually became Unita's representative in Washington. In 1990 he was recalled by Savimbi, placed under house arrest and subsequently executed for allegedly opening secret talks with the MPLA.

"Over supper Savimbi thanked me for the ray of hope I'd given his people. I said they would undoubtedly prefer the visible support of military training, logistical vehicles full of supplies, farming equipment, seeds and medicine. What I gave them could be regarded as mere words. 'Major,' Savimbi said in his rumbling voice, 'the mighty Roman Empire did not fall in a single day,' which I interpreted as a forecast of a long and hard struggle ahead.

"When we returned to our hut, the multi-lingual Amilcar reported that the Frenchman believed the situation was more serious than Savimbi wanted us to believe. When they crossed the Benguela railway, they'd been pursued by a strong Fapla force backed up by helicopters and fighter aircraft. The Frenchman reckoned it was only a matter of days before they caught up with us.

"Outside our hut the next morning, we heard a jet aircraft and through the trees saw an aging Fiat fighter-bomber in a steep bank over the base. So close that I could see the Portuguese pilot's white flying helmet, he miraculously failed to spot the base. 'Come,' said Tito, 'hurry, we must join the President.' Frantic orders were given and the entire camp marched for three hours towards the north-east to take cover in dense bush. Throughout the day fighter aircraft bombed about five kilometres west of the base. Later that afternoon we could hear the sounds of more bombing from the direction of Cacundo about ten kilometres away.

"At sunset we moved back into the base, where everyone was lined up in groups – women with small babies on their backs, cages of chickens on their heads, goats bleating at the end of leashes. The soldiers keeping order, we set off for a Unita base near the Little Cunene River, some 100 kilometres away. At about midnight I first noticed we were gradually swinging towards the south. It was a cold, clear night and a few hours later the Southern Cross constellation hung directly in front of us. When I said that we were heading in the wrong direction, Tito passed the word for Savimbi to halt the column. They conferred quickly and Savimbi came over to me.

"'Major, which direction is west?'

"'Mr President, to the south you can clearly see the Southern Cross and to the east the beginning of dawn.' I set a heading of about 280 degrees magnetic on my prismatic compass and showed it to him. 'That, Mr President, is west.'

"'Major, from now on you navigate,' he said and turned away.

"'Excuse me, Mr President, but I strongly recommend that you split this column into smaller groups.'

"He turned back. 'Why, Major?'

"'Sir, come daybreak it will be easily spotted from the air. I suggest we send the women, children and all non-combatant elements towards one of your other safe areas under a strong escort, while the rest of us continue west.' He gave the order and within minutes we were on the move again, surrounded by approximately a hundred soldiers. The second column turned towards the northwest. Daylight came and Savimbi insisted that his men carry our heavy rucksacks. As a Special Forces operator, I refused. At one point Savimbi said to Amilcar, 'My friend, you look like a donkey with that load on your back.'

"'I may look like a donkey, Mr President, but I am my own donkey.'

"Running with us was Anna, Savimbi's young secretary, a typewriter on her head, followed by one soldier with a folding chair and a second with a folding table. Whenever Savimbi stopped, Anna was ready to type whatever he dictated.[9]

"At mid-morning we heard vehicles to our immediate south and it was only then that I realized how far we had deviated during the night. The sounds had to be coming from the Ongiva–Caiundo road. 'Come, Major,' a nervous Tito said, 'or we will be captured.' Exhausted, we turned northwest, when we heard Cuban helicopters landing behind us with follow-up groups.

"A wide net was closing around Savimbi. Approaching from the north was the enemy group that had been pursuing him since he crossed the Benguela Railway line. Within earshot to the south the Cubans were deploying Swapo and Fapla stopper groups, while to the west Fapla search parties had deployed from Ongiva, Mupa and Tetchamatete. These were moving eastwards on parallel lines towards the Unita base we were trying to reach. Cuban MiG-21s were patrolling up and down the road just to our south, where we could hear helicopters landing and taking off as they dropped more teams. We were in immediate and mortal danger.

"I persuaded Savimbi to deploy delaying elements and allow me to set a claymore trap. He agreed and we laid mini-claymores in a V pattern on our trail. Hopefully, the lead enemy scout would trigger the first and when his comrades dashed for cover, they would detonate the two on the flanks. We left two Unitas to warn the delaying group of the booby trap and pushed on.

"Sergeant Gerald, exhausted, sweating and running a high temperature, was suffering a serious case of malaria. Amilcar gave him anti-malarial tablets

---

[9] Savimbi married Anna in 1983 shortly after his wife was reported to have been killed by lightning.

and injections of Voltaren to bring down the fever and placed him on an improvised stretcher with a Unita soldier at each corner. Shortly afterwards, we heard the first claymore explode about a kilometre behind us, then the other two in rapid succession. Our pursuers were only minutes away. With luck, we had inflicted enough casualties to slow the rest and keep the helicopters busy for a while with the wounded.

"At 1400 hours we made a brief stop and I quickly rigged my radio. 'Papa Oscar, this is Moby Dick.' As soon as Rundu acknowledged, I explained that Gerald was down with malaria, that the enemy were closing in and recommended a helicopter extraction that night. After signing off I was summoned to Savimbi, who demanded to know whom I had contacted. When I explained, he ordered no further communication, fearing that the enemy would locate us by monitoring my transmissions. When I insisted that our radio could not be heard by the Cubans' HF sets, Savimbi was still adamant.

"Utterly exhausted, we stopped at 1700 hours near a *shona*, a low-lying grassy stretch between high, rolling ground and sent a party to fill water containers. Gerald's condition had worsened and as I was consulting Amilcar, Abel took my rucksack to fill the reserve water bottle. Inside was my HF radio. Fifteen minutes later heads snapped up at the sounds of heavy firing about 500 metres away. A runner came in to report that a large Swapo group had ambushed the water party and killed several Unitas, amongst them Abel. My rucksack was now in enemy hands. Fortunately, all the radio codes and frequencies were in my side pocket, but not the Special Forces operational manual that proved South African Reconnaissance Commandos were with Unita.

"We were moving fast, when Savimbi asked me to contact Rundu for helicopters to extract us that night. At 1830 hours we stopped and rigged Amilcar's reserve HF set. Colonel Philips at Rundu advised that as a result of my previous message, two Pumas had already deployed to a clandestine 32 Battalion base at Omahoni, about an hour's flight to our south. They would reach us at 2100 hours and could uplift twenty passengers. When I informed Savimbi that he could take no more than sixteen of his people, his eyes narrowed. At 2045 hours he and his group arrived at the LZ. 'I cannot go without thirty one people,' he said.

"At that moment the lead Puma interrupted us. 'Moby Dick, this is Retriever, we are ten minutes out.'

17

"'Retriever from Moby Dick, I have a problem. We have thirty one passengers.'

"'Jesus, this is a chopper, not a London bus,' said a voice belonging to my good friend John Murray.

"'John, please, can't we drain some fuel and just get them out to Edward's place?' I asked, referring to the base at Omahoni.

"'OK, Henry, but it's got to be quick. There are lights closing in everywhere. Looks like you're being surrounded.'

"For the first chopper I had selected my team, Savimbi, the Frenchman and twelve others, with the balance to go in the second. The Pumas landed and the ten minutes they sat there, engines running while they drained fuel, were the longest of my life. The enemy were close enough to hear them. Then we were on board and lifting off.

"'White road coming up in one minute,' John said over my earphones. We roared across the Ongiva-Caiundo road and tracers from below and both sides flashed past us. 'Henry, where is Savimbi?' John snapped.

"'With us. What's wrong?'

"'Paul said they just took some hits in the second chopper.'

"We landed at Omahoni, where the flight engineers examined Paul's helicopter. Two bullets had struck directly beneath the tail rotor, effectively grounding the Puma until repairs could be made. This meant half of our passengers would have to wait here while the remaining helicopter flew Savimbi and his closest advisors to Rundu. But 32 Battalion was made up of ex-FNLA loyal to Holden Roberto. They had no love for Unita or Savimbi and there was the distinct possibility of a punch up between the two. I asked Edward to detail as many white NCOs and junior officers as possible to provide security for the remaining Unita officials, then departed with Savimbi, Anna and his cabinet for Rundu, where Gerald was rushed to the military hospital.

"Unita later admitted to that if I had not extracted Savimbi that night, he would have been captured and executed by the Cubans. I was proud of my rôle in saving his life and much of my thirty-years' service in the SADF was devoted to supporting his struggle for a free and democratic Angola.

"Twenty-three years after seeing him safely to Rundu that night I was hired by the MPLA government to wage war against him."

★ ★ ★

'Carlos'

As in Angola, the Portuguese colony of Mozambique was handed to a Marxist liberation movement by the communist junta in Lisbon. A strong supporter of the African National Congress, the new Frelimo[10] government provided training camps and infiltration routes for ANC fighters entering South Africa. In order to destabilize the hostile regime, Pretoria responded by dispatching covert Special Forces teams to train and advise Alfons Dhlakama's Renamo[11] anti-government rebel movement.

16 December 1981 0830 hrs, Sofala Province, Mozambique

The sun has been up less than two hours and the heat is already oppressive as we moodily strip and clean our weapons. Deep inside Mozambique, 'Mike,' the mission commander, and I are part of an eight-man Special Forces team assigned as advisors to Alfons Dhlakama's Renamo movement. To Pretoria's concern, the rebel leader has established a large base in violation of every principle of guerrilla warfare and smoke from hundreds of cooking fires rises over the sprawling base just beyond the hill. South African signals intelligence has been picking up indications of an impending attack on his base by Mozambican Frelimo and Zimbabwean forces, but an over-confident Dhlakama laughs off the threat. 'You Boers depend too much on pretty machines,' he says.

But that's not the cause of our sombre mood. Our tactical HF radio has been tuned to the BBC Africa Service, which reports that a South African special forces raid near the Angolan capital of Luanda has gone horribly wrong.

---

[10] Renamo – Resistencia Nasional do Mocambique – Mozambique National Resistance
[11] Frelimo – Frente Libertação de Mocambique – Front for the Liberation of Mozambique

We know it could only have been conducted by our seaborne comrades and we quietly wonder which of our friends have been killed.

Our signaller rushes up with a decoded message which we scan with growing alarm. The North Korean-trained Zimbabwean 5th Brigade has moved across the border and is now less than twenty kilometres north-east of our position, waiting for an airstrike by Frelimo MiGs before launching a ground attack.

Mike waits until I've absorbed the message. "What do you reckon, Carlos?"

Unlike Dhlakama, I have considerable faith in sigint. The co-ordinates of the Zimbabweans and other specific details are too precise to be ignored. "Maybe we should amble over the hill and have a chat with Alfons."

"You stay put," he orders, "I'll – ." His eyes have locked onto something behind me. "What the fuck!"

I spin around and spot the rapidly approaching dots to the north-west. Two Cuban-flown MiG-17s are turning directly towards the smoke of Renamo's cooking fires. We frantically assemble our weapons, cursing Dhlakama for ignoring our advice. The MiGs scream over our heads and let off ripples of rockets which miss the camp by hundreds of metres. Their second pass is equally ineffective and they bank away towards Beira. Their reports are probably already reaching the Zimbabweans. We know what's coming next. Mike sprints for Dhlakama's headquarters as our HF radio spills encoded messages. They tell us that the MiGs will turn around at Beira for another strike, that 5th Brigade HQ has received our correct co-ordinates and that Colonel Lionel Dyke[12] is in the Zimbabwean airborne command post. Plans for my 25th birthday in the bush are suddenly forgotten.

Andries, myself and two seasoned Angolan veterans grab our valued SAM-7s[13] and scramble 200 metres up the hill to await the returning MiGs, the balance of the team manning the HF and preparing our defences. Sigint is still pouring in and being relayed to me and Mike over our VHF radios. As we crest the hill we hear the first terrifying shrieks of in-coming 122 mm rockets. Just as I raise Mike to warn him, they start impacting and we can barely hear each other over our radios. There's a ground-shaking

---

[12] Dyke was one of the few ex Rhodesian white officers accepted with open arms by Mugabe, making him one of the most hated soldiers in South Africa at that time.

[13] During the apartheid era the SAMs were extremely difficult to procure because of sanctions and to discharge the tube one had to really justify it later.

roar when one of the rockets hits Renamo's main ammo dump outside the base. Secondary explosions rip through bunkers and trees, sending shrapnel, complete mortar bombs and huge, lethal splinters of forest spinning through the air. With the black smoke that's billowing over the dump, the enemy can be in no doubt about our position.

We receive warning that the returning MiGs are five minutes out. We hastily prep the SAMs and split into two teams, separating as far as we can to increase our chances of a hit. There they are, rolling in again. Our Russian surface-to-air missiles are switched on and shouldered, the MiGs centred in the sights. Not yet. The Cuban pilots bank hard and come around again. As they scream overhead our SAMs start emitting the warbling signal that tells us they have a lock. A missile shrieks towards the first MiG but, confused by a closer and more potent heat source, veers off and dives into the burning ammo dump.

The second MiG turns directly towards our position and we freeze. The SAMs need the heat of the jet exhaust to lock on – a head-on approach is no good. But the pilot has just realized that a SAM has been fired and he banks violently, passing so close we see him in the cockpit. He disappears, staying low until out of range, then climbs and follows his wingman towards Beira. Sigint soon reveals they have both developed "technical problems" that will prevent their return. No more jousting for them today.

The ground barrage, however, starts again, the rockets joined by 120 mm mortars. None are landing dangerously close, but it's no time to quibble. An eight-man advisory team 600 kilometres behind enemy lines is no match for a brigade. There's a sudden lull, which probably means that the Zimbabweans are preparing to advance.

Mike returns as we're decoding a message ordering us to withdraw to the south and secure a landing zone for a helicopter extraction. SAAF Mirages are on immediate standby to cover our move, which, the signal adds, *will* include Alfons Dhlakama. Mike rolls his eyes. Dhlakama has just told him that he intends to make an Alamo-like stand against the "Zimbabwean invaders". Mike turns and heads over the hill again.

The rest of us begin destroying everything that cannot be portaged out. Much of it is equipment procured at enormous cost through sanctions busting, but there's no option. Nothing may be left that can be used by South Africa's hostile neighbours as evidence of our presence. We'll keep our remaining SAM-7s.

Mike returns with the news that Dhlakama has agreed to exfiltrate with us. We immediately begin preparing to leave, wanting to leg it under cover of darkness in order to be picked up prior to first light. We're receiving inaccurate speculative fire and wondering how far the Zimbabweans have advanced, when another message from Pretoria says the enemy is having problems due to the difficult terrain and are still fifteen kilometres away.

With the precious SAMs bouncing on our shoulders, we set off running at 2000. Five hours and forty kilometres later Mike has identified an LZ just within range of our specially modified, long-range Pumas. Pretoria concurs with his choice and scrambles the choppers. If the extraction fails we're in deep shit. We only have one chance.

At 0515 we hear the sweet melody of chopper blades and talk the two Pumas into the tight LZ. The familiar faces in the cockpit lift our spirits and we start relaxing when we feel them pull power. We're just going through transition, when – *shit!* – we instinctively duck from heavy streams of gunfire streaking towards us from very close. The fuckers have laid cut-offs south of our escape route! Red and green tracers hurtle past the Pumas but with no lights showing, the enemy are targeting us only by sound. Then we're through it, staying low and checking to see if anyone has been wounded. The choppers have a few holes, but miraculously no one and nothing important has been hit.

The sun is well up when we land at the transit and refuelling spot next to the Kruger Park. Climbing out whilst the ground crew fuel the birds and tweak the engines, we start salivating at the aroma of meat on a barbeque. We strike a deal with our Puma crews: they can shoot off our remaining AK-47 ammo if they'll allow us to relax for the day and enjoy the first proper meal in weeks. Done! It was a nice little party. Take off for Pretoria was set for 0500 the next morning.

We dropped into an exhausted sleep alongside the choppers. Nerves still on edge, I woke instinctively before dawn and felt something move under my armpit. I rose cautiously on my elbow and a black mamba, Africa's most venomous snake, glided nonchalantly away after a night as my uninvited companion. "Kill it!" someone shouted. Mike shook his head. "Leave the poor fuck alone," he said quietly, "he's just hanging out with his own kind."

Nineteen years down the line and I still call this crap a job.

★ ★ ★

Juba Joubert

South African Air Force helicopter pilots were heavily involved in Angola, regularly penetrating deep behind enemy lines in support of ground forces. Though the primary target of cross-border operations was Swapo terrorists attempting to infiltrate into South West Africa/Namibia, they often faced Cuban-flown gunships and jet fighters, as well as Soviet-operated missiles. By the mid-1980s, the SADF's successes against Swapo saw the East bloc pouring thousands of additional Cuban troops and billions of dollars of sophisticated military equipment into the conflict. The immediate goal was to deny the South Africans air support by deploying the first SA-8 surface-to-air missile systems and upgraded Mi-25 Hind helicopter gunships outside the Soviet bloc.

These were extremely worrying developments, but after years under an international arms embargo, the SAAF was well versed in devising new tactics against the communists' more technologically advanced military hardware.

★

"To counter the air threat," said 'Juba' Joubert," we started air combat manoeuvres with our senior and junior space club, the Mirage and Impala fighter pilots. These exercises pitted two fighters against one or two helicopters at low level, where we could make full use of our eyes, ears and the terrain to survive. The opposition needed fourteen gun–camera frames for a 'kill', but the most they ever got on me was eight and I made them work for those. These exercises gave us great confidence and at the same time taught our fighter pilots attack profiles against enemy choppers. As far as the missile threat, there wasn't a great deal we could do beyond flying as low and as fast as the situation allowed.

"By early 1987 I was a senior Puma commander with experience all across southern Angola, but nowhere was there a better guarantee of action than around Cahama in the southwest. In February I was tasked with inserting a Special Forces team sixty kilometres north of the town. The plan called for dropping them at last light, but we didn't lift off from Ruacana until just before sunset, with the uncomfortable prospect of having to find the LZ in the dark and no assurance that it was safe. Because the other Puma commander was not night-formation qualified, as mission leader I took the No 2 position on a wide dog-leg around Cahama to avoid its AAA and suspected SA-8 batteries.

"Twenty minutes after lift-off the sun had disappeared, replaced by a full moon. Rather than maintaining position from above on the lead Puma's formation lights, I tucked into his eight o'clock. This silhouetted him against the moon, allowing me to stay just above the trees. The tallest along the route were 150 feet, and I briefed my crew to give me radio altimeter readouts when I went below 170 feet. Approaching the road from Cahama to Humbe, I descended. When my co-pilot read out 160 feet, I had a quick glimpse to confirm the height and just then saw a bright orange flame streaking towards us from the direction of Cahama. It passed astern at supersonic speed, but with rising terrain and trees flashing by, there was no time to see where it was going. I eased back up to 170 feet, continuing under radio silence. We had apparently been just far enough outside the SA-8's twenty-five-kilometre range to prevent it locking on to either of the Pumas.

"Arriving at the drop-off area, I descended to a hundred feet, switched on the landing light and came down to twenty feet on the radio altimeter. Unable to get lower, I hovered over thick bush and told the team to bail out. The first guy had a look, tossed out his sixty-five-kilo rucksack and followed it, with the rest of the team just behind. I told the lead helicopter to set heading, but to cross east of the road in case the Russians had a spare SA-8 or two. They decided not to waste another on us."

*

"Ten days after the SA-8 experience we had a casevac callout south of Cahama. A group of sappers had been ambushed while sweeping a road and taken eleven casualties, four of them serious. I briefed our two doctors, both on their first operational tour, that just before crossing the border I'd reduce speed so they could slide the doors open and keep watch for MiGs.

While I was confident of our chances of survival, the looks on their faces suggested they were less so.

"We crossed the Cunene River and were five minutes out when I tried to raise the call sign. No answer. Climbing to improve the range on the VHF radio, I looked for smoke marking the LZ. At 800 feet over their reported position I was distinctly uncomfortable; if there were a roaming missile battery in the neighbourhood we were sitting ducks. But there were Priority 1 casevacs on the ground that we had to get to hospital. Just then I saw a distant flare off the nose and turned towards it, flying another twenty-five kilometres, which placed us close to two known Swapo bases. If they saw or heard us, they were sure to radio a report to Cahama.

"I was descending, when a warning came through that five Mi-25 *Hinds* had been spotted forty kilometres to the east. I took us down fast and over the edge of the Huila plateau to get below the horizon and blend in with the terrain. We had to get in and out as quickly as possible. I finally raised the ground commander and requested smoke. A pale cloud from a white phosphorus grenade billowed out of the trees. I swore when the LZ came into view. There was only enough room for one Puma at a time. The pick-up was going to take longer than I wanted.

"I went in quickly, and as soon as we touched down the flight engineer helped the medic and the doctor out of the helicopter and I saw them disappear into the bush for the casualties. *Come on, hurry!* Long minutes went by with no one in sight. Then the report came through on the HF radio that the *Hinds* were heading in our direction. The flight engineer was standing outside and I asked him over the intercom system what the hell was going on, but his helmet microphone cord had come unplugged and I got no reply.

"The casualties were brought out of the bush and were being loaded, when there was an explosion not far away. I pulled power to warn them they must hurry up as we are under attack. Seven wounded were quickly loaded under the doctor's supervision, but there was no sight of the medic. I pulled more power to tell the engineer I was getting airborne and he just had time to grab hold of the steps and a chair leg to pull himself in as I lifted off. Because visibility was so limited in the thick bush, it wasn't until we were in the air that I realized the explosion had come from another white phosphorus smoke grenade someone had stupidly thrown. Then the doctor told me that one of the wounded was going to need more blood than he had brought. I told the No 2 to pick-up the other four casualties and the medic. They went in and there was a green spray of leaves when their rotor tips hit the trees.

"We were scanning the horizon for the *Hinds*, when another message came through that now MiG-23s were also airborne and on course for us. With their down-look radar capability, they'd have no problem spotting us from overhead. The No 2 lifted off with my medic and the last four casevacs. Because of the urgency for blood, I set heading directly for Ruacana instead of the Ondangwa hospital.

"We had just come up to speed, when the ground commander called to ask if we could return for another casualty. Gritting my teeth, I brought the Puma around, advising him *not* to throw smoke: I had no interest in giving the MiGs or *Hinds* an easier target indication. I was suddenly on top of the LZ, flaring harder than the Puma is designed for to touch down at zero speed. The last casualty was loaded in record time and we were back in the air. I turned towards the Ruacana River, using the terrain for protection and keeping the Puma's fuselage between the trees. In the cabin behind me the doctors worked frantically to keep the worst casualties alive. Another message came in that the MiGs were ahead and patrolling the border to intercept us. But I knew that first they'd have to find us, and then hit us on the first pass before having to break off because of fuel. If our Mirage and Impala pilots couldn't get me, the Cubans had no chance.

"As it was, we thudded across the cutline without interference and were soon settling on the helipad. Immediate transfusions saved three of the worst wounded. The last, though he fought for his life for four more hours after getting to the hospital, finally died."

★ ★ ★

LtCol Pine Pienaar

"A young captain a year out of my instructional tour, I was attached to 8 Squadron, 'The Flying Cockerels,' flying the Impala Mk2.[14] Aside from day after day of practising with cannon, bombs and rockets, I also learned the principles of air-to-air combat and ultra-low level navigation, using only a map and stopwatch as navigational aids. Grasping these skills ensured that, when the day came, I'd be able to deliver the required weapon accurately, defend myself against other aircraft while doing so and find my way back home again.

"It was around 14 September 1985, when we received a heads-up from SAAF Headquarters: all serviceable aircraft and flight crews on immediate standby, an indication that a Cabinet-level decision was in the making. Two days later, eight of us departed Bloemspruit for the four-hour flight to Rundu at the western end of the Caprivi Strip in Namibia, where we went straight into the ops room. The briefing revealed that a massive offensive had been launched by Fapla and the Cubans towards Unita's strategic logistics base and airstrip at Mavinga. If it were overrun, which at that point looked a distinct possibility, Savimbi's headquarters at Jamba would be within range of Angolan and Cuban MiGs.

"Were Unita to be pushed out of their self-proclaimed 'Free Angola' it would not only be a major propaganda victory for the communists, but open another 800 kilometres of border to Swapo infiltration. A grim intelligence officer revealed that South African ground units were already moving north with heavy artillery and multiple barrel rocket launchers. As soon as they were in range, waves of Impalas, Mirages, Canberras and

---

[14] A small, subsonic jet aircraft optimised for the counter-insurgency rôle, the Italian-built Aermacchi MB-326K was armed with a 30 mm DEFA cannon and could carry a combination of bombs, rockets and external fuel tanks.

Buccaneers – 41 aircraft in total – would strike the advancing enemy juggernaut. As soon as the last aircraft pulled off target, the army would add to the carnage with their rockets and artillery.

"Late on 17 September the strike launched from Rundu and Grootfontein. Everyone returned safely and the next morning we learned that the enemy spearhead had been halted. But large reserve elements were already moving forward and being frantically resupplied by Cuban-flown helicopters. Intelligence indicated that the resupply would actually gain momentum and that the enemy would continue with their push towards Mavinga.

"Our long range reconnaissance teams were reporting that the enemy helicopters, a mixed bag of Mi-8s, Mi-17s and Mi-25s, were coming out of Cuito Cuanavale, climbing to 3,000 feet to avoid small arms fire and following two tributaries to the Longa River and from there to the advancing enemy battle group. The enemy's success or failure against Unita hinged on that helicopter air bridge. It was our job to see that it failed."

With the ground reports and a stream of signals intelligence pouring in, the SAAF planners spread their maps and went to work. They looked at the distances involved and balanced them against the range of the Impalas. They calculated airspeed, time and distance for the enemy helicopters. They counted the number of strike aircraft available. They took into consideration that the Cubans had MiG-21s and MiG-23s at Cuito Cuanavale, which meant that the South African pilots, operating within the enemy's radar cover in their much slower Impalas, would definitely be playing with the lion's balls. Ideas were tossed back and forth, examined, discarded, re-examined. After endless cups of coffee, the operational plan was dropped on the boss's desk.

It was to be an ambush.

The selected target area lay thirty nautical miles south-east of Cuito Cuanavale. As soon as the Recces reported a flight of helicopters lifting off, a brace of Impalas on 24-hour cockpit standby would launch, aiming to arrive at the ambush site at the same time as the enemy. They'd have to go in low to stay under radar coverage, making navigation over the featureless terrain with only map and stopwatch extremely difficult, but that's what they'd trained for. On arrival, they had 22 minutes to spot and destroy the helicopters before low fuel forced them to scoot for home.

If more helicopters were reported, there were another ten Impalas for five more waves. Sounds good, the boss nodded. Do it.

"We spent a couple of days practising our tactics against SAAF Pumas imitating enemy flight profiles," Pine explained. "Approaching on the deck, we'd pitch up to carry out simulated cannon attacks. Keeping them in our gunsights wasn't easy, but our guys were much better than the Cubans and they knew we were coming. The Cubans didn't.

"On the 27th, Leon and I were the first two on cockpit standby. Keyed up, we settled into our seats and the flight engineers cinched the harnesses down. And we waited. Time ticked by, cuffs were pulled back to check watches, fingers drummed on the outside of the cockpit. I yawned. Suddenly, a bug-eyed intelligence officer ran out to the flight line, madly waving his arms and screaming at us to *'Fucking scramble! Go-go-go!'*

"We were airborne in minutes. I remember a very dry mouth and thinking, *'This is it. You're going to war big time. Don't mess it up.'* Under radio silence, Leon and I found our Initial Point, a bend in the Cubango River just east of Rundu. With the bush blurring less than a hundred feet beneath the Impalas' bellies, we settled down to low-level navigation, SAAF-style. Thirty-two minutes after getting airborne, we were waiting for them over one of the Longa's tributaries, eyes searching the sky.

"We were turning towards the second river, when my eyes snapped back to something. *Is that what I think it is? Yes. Halleluiah!* There they were, two helicopters in our two o'clock position, one trailing the other by approximately 1,000 metres. Leon hadn't seen them and was still turning.

"'Leon, we have two bogeys,' I said, breaking radio silence, 'two o'clock high, range three miles.'

"'Not visual.'

"'OK, I have the lead. I am pitching up to attack the rearmost guy. Watch me and I'll give you commentary on the lead bogey.'

"By now we're only thirty kilometres from Cuito Cuanavale, where I could imagine a couple of MiGs on cockpit standby. Time turned into treacle and it seemed forever as I closed the range. Then – *dammit!* – I'd overcooked the attack, ending up about 700 metres behind the Mi-25. I bunted the aircraft to accelerate to a decent fighting speed. The cannon's ideal range was 350 metres, but when I reached my next firing position, I was still about 500 metres directly behind it. I was furious with myself.

"Leon's voice came through my earphones. 'Pine, Leon, I have the lead target visual and I'm starting my pitch-up.'

"Rather than taking more time to close the range, I aimed slightly above my chopper and pulled the trigger, firing for what seemed an awfully long time. There were bright flashes, followed by an audible *whooff* and the chopper started burning from underneath. The flames stopped, replaced by brown smoke.

"'*Shit, it's not dead yet.*'

The pitch-up manoeuvre had placed us squarely within enemy radar cover and I was sure that any second now a wild-eyed Cuban intelligence officer at Cuito Cuanavale would be running onto the flightline and screaming in Spanish to a couple of MiG pilots to Fucking scramble, go-go-go!

"In desperation, I firewalled the throttle. With only empty drop-tanks under the wings, the Impala accelerated quickly. I chopped power and found myself alongside. Hunched forward in their separate cockpits, both Cuban pilots were clearly visible and very busy. Probably thinking they'd been hit by large-calibre groundfire, they were checking instruments, fighting to remain airborne as on-board systems went down. Through the three square windows in the cabin behind the aircraft commander I saw a lot of Cuban faces, all staring at me in horror. They knew.

"The Mi-25 started a gentle left-hand turn back towards Cuito Cuanavale. I pulled up and over, positioning myself on the outside for the rear-quarter attack that I had practised so many times. Allowing the chopper to pull away, I rolled in from my perch position, mentally reciting each step. It was straight out of the manuals.

"'*Airspeed: good – approaching 300 knots. Stadiametric ranging device: pegged at 350 metres. Wingspan: set. Armament master: ON. Angle-off: looking good. Aiming point: selected – the right-hand exhaust.*'"

Fire.

"There was a sparkling ripple of hits along the cowling, the high explosive shells tearing apart engines, drive shaft and gearbox. The helicopter rolled violently onto its left side, blades folding into a tangled mess and I knew this particular Mi-25 was going nowhere but down. Rolling inverted, I screamed for the deck, *very* worried about those MiGs. Down in the trees, I threw a quick glance over my shoulder. Two columns of thick, black smoke were rising into the sky. For a moment or two I became a gibbering idiot trying to get the word to our Telstar aircraft that we had just splashed two Mi-25s. The news was relayed and we landed at Rundu to a tumultuous welcome.

"Two days later we did it again – this time two Mi-17s and two Mi-25s. I hadn't joined those missions, as I was going into a night cycle in preparation for night attacks on the Fapla positions. But that's another story … ."

★ ★ ★

LtCol 'Ricardo'

At 5 Recce's HQ at Phalaborwa we'd been considering a deep penetration operation against Fapla for some time. Up until then, most of our offensive ops inside Angola had been kept within range of fixed wing close air support.

Maps and intelligence reports were spread out and we began examining the possibilities. Our eyes kept returning to Cuito Cuanavale, a strategic Fapla base that for years had been the linchpin for the annual dry season offensives against Unita. To the west of Cuito Cuanavale lay Menongue, a major logistics base. We had no intention of attacking either of these well-defended positions, but the tar road linking them was used by regular supply convoys that made very tempting targets.

The straight-line distance from our base at Fort Doppies in the Caprivi Strip was 370 kilometres. The SAAF would never consider risking Pumas that deep just for a few Ural trucks loaded with ammunition, which left us with the question of which vehicles we had that could carry a healthy strike force that distance. Someone mentioned the Unimogs that had been sitting in the motor pool for years. We'd used them in the old days; no reason why we shouldn't use them again.

We nodded agreement and returned to the maps. We all knew the well-maintained dirt road that ran from Fort Doppies into Angola and north through a succession of Unita bases. A finger traced it farther and farther until reaching the target area and stopping on the tar road between the Luassinga and Cuatir rivers. We knew the terrain well from small unit reconnaissance missions in the past. Not only was it an ideal spot for a vehicle ambush, but the road took us most of the way.

A concept proposal was put together, naming Herman as commander and me as his 2iC. The boss gave it his nod and passed it to Special Forces

Headquarters at Swartkop, which also nodded and sent it up the line to Defence Force Headquarters. It eventually came back to Phalaborwa. The boss called us in. Approved, he said. Better get cracking.

The Unimogs were stripped down and given a thorough overhaul as we debated the best weapons packages to mount. It was finally decided that we'd have two Sabres, each with a 106 mm recoilless rifle, two more with twin-pack 14.5 mm heavy machine guns and one, mine, with a 81 mm mortar. The fitting took a great deal of time and planning to make sure that after all the boxes and mounts were welded in place, the weapons could turn where we wanted to point them. In addition, each Unimog was to have a 7.62 x 51 mm light machine gun. These were mounted on a ball joint and swivel, so that you could pull it towards you and also swing it out towards the enemy. A small problem was that it was always right-handed, which meant that the driver had to turn a little left during a contact.

The force was divided into two groups. Each had two Unimogs, one with a 106, the other with a double 14.5 and each carrying a driver, vehicle commander, his No 2 and a fourth body, plus a Samil 50 support vehicle with ten infantry soldiers per group. In addition, there was my vehicle with the 81 mm mortar and Herman's command vehicle. All of the approximately fifty black and white operators were Special Forces qualified.

We practised at Phalaborwa to get the feel of our new equipment, then flew to Fort Doppies, where we rehearsed group manoeuvres, laagers, attacks, ambush drills – stop, shoot, infantry dismount, fire heavy weapons, shoot mortars, start with either infantry or vehicle attack. Satisfied that we were working as a team, we set off, moving during daylight from one Unita base to the next. The rains had just started, but Unita's logistical route was good and so well camouflaged that we could drive most of the day without worrying about being spotted from the air. Just to play it safe, as we got closer we switched to driving at night. There was no worry of the enemy spotting us, because they just didn't fly at night, but 'Big Daddy' of 32 Battalion once told me that in the unlikely event they did, all you had to do was put on your right indicators, turn to the left, and they'd be convinced it was Fapla.

Ten days after setting off we reached the tar road between the Luassinga and Cuatir rivers. Herman asked me to select the killing ground and ensure that everybody knew exactly where he should be. I picked an area where the ground sloped gently towards the road, trees breaking about a hundred metres from my position, with long grass and scattered bush about fifty metres from the road. This was where the infantry and Sabres would take their attack positions. The 14.5s had to support the 106s, and the infantry support both of them. About thirty metres on the other side of the road was a shallow trench where the enemy were sure to take cover when we hit them.

Satisfied, I stepped off 132 metres back to my vehicle. I'd open the ambush with the mortar, the signal for everyone else to open fire. The early warning groups were placed in their positions 300 metres to the east and west, and then we waited. Christmas was only a few days away.

It was Christmas Eve 1986, when José, the commander of the western early warning group, came on the air, whispering that he had infantry moving between his team and the road. We waited, poised over the radio. There was a long silence. Unknown to us, more infantry had appeared behind him, sandwiching José and his team against the road. A supply convoy of Ural trucks with an infantry company suddenly rolled into view in front of him, heading towards Cuito Cuanavale. When we heard him press his mike switch twice, hand signals were relayed to the ambush group. *Standby.* Then I heard him whisper, 'Five vehicles, five vehicles'.

This was exactly what we were hoping for. The time was also perfect: about 1830 hours, the light starting to fade. When the last Ural had passed José's position, I told him to get back to the assembly area and ordered our own vehicles to start. The Samils advanced to within thirty to fifty metres of the road, where the infantry debussed and took positions between them.

Standing in my Unimog with line of sight to the road, I waited until all the enemy vehicles had entered the killing ground, then dropped the first mortar bomb down the tube. The high-explosive round impacted on the road and the Sabres surged forward, 106s and 14.5s knocking out all five Urals in seconds as the LMGs ripped through the Fapla ranks. Those who hadn't been killed pulled back and dropped into the trench and I threw another twenty-five mortar bombs along the trench line and the tar road, killing more who were taking cover or running to escape. Small arms fire continued for another twenty minutes and then everything went quiet.

A quick check confirmed we had no casualties and we began inspecting the Urals. As far as we could see, they were carrying ammunition, food and crates of champagne, whiskey, wine and beer. It was the Christmas convoy for the senior officers at Cuito Cuanavale. Deciding that we were far more deserving, a few cases of booze were liberated. About two hours after the contact, Jenks was on top of one of the Urals and waving a box full of wrist watches, when the enemy suddenly counter-attacked our command vehicles from the west. At first I thought they were going to break through, but my crew and Herman's crew kept them busy until the infantry ran back from the ambush site to help. The enemy withdrew an hour after it started.

About twenty minutes later a second counter-attack started from the killing ground side. This time their heart definitely wasn't in it. The shooting was high and quickly tapered off, but gave me a good indication where to throw more mortar bombs. While all this firing was going on Gert was taking cover next to one of the shot-out Urals. A Fapla troop looking for his own cover dived to the ground next to him and Gert had a prisoner!

It was now approaching midnight. With less than six hours to put some distance between us and the ambush before dawn, there wasn't time to examine the rest of the cargo. We tried to set the vehicles alight, but they stubbornly refused to burn. In the end we placed mines under them and built fires on top of those, before hurriedly loading everyone and clearing the area. Ten kilometres down the road we picked up a group of waiting Unita and continued another twenty kilometres to one of their safe bases, from where we could still hear explosions coming from the burning convoy. That was when the first bottle of whiskey appeared and it didn't live long either.

The official score, as learned from radio intercepts, was forty-two enemy dead. Added to that was our one prisoner and five trucks destroyed for no losses or wounded on our side. The bonus was that we had booze for Christmas and New Year.

Just for the record the 14.5 gunner on my right was Lafras Luitingh, who seven years later became a director of Executive Outcomes, and the 106 gunner next to him was Sunshine, who, as an EO instructor, would train the special forces group for FAA.

★ ★ ★

SOYO

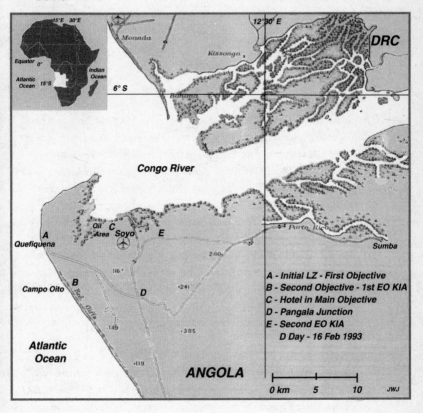

A - Initial LZ - First Objective
B - Second Objective - 1st EO KIA
C - Hotel in Main Objective
D - Pangala Junction
E - Second EO KIA
   D Day - 16 Feb 1993

Soyo

An Iron Age fishing village probably sat there long before the first Portuguese explorers sailed their caraques down Africa's coast. Lying sheltered where the mighty Congo stretches ten miles across and seven from the Atlantic Ocean, it's a natural site, though the mosquitoes, heat and surly natives are much the same today as when Diogo Cao's tired crew dropped anchor in 1483.

Some things have changed, however. In the decades since oil was discovered off Angola's coast, the cluster of primitive huts has been replaced by the concrete block and sun-baked steel of a modern oil exploration support facility. Today, Soyo services off-shore platforms pumping the black gold that Western civilization demands for its plastics, SUVs and endless miles of super highways. It should come as no surprise, therefore, that American companies are well represented.

The irony is, that since 1975 the fields tapped by these giants of industry have belonged to a Marxist state eager for the wealth their capitalist enemies provided. Even more ironical is the use to which that wealth was put: for the MPLA government of President José Eduardo dos Santos it purchased weapons and the services of thousands of Soviet and Cuban advisors to fight Jonas Savimbi's Unita rebel movement; at the same time American oil companies were paying US taxes on their share of that wealth and Washington, drawing from those taxes, was sending weapons and CIA advisors to Unita in its struggle against the Marxist state. It's a funny old world.

As an added complication, the South Africans, initially encouraged and later officially disowned by Washington (though perhaps with a nudge and a wink), maintained a military presence inside the country to support Unita's war against the MPLA and protect Namibia to the south. And while both Angola and America, locked in their paradoxical *pas de deux,* excoriated the other in public, neither was prepared to interrupt the flow of oil on the one hand, nor violate the geopolitical imperatives of the Cold War on the other, even if both hands were rudely groping the other's most private parts in between. In the world of *realpolitik*, economic self-interest must always prevail, regardless of the music to which it sways.

But when the Berlin Wall toppled in 1989, followed soon thereafter by the rest of a corroded Iron Curtain, something approaching common sense raised its head from a fusty bomb shelter and blinked. Is it over? My God! that was an expensive forty-odd years. Hey, you over there. Yeah, you. Let's make a deal. And they did. Quiet, friendly words, a little arm-twisting of old dance partners where necessary, and in exchange for South Africa ending its waltz with Unita, Moscow and Havana, without even the welcoming notes of a military band, brought their boys home. At the same time, Washington trumpeted that its own largesse was at an end: Savimbi had the option – join the proposed democratic process or lose political support on Capital Hill as well. If the American eagle and Russian bear could skip the light fantastic after almost two generations of waiting for someone to trip over The Button, then their Unita and MPLA proxies could damn well do the same.

Both parties sullenly agreed, negotiations went forward, truces were signed and the MPLA ordered its army – re-christened a more neutral *Forças Armadas de Angola* – to stack arms under the watchful gaze of United Nations monitors, while Unita did the same, more or less. The UN smiled happily for the cameras, took a deep breath and crossed its fingers.

But Third World governments and rebel movements are nothing if not paranoid, and Savimbi may have been less than forthcoming in the decommissioning process, handing over more pig iron, it's been suggested, than cold steel. Compliance? asked pink-cheeked Blue Berets dreaming of Surrey and a decent pint at their local. Look for yourselves. Here's what Dr Savimbi's chaps gave us; how can *we* know what *hasn't* been turned in? Still, for the first time in almost fifteen years the guns had gone silent. Peace at last.

Until the 1992 elections.

Though no one will ever know the true count or the extent to which both sides fiddled the vote, Unita lost by a mere one percent. In a BBC interview Savimbi claimed the elections were rigged, an indignant dos Santos accused Savimbi of pretty much the same thing, and within hours of the interviews, tanks were shelling Unita's political headquarters in Luanda's Rovuma Hotel. Savimbi was spirited out the back to a waiting 4x4 and sped to Negage airfield, whence his Fokker F-27 flew him to Jamba in the south-eastern corner of the country. Angolan state radio reported that he had been killed, but a few days later Savimbi gave an interview by satellite phone and the nation geared itself for the inevitable.

The war, if ever it had truly ended, had a new lease on life. But this time Savimbi held the high cards – and the military high ground too. The Cubans and Soviets were gone, he'd hoarded the best of his arsenal and, with diamonds perfectly acceptable to Russian arms dealers looking for new business (another of those little ironies), was upgrading and restocking at a furious pace.

It is axiomatic that, with rare exception, African politics grow from the barrel of a gun, the will of the people an ephemeral concept. To hold power is everything; to be without a condition traditional chiefs such as Savimbi ill-tolerate. His goal of paramount chieftainship not just of Angola's majority Ovimbundu tribe, but of all Angola still glittered.

So, prepared for just such an MPLA perversion of the democratic process, an already poised Unita attacked and overwhelmed weakened FAA garrisons. With the war in Bosnia boiling on Europe's doorstep, Western governments and the media looking for a new dramatic series lost sight of Angola, where the battle for the city of Huambo alone saw tens of thousands killed and even more made homeless.

As ruthless as he is charismatic, Savimbi's strategy was to capture as much territory as quickly as possible – particularly areas of crucial economic importance to the MPLA. The first target was the diamond-bearing areas along the Cuango River in Lunda Norte Province, centred on the town of Cafunfo. The next was Soyo.

In late 1992 Unita overran the petroleum complex, promising the MPLA that any attempt to recover it would result in its complete destruction. The government was stunned into inaction. Already on the defensive under Unita's long-planned assault, the loss of petro-dollars threatened the collapse of an already sclerotic economy, which, if it went into terminal arrest, would lead to the inevitable victory of the arch-enemy. To rebuild the facility could take months, possibly years, by which time the country would be bankrupt. Not since the withdrawal of their Soviet bloc allies had the MPLA faced a crisis of such magnitude. The international consortium which had built Soyo was pressing for action but the generals dithered. Not on their watch. Not on their heads. They could see no solution.

But indecision is not what makes corporate giants. The consortium – thought to include Texaco, Chevron, Gulf and Fina, among others – was less a-flutter than incensed by the millions in lost production each day. Not to mention the nightmare of seeing their almost half-billion-dollars of assets turned into smoke and ash. Banks and stockholders were breathing down their necks. Bonuses were at risk! Something had to be done. Now. Among those affected was Heritage Oil, a relatively small London-based company and the owner of some very expensive custom-designed and - built equipment now rusting under Unita control.

With fortunes being lost, a conference attended by Sonangol, the state-owned oil company, and a representative of Heritage Oil reviewed the situation and agreed in principle on a course of action. Heritage, run by a man of impeccable buccaneering spirit, would introduce the Angolans to a suitable contractor for the back street job, a job that hadn't been seen in Africa for three decades, and never as a private initiative: the hiring and deployment of a professional mercenary force.

★

Though the principals remain somewhat coy about the process, networking revealed a small firm in South Africa that provided operational intelligence training for South African Special Forces and advised private firms on security matters. Eeben Barlow, a former officer in the South African Defence Force's elite 32 Battalion and later the super-secret Civil Co-operation Bureau, was the founder of Executive Outcomes.

"In early 1993 I was approached by an international oil company[15] who wanted to know whether we could assist the Angolan government in recovering equipment that had been lost," he told the author.[15a] The deceptively mild-mannered South African agreed to examine the feasibility of the project, but laid down a number of hard and fast criteria. Any former professional soldier worth his salt would have fought the

[15] London-based Heritage Oil in a joint venture with Ranger Oil of Canada
[15a] Carlos and a number of international journalists believed the 'international oil company' to be Heritage Oil.

Angolan army between 1976 and 1988; thus, he wanted an ironclad guarantee that, if the project were taken on, none would be harassed by the MPLA government or the army. The second condition was that payment must be in advance. Sonangol agreed to the terms, assuring him that Unita had withdrawn from Soyo and it was but a week's work to secure the compound and allow the expats to get it up and running again.

Barlow immediately began recruiting, giving preference to former members of South African Special Forces, 32 Battalion and the Koevoet police counter-insurgency unit. With the client pressing him to hurry, the vetting process perhaps wasn't as comprehensive as it might have been: among the sixty alleged veterans of South Africa's various border wars were one or two charlatans and fantasists, while others would not live up to the reputations of their former units.

A twin-engine Cessna 402 was leased from Crause Steyl of Pro-Pilot in Windhoek. A former drug-running aircraft purchased at a DEA auction in Miami, 'Ghost Rider' shuttled the South Africans by twelves from Lanseria airport outside Johannesburg to Cabo Ledo, a former Cuban air force base in Angola. It wasn't until the EO leadership element had arrived and begun discussions with senior Angolan officers that the true tactical situation was revealed: Unita still held Soyo in force. Right. Planning and preparation for the operation began, with an emphasis on house clearing.

Although an understandable degree of distrust plagued their early meetings with the Angolans, joint planning was undertaken. It was known that Unita had established bases at the Campo Oito pumping station south-west of Soyo, and at Sumba to the east, where they expected any attempt to retake Soyo to come from. Never do what the enemy expects, the South Africans cautioned. Better a heliborne assault on the lightly defended repair facilities at Quefiquena, west of the Soyo complex. This could coincide with an amphibious landing by Angolan infantry and armour on Quefiquena's Atlantic beach. The FAA officers agreed, adding a Mi-25 helicopter gunship and MiG-23 jet fighters to attack Unita positions immediately prior to the landing, after which their forces would join the South Africans to liberate the rest of the complex. D-Day was fixed for 16 February 1993.

A little internal politics had to be addressed first. "We hadn't been entirely happy with the individual first named to lead us," said Carlos, a former Special Forces officer, "and we'd made our views known before departing South Africa. Thus, we were much relieved when told that he had been replaced by Lafras Luittingh. Tall and lanky Lafras had a solid record in Special Forces and his various wounds testified to his having tasted more combat than most. He was a sound choice to lead us to war."

Crates of new AK-47 assault rifles were delivered, along with PKM machine guns, a 60 mm mortar and boxes of ammunition.[16] The Angolans set off by barge from Cabo Ledo and the EO group boarded an Antonov AN-26 for Cabinda, where they were accommodated in a remote corner of the airfield. The last night was spent under torrential rain. Before dawn, pulses building, they donned webbing heavy with ammunition and water bottles and boarded the three Mi-17s for the twenty-minute flight south to the objective.

The Congo River slid under them, the helicopters' shadows keeping pace across the muddy water. Feet dry again, following the beach, the dirty-green Atlantic off to their right. Riding with them were all the emotions of going into combat: pounding hearts, dry mouths, wondering if this was the day it finally happened, and the sheer adrenaline-charged excitement of playing the ultimate game once more. And then the warning from the cockpit: five minutes out. Wrists overlap to pull those still sitting to their feet. A quick check that rounds are chambered, safeties on. Shoulders roll to ease necks and settle webbing; tense smiles, nods and thumbs up and they assemble into two ragged queues inside the Russian helicopters, poised for the open door. They balance themselves as the choppers flare for landing, flashes of elephant grass growing larger through the round portholes. Then the bump of solid ground and they spill out, eyes squinting, weapons sweeping bush that shakes in the maelstrom of downwash as the helicopters lift off behind them.

Training and rehearsals take over. Forming into three groups, they headed south, cut through a security fence and reached the first tar road. Muzzles jerked up and centred as an engine roared into high revs and a maroon Mitsubishi pick-up truck screeched away. Windows disintegrated, paint chips flew and tyres hissed under the concentrated fire. The vehicle lurched to a stop, both occupants slumped forward. Doors were snatched

---

[16] "One new employee who had been boring everyone with elaborate war stories drew a Dragunov sniper rifle, a 12 gauge shotgun, a PKM and an AK!" Carlos said. "He was politely asked where the wheelbarrow was. Another chap was firmly denied the right to bear arms when he was caught sticking a needle in his arm. Soon dubbed 'Apocalypse,' it was later established that he had been rejected for service in the SADF due to substance abuse."

open, the bodies quickly searched for documents, weapons taken. The men spread themselves along the side of the road, sprinting across in small groups. Just ahead a prefab house formed part of an accommodation–cum–workshop. From it a curious but very relaxed Unita soldier appeared, did a celluloid double-take, before spinning around and escaping under a hail of bullets. Inside, a thread of smoke rose from a marijuana joint.

Without ground-to-air communications or marker panels to confirm their own position, the promised close air support was a dubious and worrying exercise. A few hours late, the Mi-25 thudded over, orbited aimlessly for a while, then, as if remembering why he was there, the pilot rolled in and triggered his rockets. At something. At least nowhere near them, the men on the ground thought with relief. The gunship was followed by a MiG-23 fighter-bomber streaking in to bomb the Unita base at Campo Oito. The South Africans watched the bombs sail harmlessly into the Atlantic, raising tall spumes. If the Angolan pilots did mistake them for Unita, at least the chances were pretty good that nobody was going to be hurt.

They spread along the southern perimeter. Beyond the high, chain link fence elephant grass grew an impenetrable curtain. Watches were checked. Where were the FAA reinforcements? Under a wicked sun the temperature nudged a hundred degrees and the humidity thickened, clinging like a wet sauna. One section found shade under an outdoor workshop, when a grenade sailed over the perimeter fence, followed by heavy automatic weapons fire from their twelve o' clock. They had good cover behind a low wall from the AK-47 fire and what appeared to be a single RPD light machine gun. The rebel force of about thirty had chosen their position poorly, the thick elephant grass making accurate fire impossible. The South Africans' Russian assault rifles, bolstered by machine guns and the 60 mm mortar, kept the rebels down. Thirty minutes after the contact started, whistles signalled a withdrawal. There were knowing looks at Unita's use of referee whistles in combat, a tactic learned from South African instructors, some of them right here. An ops medic was daubing a scalp wound from ricocheting debris. Their first operational casualty!

An hour later there was the crack of a distant shot and a platoon commander spun around, clutching his arm and swearing. A Unita sniper abseiled nimbly down a baobab tree and disappeared into the elephant grass. EO had it's first casevac.

The group on the southwest corner held their fire when a face appeared cautiously at the perimeter fence – FAA had come to the party. The newly-arrived company was left to hold the position and EO moved the 1500 metres to the beach, where Colonel Pepe de Castro, who would later play a prominent rôle in EO's Angolan adventures, was supervising the amphibious landing. The barge was bow on to the beach and the first tank rolling off at the surf line, when the driver backed off to shift gears and the T-62 settled. Under full power, the tracks spun, throwing sand and water, digging themselves deeper until the belly touched bottom. It was abandoned, the first of many examples EO would see of FAA's indifference to the loss of equipment.

The second tank came off safely, growled up the beach and immediately drove inland, accompanied by the other two infantry companies. A courteous but cautious Colonel de Castro invited the EO officers to join him at his tactical headquarters northwest of the complex. While they discussed their next move, another South African was wounded by a sniper and a third, running to his assistance, fell into a concealed ditch and fractured his hip. Not a good day so far.

Taking the western side of the complex, the ocean at their backs, the South Africans dug in at the top of a gentle slope and laid out fields of fire either side of the T-62. The sun sank into the Atlantic, but the darkness provided little relief. The smell of rotting vegetation hung in the hot air, sweat ran into eyes and clouds of mosquitoes hovered and dived. Leaning forward in their positions, they stared into the night, listening for sounds of movement over the hum of biting insects.

The attack came an hour after sunset, yellow-white muzzle flashes and small arms fire ricocheting off the tank and cracking overhead. Tracer and ball crossed in the dark. An hour later the in-coming fire ceased as abruptly as it had begun. Sudden silence. A quick check up and down the line confirmed no casualties. Uneasy rest followed until 0400, when another grenade came arcing out of the night and exploded harmlessly.

Just before dawn a recce team slipped forward and returned to say that Unita had pulled back. After stand-to, a helicopter delivered their rucksacks and a resupply of rations and badly needed water. There were curses on discovering the rucksacks had been rifled and the water tasted of diesel. Enemy resistance, the heat, stink, mosquitoes and unpalatable water were already raising mutterings in the ranks. This wasn't what they'd expected.

"As it turned out," said Carlos, "some of our guys were better talkers than fighters and hadn't quite grasped what they'd been hired to do." Their discomfort was heightened by another attack that night. The next morning the malcontents demanded a meeting with Lafras. We've had enough, they told him, we want to go home. Well, yes, it was decided, it probably *would* be in everyone's best interests if they left, and resignations were accepted. They were promptly helicoptered back to Cabinda and then on to Cabo Ledo, where in the interests of operational security, and to their considerable displeasure, they would remain until the Soyo project was concluded. When the sounds of rotor blades faded, those still on the ground silently counted heads. Less than half of the original complement remained. This wasn't what they expected either.

★ ★ ★

Completing the Job

"With Quefiquena secured, our next objective was the Campo Oito pumping station due south of us," Carlos said. "This was their command and logistics HQ for the area and had to be neutralized before we could confidently take and hold Soyo without the constant threat of counter-attacks."

But they were faced with two tactical dilemmas. The first, aside from being dangerously under-manned and out-gunned, was the one avenue of approach, a narrow coastal road flanked by thick bush and eight-foot-tall elephant grass. They could forget about surprise. The second dilemma was that the client wanted as little damage as possible to the infrastructure, which meant restraint in the use of heavy weapons.

"Supported by the T-62 and one of Colonel de Castro's companies, we decided to hit it at first light," Carlos said. "Part of the plan was to land a mortar team by inflatable boat. They would sow some confusion with a pre-dawn, 60 mm wake-up call that would continue until we were ready to hit the place."

Faces blackened, the amphibious team left at around midnight and slipped a few kilometres out to sea. Outboard engines throttled down to reduce noise, the boat turned south, riding the greasy swells until they were circling off Campo Oito in the dark. They swung the engines and headed slowly towards the beach, the sound of heavy surf growing louder. Coming closer, they could make out massive waves breaking well off shore. The likelihood of getting through them without capsizing, losing their equipment and being at the mercy of a much larger force was too small to risk the landing. Disappointed, they returned to Quefiquena to join the main force.

As the eastern sky lightened the tank rumbled into life, belching black exhaust. There was the clatter of tracks as it lurched forward. Twenty-eight South Africans fell into step with it until they were in range of the camp, then slipped off the road, spreading out in line abreast to push through the dense undergrowth. Their Angolan allies followed nervously. Mosquitoes swarmed, sweat darkened camo shirts and visibility fell until they sometimes lost sight of the man next to them. "We were completely blind to what lay ahead," Carlos said. Unita were blind too, but not deaf to the approaching tank.

They had just reached a dry river bed a hundred metres outside the camp, when gunfire exploded across their front. Impossible to pinpoint the sources, they dropped and laid down suppressive fire. Behind them, their Angolan allies fled. A Unita machine gun gave itself away by the swathe it was cutting through the grass. Weapons swung automatically and the concentrated fire quickly silenced it. "It was all pretty loud and chaotic," Carlos remembered, "but no one had been wounded so far and we were giving better than we were getting. Then one of our ex-32 Bn blokes scrambled onto the tank and in full view was shouting at the crew to engage the enemy, when he was hit with a rifle grenade and killed instantly." They were emptying magazine after magazine, enemy fire clipping grass and trimming branches around them. Then from ahead came shouts and whistles. The enemy fire slackened, faltered, then ceased as the defenders, outnumbering the attackers by at least four to one, disengaged and retreated.

"We broke out of the bush and swept through the deserted pumping station," Carlos said. "Evidence of Unita occupation lay everywhere. Smoking campfires, empty ammunition tins, food, bloodied field dressings, discarded caps and propaganda leaflets. One of our guys shouted and picked up a headband. Clinging to it was the partial scalp of a blond Caucasian. Although the body had been taken by Unita, it was quite clear that we had killed a white mercenary on their side. We never found out who it was, but we wondered if it was his death that prompted their withdrawal. Not long after we'd secured the place, our gallant allies pitched up again, acting for all the world like they'd just stepped out for a pizza. Wasn't it a good thing they got back in time to give us a hand? they told us. We left them in charge and returned to Quefiquena."

A pickup truck liberated by three Angolan soldiers raced past a knot of South Africans carrying their dead colleague. The laughing driver spun around and came back with the offer to transport it. This was gratefully accepted, after which the driver, still laughing, began swerving violently back and forth across the road, oblivious to the body being thrown from side to side. Furious, the South Africans ordered the driver to stop. The ensuing argument saw the two sides on the verge of blows, when Lafras and de Castro arrived to defuse the situation.

A delighted General João Baptiste de Matos, FAA's supreme commander, flew in. For someone who'd seen his forces decimated in every encounter with the South Africans in the old days, de Matos was the model of courtesy, he and his staff repeatedly expressing astonishment at what so few had accomplished. His apparently genuine condolences over the death of their brother-in-arms and his heartfelt thanks set the stage for a gradual warming between the former enemies. The South Africans were stood down and given a few days to relax before the assault on Soyo itself.

For something to do, they looked at repairing the basic infrastructure and getting to know their new allies. "A big guy with a bit of a paunch, Colonel de Castro seemed okay," Carlos remembered, "but he could be quite ruthless when it suited his purpose. One morning I accompanied him and a few of his staff to examine a broken pump that supplied drinking water. We were still being pestered by Unita harassing fire from the eastern side of the Quifiquena complex, and as I was examining the pump we started receiving fire from some distance away. It was fairly ineffective but clearly frightened de Castro's batman, who began edging towards cover. 'Where do you think you're going?' he snarled in Portuguese. 'Move another step and I'll kill you.' Whether his batman just faced away or had turned to bolt, I'll never know, but without hesitating or another word, de Castro drew his pistol and shot him in the head. He holstered the smoking Makarov and carried on talking as though nothing had happened."

Almost immediately, the controversy that would follow EO began with newspaper headlines about the latest "Dogs of War". According to Barlow's sources, the leak was orchestrated by staunch supporters of Unita within the South African Defence Force. Vehemently opposed to the Soyo venture, they are alleged to have passed intelligence about the operation to Savimbi. Closer to home, they orchestrated a campaign to intimidate next of kin with anonymous, threatening phone calls.

This was a complication that Barlow, working twenty hours a day from his home in Pretoria, didn't need. "[We were] supporting the whole operation - logistically, medically, transport, everything," he said. "At no stage in a twenty-four-hour period was there a plane on the ground; there was always a plane in the air. Without trying to give ourselves too much credit, we ran a very solid operation despite all the media hype going on and the police sitting on our doorstep, and our phones being monitored by South African military intelligence, and Unita attacking us, and MI using all their front companies … to put out propaganda against Executive Outcomes. We still ran this damn thing."

Run it they did, and now it was time to finish the job. To their surprise, a night reconnaissance returned with the welcome news that Unita had withdrawn. Expecting an overwhelming heliborne, amphibious and air attack, the rebels had made a tactical retreat to Sumba, some twenty kilometres farther up the Congo River. The South Africans secured the airstrip just south of Soyo, then moved cautiously into the town. One of their abiding memories was the sight of wild dogs scavenging the bodies of young men executed for refusing to join Unita.

They commandeered the Soyo Hotel as their headquarters and were rolling up sleeves to start cleaning it, when a breathless Colonel de Castro arrived to warn that a group of journalists had just touched down at the airstrip. Eager to score a propaganda victory, the MPLA had brought them in to verify that Soyo was back in government hands. Everyone scattered. "Some of us ducked into a private residence, where the owners hastily removed a portrait of Unita's leader, Jonas Savimbi," Carlos said. "Whether it hung there out of sympathy for the rebels or simply to survive during the occupation was of no concern to us. Once we assured them of our good will, we were treated for the first time in a week to a meal that didn't come out of a can."

As soon as the press departed, they returned to the hotel. It had been used by Unita as a hospital and the first task was sweeping up septic bandages and scrubbing blood from floors and walls. Unita's withdrawal was so sudden that they'd not had time to destroy everything; to EO's immense delight the showers and air conditioning still worked. There was even a washing machine and dryer. They revelled in the unaccustomed luxury, but it was tempered by the malaria that soon hit everyone.

The oil facility and harbour bordered the western side of the town, where a small ship lay alongside the quay. It had arrived from Matadi up-river with supplies and the skipper apparently hadn't known the town was in rebel hands when he docked. No one knew the fate of the crew, but

Unita had stripped the inside bare, everything, to include engine accessories. Elsewhere, a D-30 122 mm howitzer and ammunition bunker were found abandoned and, rather unsportingly, turned around and used for harassment and interdiction fire against its former owners.

"We liberated a Toyota sedan for use as a command and resupply vehicle," Carlos said. "For tactical purposes, the doors and windscreen were removed and the white paint job broken up with duct tape. It wasn't particularly rugged, but we didn't have to do any bundu-bashing and it served our purpose. In conjunction with our FAA allies, a security perimeter was established and a round-the-clock observation post manned atop a microwave tower. Our daily routine included regular security patrols, starting with the airfield, then driving the twenty-five kilometres to check Quefiquena and Campo Oito, where we delivered supplies and assured the Angolan troops that they hadn't been forgotten.

"As a gesture of appreciation from General de Matos, we were flown a few at a time to Cabinda and given an all-expenses-paid day and night in the hotel there. I was in the bar watching the local television news when there was a bulletin announcing the liberation of Soyo. All the Angolans broke into spontaneous applause, shouting *'Bravo, Africa de Sul!'* [17] They insisted on shaking our hands and buying round after round of drinks for us. That our efforts were appreciated and raised the morale of the locals was a boost to our own, though we were mortified that they knew it had been us. So much for security."

A limited number of Texaco and Chevron personnel returned to conduct a damage assessment, along with representatives from Unesco and the World Food Program. Appreciating that the South Africans were their only defence, they accepted EO's request to stay close to the harbour. In the event of another Unita attack, EO's plan was to load them on a waiting tug boat and send it to the closest Texaco oil rig, some three miles from the mouth of the Congo River.

"A joint briefing was conducted each morning, where we gave them our latest security assessment and they advised us of their intended movements. The relationship might be likened to a Texaco-Chevron-NGO hand inside EO's chain mail glove and worked exceptionally well. They all admitted feeling far safer with us than FAA, which had folded under the first Unita advance, leaving them to get out in their socks."

---

[17] "Bravo, South Africa!"

To EO's surprise, the oil companies had their own high-grade intelligence, which suggested that over the last two years they had dealt with Unita at some level to protect their assets at Soyo. Over a few beers one evening Carlos joked that their information could only have come through a degree of contact with the rebel movement. A company rep handed him another Bud, smiled and said, "No comment."

"Our liking for the Yanks wasn't hurt by the masses of such crucial items as Marlboros, fresh meat and stacks of Budweiser they brought with them. We got along extremely well. The WFP and Unesco reps, on the other hand, played a very careful game, maintaining a formal and distant relationship during the day, but staying damn close to us once the sun had set.

"Eeben decided to try countering the negative publicity back home with some coverage of us being feted by the adoring locals. A petite and stunning blonde reporter arrived from Windhoek for a story and within minutes of meeting some of the lads, already had at least two more-or-less serious proposals of marriage."

As part of their contract, EO was to secure the site for a minimum of six weeks so that various pieces of equipment could be recovered. Which meant that the continuing rebel threat from Sumba had to be dealt with. The terrain, choked with elephant grass and swamp, offered little scope for manoeuvre. They'd have to use a road cut by the oil companies, a dirt track leading east from Soyo to the tarmacked Sumba road. To boost their firepower, they mounted a Russian ZSU-23 twin-barrelled anti-aircraft gun on the back of a DAF lorry and on the morning of the advance formed up around the DAF, the only black faces belonging to two of their fellow South Africans. They were in this by themselves; their Angolan allies, it seemed, had more pressing business elsewhere.

Lafras waved them forward, the DAF began to roll and they fell in with it. They were barely out of sight of the gate, when they came under massive fire from a small hill fifty metres to their right. Two men went down immediately. The 23 mm was firing, but another Unita position opened up, making the road a death trap. The South Africans, putting down suppressive fire, looked for cover that wasn't there. Others ran forward to pull the two wounded to safety, but were driven back. The air seemed solid with the sounds of bullets cracking past and the whines and warbles of ricochets coming off the road. Impossible to advance, nowhere to find cover, they were forced to withdraw, alive, no one else wounded, but devastated at leaving two of their number behind. "Oh, *fuck!*" someone said in anguish. They pulled back to Soyo, pleading with FAA for reinforcements to return now-now! – but the Angolan troops wouldn't budge. Men sank to the ground, head in hands, sick with concern for their friends. *Let them be dead,* some thought. For one it was not to be. Not immediately.

"As the intelligence and signals officer, my room in the Soyo Hotel doubled as the radio room," Carlos said. "We were using a standard HF set linked by commercial frequency to the ex-pats' radios. At about seven o'clock the next morning Marcel, one of the Texaco employees, came in for the morning comms check. He had just offered his condolences for our two guys, when an unfamiliar voice broke in on the radio. 'To the dogs in Soyo who are missing a friend,' it laughed. 'Listen carefully, your friend is going to sing for you.' The microphone was keyed and a piercing scream came through the speaker. The scream went on and on. Marcel's eyes met mine and he bolted from the room. Helpless, I switched off the radio. Marcel was so shaken that he requested immediate relief and was gone that day."

They were now twenty-five lightly armed South Africans, all suffering malaria and vastly outnumbered by a more heavily armed enemy. Following the death at Campo Oito, the two fatalities had had a drastic effect on morale and, as Carlos admits, there was much individual soul-searching. But all of them had been in similar, or even bleaker, situations in their military lives and they drew closer together as a team. It was towards the end of this period when the miraculous escape of EO's ferry pilot lightened everyone's mood and entered EO folklore. It also reminded them of how much luck is involved in living or dying.

"Our resupply flight from Luanda was due that day and we were looking forward to mail and South African staples not included in the Yank's inventory. The Cessna 402 wasn't expected until the afternoon. Without advising us, however, the pilot departed Windhoek much earlier than scheduled and arrived just after sunrise. Which wouldn't have been a problem, except that we hadn't made our morning sweep of the airfield."

The aircraft taxied up to the apron, shut down and the pilot climbed out, coming face to face with a Unita penetration team. Not a word was spoken. The pilot looked at them, they stared back. Deciding they weren't who should be meeting him, he climbed straight back into the aircraft, started the engines and took off.

"When he rather excitedly called us on the radio, we raced for the airfield, but the rebels had disappeared. Why he wasn't captured or killed remains a mystery. As he was shaking his head over a cup of coffee and repeating the story for the tenth time, we were convulsed with laughter. We couldn't help asking why he hadn't used them to off-load the supplies, rather than waiting for us to do it."

The rest of their time at Soyo was relatively uneventful and at the end of the six-week commitment they returned to Luanda and then home.[18] Not everything had gone perfectly, but what was seen as either farcical or suicidal by more conventional military minds had been successfully executed by a handful of men. It also left a lasting impression in the minds of the Angolan government and its generals – people who had been their sworn enemies barely five years previously. The result would strain the credulity of the most imaginative novelist, and their own wildest dreams.

★ ★ ★

---

[18] A week after EO withdrew, Unita overran Soyo. Barlow was asked to retake it again, but a dispute over the fee saw him decline. "Sonangol had decided that we were too expensive for them," Barlow told the author. "They had hired cheaper people and they now had the result of cheap labour. We weren't prepared to go in and put our people at risk again to fix what was [their] tactical fuck-up."

"Will you train our army?"

Three months after the end of the Soyo contract, EO's founder Eeben Barlow picked up the ringing telephone. The caller identified himself as General Luís Faceira of the Forças Armadas de Angola and said he would like to meet to discuss a proposition. Taking his number, Barlow promised to get back to him, then dialled another number in Luanda. "I didn't know ... if it was a set-up or not [so] I called first of all Sonangol to ask them who the hell was General Luís Faceira. And they said to me that he was a very senior officer in the Angolan army."[19] Barlow returned the general's call and said he would be willing to meet, but not in Angola and that it would have to be in the company of another EO employee, as well as a senior member of Sonangol and "a representative of the international oil company [Heritage Oil]. If this was a set-up," Barlow told the author, "there would be a lot more people embarrassed than just Executive Outcomes."

Barlow and Lafras Luittingh flew to the Etosha Game Reserve in northern Namibia, where they met Faceira and his party in a remote lodge. The Angolan general began by complimenting Barlow on the organization, planning and logistical backup that had been evident in the Soyo contract. When the small talk was out of the way and they had settled with coffee, Faceira came straight to the point. Would Executive Outcomes be prepared to train the Angolan army?

If Barlow was rocked by the question, he didn't show it. After a moment's thought he explained that he'd first have to write a concept proposal. If they liked that, then a more detailed proposal would be drafted and submitted for approval. But General Faceira shook his head; there wasn't time for that. He wanted the proposal now. "I said to him, well, this type

---

[19] General Luís Faceira was in fact Chief of the Army. His brother, General Antonio Faceira, commanded FAA's Special Forces 'Commandos'.

of thing doesn't take ten minutes to write. He said, 'Fine, please bear in mind we are in a bit of trouble, and you can give it to us tomorrow morning or, better still, tonight at about ten o'clock.' And this was about ten o'clock in the morning. I said to Lafras, basically we're in the shit here; we haven't got a typewriter, we haven't got a computer. So we got paper from the owner of the lodge, carbon paper, and I set out writing a proposal for retraining the whole Angolan army.

"Lafras and I sat down and I said to him, well, to train the whole army we'll have to start from grass roots-level with basic training, because there is no way we are going to change the mindset of the Angolan soldier until he wants it changed. If we could train a green brigade, as in green, raw brigade, and they could achieve success, the other troops would want to have the same – and that was the idea we approached the Angolan army with: to set up a team for them and train a brigade."

Barlow presented the proposal that evening. Faceira examined it, then sent him away again to work out costings. "We sat down and worked out the military rank structure within the company in Angola, how we'd struc-ture the training team, how we'd award salaries[20] to them, and what were our prerequisites for any guy going in, and we went back to him and said, this is what it's going to cost. He looked at it and said he had to do some work on it himself, but he would let us know the next morning.

"The next morning he said, 'Fine, when can you start? I would like your first men on the ground sometime next week.' I said to him, 'Well, General, there is no way we can start that soon. First of all, I need to know if we're getting the money, because we will only work if we are paid in advance – every three months in advance, and after a month or two, if the next lot has not come in we withdraw'.' He said, 'No, you have my word on it. You will be paid as you stipulated, and the first money will be paid into your account within the next few days.' We shook hands on it.

"I then said to him, well, forgive me, but this is a highly unusual way to do business and I'm a bit hesitant about the whole thing. He said, 'Fine, we'll write you a letter to say you've got the contract if that's what you want.' I said, yes, that is what I would like. He said, 'That might take a few months to get it off the system to you, but we haven't got a few months to wait, but you can start recruiting your people when you are satisfied the money is there.' I said, the sooner you have the money there,

---

[20] Salaries ranged from US$2,000 to US$10,000 per month.

the sooner I can start recruiting. That was where the Angola project started."

★

While waiting for the agreement to be finalized, Barlow checked the legality of the proposed venture. "I went to the Reserve Bank of South Africa to find out how we must do everything so that it is in line with their rules and regulations. We went to the Receiver of Revenue to discuss it with them, and I went to the South African Police, who I got to know from them sitting on the veranda for two months during the Soyo contract. I said to them, 'This is what we're going to do; are we breaking any laws?' They were quite happy with what I told them. I approached attorneys both in South Africa and outside of South Africa to ask whether we were breaking international laws, and everybody said no. They quoted companies to us who were doing exactly what we intended to do, who were regarded as being totally above board and legitimate companies."

Recruiting began, each man given a year's contract, renewable on review, with a clause stipulating that should he divulge information about Executive Outcomes, the company would sue for 100,000 rand. "I didn't want people training the Angolans and coming back and telling Unita what we were doing because it would be bad for the company and it would place our people's lives in danger."

Barlow and Luittingh spent long hours debating how and what the Angolan soldiers would be taught. "We pooled all our experience, because the guys in Executive Outcomes came from the diverse fields of the old South African Defence Force: from Special Forces, from the parachute battalion, from 32 Battalion, engineers, armour, artillery, normal line infantry, signals, medics – we had all the skills. We even had pilots who could train their pilots. So we threw all our experience into the hat and said, 'If we were commanders, and we were looking at this as a true South African unit, how would we train these guys?' And we took what we thought was the best out of everything we had, and we put that together as our curriculum."

★ ★ ★

Developing the Concept

"Once the Angolans had made an initial payment to demonstrate their commitment to the project," Carlos said, "an advance party consisting of myself as intelligence officer, a medical doctor, signals, logistics, and Special Forces experts were selected. On 23 August 1993 we discreetly departed Grand Central airport in Crause's overloaded Beechcraft King Air and flew to Cabo Ledo via Windhoek in Namibia. On arrival at the former Cuban air force base we set up HF communications and began cleaning the place in anticipation of using it as our headquarters and reception base. Our arrival was easier than six months earlier, due to the help of a few Angolan officers we'd met during the Soyo operation. Within a week we were welcoming the first complement of EO personnel."

*

Forced to think at both the tactical and strategic level, Barlow and Luittingh immediately understood that logistical and operational air support would be crucial to fulfilling the contract: shifting personnel and equipment for an operation of this size and complexity would surely require more than a couple of light, twin-engined aircraft. "That entire Soyo operation was supported logistically, medically and in terms of transporting our people by those two aircraft flying between South Africa and Angola," Barlow explained, "but this was something on an entirely different scale."

Indeed, the problems of supporting the Soyo strike force had been minuscule compared with the requirements the company faced in establishing a long term presence that would eventually include up to 600 instructors and administrative and frontline personnel. Although the client agreed to supply all weapons and ammunition,[21] South Africa was the only guaranteed source for the balance of their requirements, which presupposed a major logistics effort.

Crause Steyl was asked about the possibility of leasing a commercial airliner. Yes, it could be done. It wouldn't be cheap, but it could be done. Why lease? they asked themselves, and Steyl flew to the United States to investigate buying something that would adequately support the operation. In the end, two Boeing 727s[22] were purchased from American Airlines for a new charter company called Capricorn Systems. As the financing and paperwork was being sorted a second King Air was purchased in the US and new employees were shuttled to Cabo Ledo in the pair, jammed in with food, medical supplies, radios, rucksacks, battledress, tents and the myriad other requisites for a professional military unit.

For the Soyo contract only two black, former 32 Battalion soldiers had been recruited. Now, with the SADF being down-sized, and the inevitability of Nelson Mandela's African National Congress coming to power, blacks serving in the Reconnaissance Commando regiments and 32 Battalion saw the handwriting on the wall. The government and the new senior military officers that would be assigned to command them would not look favourably on those who had fought so well and courageously for the previous white government. So when former members of their units made discreet contact and asked them to join EO, hundreds of the best accepted and resigned from the SADF.

Because a mechanized infantry element was also envisaged, Namibians who had served with the fearsome South West Africa Police Counter-insurgency unit – Koevoet – were also recruited. As the flights brought more and more of these veterans to Cabo Ledo, there were grins of delight as white and black professionals, men who had probably shared more combat in the previous ten years than anyone else in the world, were reunited. Hugs, clasped hands, backs slapped, laughter, all done without pretence or affectation – they were scenes beyond the imagination of outsiders fed on stories of hate and antipathy between South Africans of different colours. For the new employees of Executive Outcomes, there was nothing unusual about it at all.

---

[21] While Executive Outcomes did maintain an inventory of specialized items such as secure communications equipment and NVGs, it never had its own armoury, relying exclusively on the host government to provide all weapons.

[22] To appreciate the scale of EO's logistical requirements during their subsequent 28 months in Angola, which averaged almost 56 tonnes per month, one need only look at the aircraft and flight hours eventually involved in transporting men and *materiél*: Boeing 727 – 2100 hrs; Beechcraft King Air – 2600 hrs; Antonov AN-32 – 100 hrs; Antonov AN-12 – 70 hrs; Ilyushin IL-76 – 46 hrs; Lockheed L-100 – 30 hrs.

Though designated as serving members of the Angolan armed forces by General de Matos, all were met with considerable distrust and suspicion by some of the Angolan officers assigned to work with them. Given the many defeats the Angolans had suffered during the years of war with South Africa and the daily barrages of anti-Boer propaganda, it was an understandable reaction. The hostility was such that FAA initially refused to issue them weapons, despite approval from the higher echelons.

"I think everybody understood [the reasons]," Barlow said. "However, that didn't help with the frustration, because the guys found themselves in what they considered a hostile area with no means of protecting themselves if they had to, but relying on the Angolans, and the Angolans weren't prepared to speak to them. It led to a lot of frustration. So much so that at that stage people wanted to revolt, just to do something."

Fortunately, the man selected to head up the project understood the Angolans and their culture. A recently retired colonel, Hennie Blaauw had been recruited to oversee the training of the new brigade's senior staff officers. With a background in the parachute battalion, Special Forces, military intelligence and seven years as an infantry divisional chief of staff, he was more than qualified for the job. Six-foot, florid and modest to a fault, he had earned the nickname of Oom (Uncle) Hennie for his avuncular manner. Under that wispy halo of ginger-blond hair and behind those thick spectacles, he looked, well, like everyone's favourite uncle. His self-effacing manner notwithstanding, he also had a reputation for expressing his views without regard to the opinions or sensitivities of senior officers. He would soon add to his already impressive legend as a combat leader.

"The Angolans were in a rush to get the programme underway and a location for the training camp was selected near Rio Longa, some seventy kilometres south of Cabo Ledo," Oom Hennie said. "They insisted that training commence immediately, ignoring the fact that the supporting infrastructure was non-existent. Our newly-arrived infantry, heavy weapons, medical, engineering and armour instructors were dispatched to hack out a clearing in the bush and erect tents for themselves and the expected recruits."

"Though the camp commandant, Brigadier Vileriano, proved to be an easy-going officer," Carlos said, "we were soon at loggerheads over the quality of our first intake. As far as FAA were concerned, recruitment involved press gangs roaming city streets and rural villages, abducting any youngster they happened to see, regardless of age or physical fitness. If he was big enough to carry a weapon, into the lorry he went. We very quickly made it clear that we would not train anyone under the age of sixteen, or whose physical or mental capabilities we deemed unacceptable. Vileriano was initially bewildered and then incensed by our firm position on this, seeing the conscripts simply as part of the annual quota to be fed into the Unita buzz saw. Explaining the immorality of sending thirteen to fifteen year-olds against the battle-hardened guerrillas would have been pointless. Instead, we emphasized the public relations damage should the media begin comparing the Angolan government to Liberia's Charles Taylor, who had no compunction about throwing children into combat. It took a meeting with General de Matos before our stance was reluctantly accepted."

"Most of the recruits were very frightened of the war they were being trained for and also distrustful of us – despite most of our guys being black," Uncle Hennie added. "We were the South Africans who had fought their fathers and their brothers, they'd heard all the anti-Boer propaganda, so obviously they were frightened of us as well. All of which was perfectly understandable. But the guys at Longa did a fantastic job of establishing a rapport with these youngsters in whatever way they could.

"For example, we set up a clinic where they could be treated for malaria, intestinal parasites, malnutrition and whatever other medical problems they had. Even basic dental work. Our engineer detachment started purifying water for the locals, and instead of them having to buy clean water, which is the case in Angola, they could get it from us for free. The recruits started seeing us in a different light and the locals saw us, in a sense, as saviours, because this was the first time anyone had ever done anything for them for free."

As the relationship between FAA officers and the South Africans settled down, interesting doors began to open. "[W]hen I was in 32 Reconnaissance," Barlow said, "I led a raid on a town called Cahama, and one of the generals I was speaking to frequently in Luanda had been the commander there. We got on so well that we actually sat down and analysed what went wrong on their side and how we were able to achieve what we did. I think it got to a stage where the Angolans recognised us as professionals, that we weren't there with a hidden agenda, that we were trying to give them our very best in return for the money we were being paid.

"We finally started getting bits and pieces of weaponry in, but initially we trained the recruits with a stick as his rifle. The guys at Longa taught fire and movement with recruits who had never held a rifle. We carried on in this manner with limited equipment, very limited resources under very difficult conditions. We were knocking on the doors of the generals in Luanda, trying to sort things out from the top down, but eventually we got it right and weapons started arriving, and better recruits started arriving, and we started whipping these guys into shape. It was then said to us:'What you are training now will become the 16th Brigade. You destroyed the 16th Brigade, now build the 16th Brigade.' It was said very good naturedly, but we understood the importance of it."[23]

"With only the most rudimentary facilities available, all the normal teething problems associated with new units were magnified ten-fold," Hennie said. "Nonetheless, we settled into a routine and began producing trained troops. By South African standards, their skills were fairly basic, though far in excess of what FAA produced themselves. We concentrated on a variety of disciplines, with an emphasis on offensive rather than defensive deployment due to the limited time we had been given to prepare them for combat. Unfortunately, the original concept of amalgamating them with EO and continuing their training 'on the job' was never realized."

Because of the paucity of competent soldiers within FAA, each class was immediately sent to the front, where Unita grudgingly admitted that the South African-trained troops they encountered were far better than the run-of-the-mill government soldiers they normally faced.

"It hadn't taken long to establish ourselves and bond with our Angolan counterparts," Carlos said. "That Executive Outcomes had roughly a five-to-one racial mix between black and white employees surprised senior Angolan commanders, who had been unaware that all the South African Special Forces units they had faced in previous years were predominantly black. Koevoet, the most successful counter-insurgency unit to have

---

[23] During the last major battle between the SADF and FAA, 16 Brigade was attempting to ford the Tshumbinga River as part of a determined effort to reach Unita's strategic town and airstrip at Mavinga. South African Reconnaissance Commandos, watching from the far bank, called in a massive artillery strike that virtually annihilated the brigade and its Soviet advisors.

operated on the Namibian-Angolan border, had been almost 90% black, while most of the black Recce and 32 Bn veterans were Angolans who had joined the SADF following the communist takeover of the country. All had fought with distinction side by side with whites throughout the 1976–1989 South African-Angolan war. For our former Angolans, this was the first time since 1976 that they'd had the opportunity to look for their families. There were quite touching scenes over successes and failures to locate long-lost relatives. For those who were successful, EO made a special effort to give them as much time as possible with their families."

★

Under the terms of the new contract, EO was to provide aircrew and the MPLA government to provide both helicopter and fixed-wing assets. In early October 1993 the first ex-SAAF helicopter pilots boarded the King Air at Lanseria. Five hours later the Cabo Ledo runway appeared out of the low coastal cloud base. "When we stepped out of the aircraft," Carl Alberts said, "we had no idea that it would become the scene of so much drama and tragedy." Wasting no time, they immediately wrote down their requirements for conversion onto the Russian Mi-17 and Mi-25 helicopters, then drew up a list of essential equipment such as Kevlar and ceramic chest protectors, personal Global Positioning Systems (GPS), night vision goggles, VHF portable radios, cockpit voice recorders and gyro stabilised video cameras.

One of their first appointments was with Air Force Chief of Staff General Pedro Afonso, who told them that they would soon receive conversion training on the Mi-17, but that the Mi-25 gunships had engine problems that were unlikely to be solved in the foreseeable future. It was an admission that left them crestfallen.

★

A month after the chopper pilots had their first view of Cabo Ledo, four former South African Air Force jet pilots stepped onto the tarmac, itching to get their hands on the Angolans' Sukhoi SU-22 fighter-bombers. Among them was Lieutenant Colonel 'Pine' Pienaar, who had seen his chances of promotion and getting his own squadron plummet with the cut backs in the

SAAF in the early 1990s. A Mirage and Cheetah[24] instructor, his logbook recorded over 3300 hours, with 2000 hours of operational time in Impalas, much of it over Angola in the 1980s, as well as 630 hours in Mirage IIIs and Cheetahs. "I heard that EO had openings and took some leave to have a look at the set up," he said. "The pay they were offering was good, and it looked like an interesting job so I submitted my resignation to the SAAF."

When it was obvious that they weren't going to be climbing straight into a SU-22 ground attack aircraft, the former SAAF pilots tried to convince the Angolans to give them Pilatus PC-9s. Unfortunately, the engines on all of them were time-expired and there were no new ones or overhauls coming, so they were given one unarmed Pilatus PC-7 to play with. By the end of the month they had mounted a rocket pod under each wing. "The Angolans gave us a bombing range south of Cabo Ledo and we started working out attack profiles for the rockets. We started off with high explosive warheads, tried flechettes, decided they weren't that effective and settled for the HEs.

"With only seven rockets per pod, however, it just wasn't enough fire power and we started pestering the air force to mount four pods. The problem was that though the models they had carried four stations, they didn't have the wiring to the outboard stations. Fortunately, there was a Pilatus rep in Luanda, who provided technical assistance and advice. He gave us the proper wiring diagrams, and it was just a matter of running wire looms from the dead stations back through the wings to the bus on the arming panel in the cockpit."[25]

They were eventually given access to four aircraft, two of which they mounted with four pods, one with two pods – there being no more available – and an unarmed fourth that would be used as a Telstar radio relay and command and control platform. "We spent those first months getting used to the PC-7s and the ordnance packages and getting a feel for the area, though with no helicopter search and rescue available, we didn't stray too far inland."

★

---

[24] In collaboration with Israeli Aircraft Industries, the Cheetah was the South African version of the Kfir, a modification of the Mirage III ground-attack fighter-bomber.

[25] If the world could work together as well as the various components of their PC-7s, they decided, they'd be out of a job. "We dubbed it the 'United Nations lorry'," Pine said. "It was a Swiss-built aircraft with a Canadian engine, American underwing pylons, Brazilian rocket pods, North Korean rockets, flown by a South African crew and carrying Angolan air force insignia."

Almost a month had passed before the EO helicopter contingent of Arthur Walker, Sonny, JC, Juba Joubert and Carl Alberts found themselves eagerly awaiting their first flight in a Mi-17. General Afonso flew in with instructors John Vierra and Tino Nuñes. Vierra, who had been a Mi-l7 commander for ten years, was the Angolan version of Tom Cruise, dressed in designer jeans, leather flying jacket and the obligatory Ray Bans, an ensemble he wore day and night.

"After a brief introduction, they showed us around the helicopter," Alberts said. "The fact they could speak only Portuguese was probably a good thing, as we were too dumbfounded by its condition to listen to what they were saying. Besides being filthy, there were bits and pieces that seemed to be missing, the main rotor blades were in terrible condition, and the amount of grease and oil covering the gearbox and engines guaranteed that they'd never rust!" With promises that John and Tino would return the next day with more instructors, the South Africans watched them depart, blinking in amazement that something so ill-treated could still fly.

"We were up at six the next morning, eagerly watching the sky, but it wasn't until lunch time that John and his team landed with Tomas Arbo, whose finely sculpted features reminded us of Michael Jackson. Tom didn't speak English either, so we press-ganged one of our Angolan-born Special Forces members as an interpreter, but he knew nothing about aviation and was completely baffled when it came to translating technical terms."

To the consternation of South Africans accustomed to state-of-the-art training aids, Tom began his lecture by drawing on a chalkboard a "picture perfect" image of the cockpit panel, complete with Russian instrument labels. The primitive presentation notwithstanding, Tom soon impressed his students with his technical knowledge of controls, engines and sub-systems, though his regular references to "Natasha" left them and the translator stumped. They had no idea what this mysterious woman or system was, or what she or it did. Someone with a better grasp of the language eventually explained that Natasha was a female voice tape that warned of emergencies. In Russian, naturally. They would become quite intimate with her in the coming two years.

As the South Africans and Angolans warmed to each other, the conversations inevitably turned to the previous war. There were some surprising coincidences. During the SADF's Operation *Askari* and the cross-border attack on Cuvelai, Alberts was flying an Alouette III gunship, while Tino Nuñes was crewing on a Mi-17 that evacuated the Russian contingent from the town. Two of Tom Arbo's friends were killed when squadron-mates of Pine shot down a pair of Mi-17s over south-eastern Angolan in 1985. The Angolans also mentioned the shooting down of Major Ed Every, a Mirage pilot who had been Alberts' flying instructor.

Thrown together, they soon became friends, with photos of girlfriends, wives and children passed around and admired. It was a classic example of bonding between men whose first love was flying. One of the many ironies was that, while they could laugh, joke and drink with the demon Boers, the Angolan pilots felt they could never find common ground with Unita. Regardless of any agreements that might be made between the MPLA and Savimbi, they were convinced the two sides could never live in peace.

Turning serious, Tom warned that because his new friends had joined them Unita would surely apply the pockets treatment if they were captured. Pockets treatment? Tom smiled thinly and lifted an arm. With the other forefinger, he scribed a line from the bottom of his ribcage to the hipbone. They cut you here both sides, he said through the interpreter, then push your hands inside so it looks like you have them in your pockets. The South Africans glanced at each other, cleared their throats and ordered another round of beers.

Two weeks of lectures absorbed, they were ready for their first dual instruction. After lots of hugs and hand shaking, Tom, John and Tino left for Luanda, promising that a senior instructor would be with them the next morning.

"The unmistakeable sound of a tractor was heard in time for lunch," said Alberts. "In the driver's seat of the Mi-17 was Colonel TC Abel, a short, stocky squadron commander from Luanda. After lunch, he waved us towards the helicopter and as everyone climbed into the back I was selected as his first victim. Strapping myself into the co-pilot's seat, I watched the flight engineer go through the start-up and then, with everything whipping around overhead, I waited for my first instructional command from Colonel Abel. Arms folded, he gave me a bored, heavy-lidded glance as though the world really was too difficult. 'Take off now,' he sighed. So I took off. Thirty minutes later he pressed his microphone switch a second time. 'Land now.' So I landed. Thus ended my first and last dual instruction. I moved to the back and my place was taken by the next candidate."

Two hours later the five newly-qualified Mi-17 pilots were congratulating each other, when a glowering major sitting in the back slurred, 'Me now fly'. Trailing whiskey fumes, he stumbled up to the cockpit and pulled the colonel from the left seat. When he started strapping himself in, the South Africans headed for the door, with Colonel Abel and most of the Angolans right behind them. Before Peet, the South African flight engineer, could escape, the helicopter was wrenched off the ground and began hurtling over the dispersal area.

"As he was booting in yards of rudder, throwing the cyclic around the cockpit and parking the collective up in the roof somewhere, the complaints coming from the gearbox and tail rotor were awesome," Alberts said. "Both engines started emitting thick black smoke in an effort to push out a constant 2,500 horsepower. Convinced that he was going to spread the aircraft across the tarmac, everyone bomb-shelled. He narrowly missed our Chevrolet pick-up truck where Louwrens and Juba had taken cover. When he eventually decided we were suitably impressed, he planted the aircraft on the tarmac and dragged the wheels sideways for about six metres before coming to a quivering standstill. An ashen-faced Peet stumbled out, spluttering that old 'John Wayne had been yahooing like a cowboy' while the co-pilot was cringing in his corner with his eyes closed.

"On 8 November, 1993, I went solo and what a magic aircraft it is to fly. Having loads of excess power, the Mi-17 is a very forgiving machine, smoothly powering its way through exaggerated manoeuvres that in most other helicopters would demand corrective action to recover. Juba and I flew a few circuits with Colonel Abel, followed by myself with a couple of circuits, and that was it. Later that afternoon, I was the colonel's co-pilot to our Rio Longa base to collect two generals. It was my first VIP trip after only ninety minutes on the aircraft! Our passengers said that the training at Longa was on schedule and we were still on track for our D-Day."

★

They finally received their first Mi-17, an Mi-8 MTV-1 civilian version in Aeroflot livery. EO's pilots were somewhat bemused by the idea of going into combat in a blue and white, unarmed Russian airline helicopter but remained in awe of its brute strength. When Alberts and newly-arrived Charlie Tait used it to uplift a shipping container for use as a lock-up store at Rio Longa, the cargo swing load metre registered 4,000 kilograms, a mere 1,000 kilograms over the maximum permissible load. They were impressed.

As their flight hours accumulated the South Africans became increasingly taken with the Russian helicopter in comparison to what they had flown in the SAAF. "The Mi-17's performance could be enhanced somewhat by removing extra weight intended for cold weather operations," Tait said, "and it could do with Western avionics and a more ergonomically-designed cockpit lay-out, but it is far superior to just about anything else in its weight class in a hot and high environment, and is capable of carrying heavier loads.

"In some respects the Oryx[26] compares favourably to the Mi-17. It is approximately 10,000 pounds lighter at maximum all up weight and can carry comparable loads at reasonable distances. The Oryx's shortcomings versus the Mi-17 are its limited cargo space and the need for many more skilled technicians to keep it maintained properly. Whereas the Mi-17 is a very rugged and robust helicopter with good serviceability in the field and capable of taking a real hammering – qualities that saved our lives more than once – the Oryx needs far more pampering and TLC. The reliability of these Russian helicopters was fortunate, as the maintenance facilities in Angola were of a very poor standard, or non-existent."

As soon as the South Africans received their three civilian Mi-17s they replaced the rear clam-shell doors with cargo gates and installed trooping steps and external GPS antennas. Two helicopters were fitted with 7.62 mm PKM machine guns in the door and starboard hatch as defensive weapons, and the third with a 12.7 mm DshK heavy machine gun. As a commentary on the poverty of the country, they also had to install lockable fuel caps to prevent the Angolan sentries from siphoning the tanks.

"Arthur and I flew some Angolan staff officers down to Funda to observe an EO-trained infantry battalion being put through its paces," Alberts said. "The stars of the show were four new Russian BMP-2 armoured vehicles – real bushveld Ferraris packing a rapid-fire 30 mm cannon and capable of racing through the bush at seventy kilometres an hour. To add a bit of realism, the Angolans decided to simulate incoming mortar fire by planting small blocks of command-detonated TNT. The first one was triggered just as a Russian GAZ-66 truck passed next to it, blowing all the occupants out of the vehicle.

---

[26] The Oryx is a South African upgrade of the Puma SA-330.

"The second was even more disastrous for a BMP. When the dust settled, you could see that things had not gone according to plan. The blast had blown the driver into the overhead armour plating, depositing his brains on the floor, and killing the car commander and gunner as well. It was later discovered that the Angolan explosives expert had prepared a charge of twenty-five kilograms of TNT instead of the required 250 *grams*. Although the generals were not too pleased about the fate of their new BMP, they thought the exercise was pretty nifty."

★ ★ ★

Operational Planning

In a continent where roads are scarce and the terrain difficult, conventional, European-style warfare faces additional challenges. This had been evident since the days of the Anglo-Boer War, when the horse-mounted Afrikaners developed small, hard-hitting guerrilla units that regularly humiliated the better equipped and much larger British forces. The concept was modernized and further honed from the mid-1970s by melding Special Forces with compact mechanized infantry units supported by helicopter and fixed-wing assets.

Nowhere was the concept more successful than in Angola, where the SADF consistently out-fought numerically superior forces heavily supported by Cuban infantry and armour backed by Soviet advisers and technicians. Ignoring mistakes made by the Americans in Vietnam and their own subsequent experience in Afghanistan, the Soviets never discarded the Fulda Gap mentality, relying on overwhelming numbers to destroy their enemy. If it worked for Zhukov on the way to Berlin, they reasoned, it should work in Angola.

But Angola was not the flat farmland of Germany crisscrossed by modern roads. Instead, it was as much the enemy as the South Africans, destroying or rendering useless much heavy equipment that the poorly-trained and - motivated Angolan conscripts were often incapable of maintaining. The Angolan army was also dependent on torturous, off-road logistics routes that were vulnerable to hit-and-run attacks by Unita and South African Special Forces. These problems were further exacerbated by rigid doctrine and a ponderous, poorly integrated command and control structure ill-suited to making quick, tactical decisions. At the time, all of this had played into the hands of the SADF and their Unita allies. But it was also a legacy inherited by FAA and one that Executive Outcomes now worked hard to reverse.

"We began joint intelligence and operational planning in Luanda with the Angolan high command," Carlos said. "Everything took place in 'The Fort', built by the Portuguese a few hundred years ago and used as FAA headquarters. They had a museum with various bits of kit captured from the SADF during the 1976-88 war, which they took great delight in showing us. One of the more grisly examples was the boot of a Recce who'd been killed when a charge he was setting exploded prematurely. His foot was still inside the boot."

"Amongst their various trophies were a number of South African vehicles they had captured," Ricardo added. "I was amazed to see a nearly spotless recovery vehicle which had belonged to an old friend of mine. Also on display was the camo battle dress taken from Wynand du Toit, another former colleague from the Recces, who had been wounded and captured in Cabinda.

"I was involved from the beginning in the planning, and it was an amazing experience in that I was drawing on everything I'd learned from combat experience and lessons at the staff college. We started off very much in the dark. There were no details available regarding enemy strengths, locations or capabilities, no order of battle, no intelligence assessments. Not even details of FAA's own forces were immediately to hand. We really had to squeeze everything we could out of the generals to bring everything together and come up with a workable plan. To give them credit, they gave us their total co-operation and ensured that we had more than enough space and equipment to do our task. The plan we finally presented was one Hennie didn't like at all, but the generals loved. However, once I started getting him, Rolf, Mickey and a few other senior chaps to help with the planning it was a bit easier and everybody became more positive."

To the surprise of the EO management team, a crucial asset not available to the Angolan planners was a dedicated photo-reconnaissance unit. Deciding that it was a must-have arrow to their bow, Carlos was tasked with briefing General de Matos and Sonangol's managing director Joachim David. Using examples from the previous war to illustrate the concept, he explained that the SADF almost never embarked on operations without the crucial intelligence provided by aerial reconnaissance. The proposal he put forward was to modify a Beechcraft King Air 200 by installing stills cameras, a high resolution colour television camera, as well as a Forward Looking Infra-red (FLIR) system. The latter would be capable of penetrating the very hazy conditions caused by the slash and burn farming methods in Angola, and locating targets at night. Convinced by the presentation, the two Angolan officials gave their approval and a dedicated King Air was purchased, while EO's British contacts began sourcing equipment in Europe. The installation was done under great secrecy in South Africa to prevent Savimbi's sympathizers from passing the information to Unita. As soon as it was completed, "Papa Whiskey" was flown to Luanda, where it was to be based for easy access to a film processing laboratory and video editing equipment.

In order to have a solid foundation from which to work, the South Africans spent long days putting together an armed strategic appreciation, complete with maps, graphs, intelligence summaries, levels of threat and a list of priority counter-measures. The astonished generals admitted it was the first time they fully understood the problems they faced; not even their former Soviet or Cuban advisors had come close to giving them a similar assessment of the war.

Beginning with an analysis of the threat, EO was at pains to point out that, whereas Unita were well established within their traditional areas of Jamba, Huambo, Kuito, Bailundo and Andulo, and held isolated areas of less strategic significance, they did not control the two-thirds of the country they liked to claim. The fact was, that government forces held more cities and ground than their enemy, but were constantly reacting to Unita's more aggressive hit-and-run guerrilla tactics.

One of Unita's major strengths was its control of most of the primary east-west land route that bisected Angola from Luanda on the Atlantic coast to the Zairean border. This 1,000-kilometre strategic highway was moderately safe only as far as N'Dalatando, 250 kilometres to the east, where Unita occupied the high ground. Should a convoy fight its way through the permanent ambush mounted there, it could proceed with only marginal confidence to the besieged city of Malanje, situated roughly in the middle of the country. Another 130 kilometres beyond Malanje lay the Lui Bridge at the narrow mountain pass at Xa-Muteba, also controlled by Unita. Thus, the FAA garrisons in the eastern provinces of Lunda Norte and Lunda Sul were surviving only by air resupply. The brutal fact was that most of the country was cut off from its capital.

The second strategic problem was that Unita funded its war efforts through the sale of diamonds taken from the Cuango River area in Lunda Norte province. Cafunfo, the centre of its diamond operation, was also where Savimbi received essential war *materiél* flown in by mercenary pilots from Zaire, Zambia and Uganda. Until that source of funding was denied them and the airstrip captured, they would remain a potent force.

However substantial these problems, they were not irreversible. "We recommended that EO and attached FAA units be given the task of opening the route from Luanda to Malanje," said Carlos. "At the same time, a second mixed force should be flown to the encircled Lunda Sul provincial capital of Saurimo. Once the threat to Saurimo and its airfield was neutralized, they would advance towards Cafunfo from the east, while the first task force would drive towards Cafunfo from the west."

When the FAA high command endorsed the overall plans for the offensive, a list was examined to decide who would serve as the senior EO advisors and combat leaders for the eastern and western fronts. 'Rolf', a former lieutenant colonel and highly experienced mechanized infantry officer, was selected for the advance to Cafunfo from Saurimo, while Hennie Blaauw would lead the drive to Malanje and from there to the objective.

"In early January I was told that a joint EO-FAA planning session was already underway," Hennie said, "but it wasn't until 24 January that Rolf, Mickey and I were summoned to Cabo Ledo and asked for our ideas. I had already examined the problem and recommended that 16 Brigade move to Malanje, establish a firm base and then launch a massive air strike on Cafunfo, followed by a heliborne assault. Brigadier 'Dolphin', the EO project leader, and 'Ted', EO's chief of staff, rejected it out of hand. A week later we were again ordered to Cabo Ledo, this time to be briefed on a plan to airlift 16 Brigade and its equipment to Saurimo, while a second combat group advanced from Luanda to Malanje. The two independent forces would then drive from east and west in a pincer movement towards the town of Cacolo, consolidate and then advance to Cafunfo.

"I had serious doubts about its feasibility. Because the diamond fields were vital to financing its war efforts, Unita would do everything it could to defend them. Savimbi's guerrilla and semi-conventional forces were masters in the use of mines, small unit penetration attacks and stand-off bombardments – tactics we had taught them during the South Africa-

Angolan war and which had proved successful time and time again against FAA's annual dry-season offensives. As far as I could see it was a plan that allowed Unita to use what it had so ably learned from us to its best advantage. 'You're trying to put a drip on a corpse,' I told them. Not amused, Dolphin said this was the plan and it was my job to work out the details.

"Unfortunately, personalities, egos and branch rivalries were at work here," Hennie said. "The major problem within the EO management structure was the preponderance of former members of the parachute battalion. During the Namibian bush war against Swapo insurgents, 1 Parachute Battalion had typically been used in a fire force rôle for stringently limited follow-up operations after contact had been made. Their knowledge of conventional warfare was limited to what they'd learned at staff college, while they had no experience whatsoever in long-term clandestine guerrilla operations, of which the Reconnaissance Commandos and 32 Battalion were absolute masters.

"Another limiting factor here was that, unlike the Reconnaissance Commandos, 32 Battalion and Koevoet, 1 Parachute Battalion was an all-white unit and, except for the Permanent Force cadres, was composed of national servicemen called up for their annual service. Thus they had no experience in working alongside black soldiers or in joint planning or co-operation with senior black officers as many of us had with Unita in years past. Because they didn't understand the culture or mindset, there was often a lack of consideration and diplomacy towards the FAA high command, resulting in frustration and friction on both sides."

★

More than internal politics was giving the company headaches. A concerted effort was still being made by the South African Department of Foreign Affairs and Military Intelligence to neutralize or close them down altogether. To their surprise, a number of South African journalists in Pretoria, Johannesburg and Cape Town found themselves treated to expensive lunches where they were fed exclusive stories from unattributable sources. Despite the absurdity of the stories, they nonetheless caused EO a certain amount of indigestion.

"The first story that came out was that we were out to assassinate

Savimbi," Barlow said, "and that I'd been paid - personally been paid - I think it was twenty million dollars to kill him. When I was asked for comment on that I had to laugh, quite honestly, because at no stage did the Angolan high command even suggest that Savimbi had to be killed. Their aim was to end the war on the battlefield. However, what people don't realise is, that if we were paid twenty million dollars to kill Savimbi he'd have been dead a long time ago and we would have had a lot of change in our pockets. But that wasn't what we there to do, and it wasn't what the company was established to do.

"Then came the story from the military on a secret document [sent] to unit commanders at battalion or regimental level, that Executive Outcomes was of grave concern to the SADF; that we should be shut down as quickly as possible; that we were lying to people in our recruitment by saying they were going to protect oil wells; that we were contravening exchange control laws, income tax laws, international laws, every possible law; that unit commanders must advise all members of their units not to apply for work with Executive Outcomes; and that it was in the best interests of the SADF that we were taken out of Angola. Now, I don't know where the SADF's interests lay in Angola in late 1993, but that was, in brief, what the signal said. Of this so-called 'secret' signal, we got 32 copies. We had to phone the police to come and take possession of them [because] I thought we were being set up for being in possession of classified military documents.

"Then an article appeared in the Afrikaans paper *Die Rapport* stating that we'd resorted to cannibalism and were eating our comrades and that our people out there were forgotten, that we'd just left them to fend for themselves. The *Sunday Times* [of South Africa] intimated that we were smuggling diamonds and weapons out of Angola into South Africa. One of the Afrikaans papers - I think it was *Beeld* - stated that we were training [white supremicist] hit squads. Another article subsequently stated we were training the ANC's hit squads. We were then accused of being a destabilising force in Angola, when, in fact, we eventually brought the war to an end, but they wanted us out of there immediately. It was then stated in an interview that a journalist allegedly had with me in a hotel in Paris – I wasn't even there at the time he mentioned – that we'd suffered serious casualties in Angola and had to hide that from the people in South Africa; that we were in Angola purely to take over all the diamond and oil concessions, and making ourselves very rich. Then there was a story that Lafras had skipped South Africa with all the money that had been paid to us for the contract in Angola, and that I at some stage had also skipped the country with all the money."

"In the lead-up to the elections in South Africa," Carlos said, "which everyone knew would be won by Nelson Mandela's African National Congress, the old SADF pension-watchers were queuing up to ingratiate themselves with their soon-to-be new masters. The man tipped to be the new minister of defence, Joe Modise, was briefed by military intelligence that we were actually the Third Force, a super-secret organization dedicated to disrupting the approaching elections. Furthermore, that we were in Angola preparing a counter-revolution that would take place after the ANC had taken power. Fortunately, Eeben is a very capable intelligence officer himself, and had frequent talks – I wouldn't go so far as to say he *recruited* anyone – just friendly chats with people inside military intelligence. As a result, we were kept up to speed on some of the machinations going on behind the scenes. In an inspired move, he took the bull by the horns by approaching a senior ANC official and inviting him to inspect our operation in Angola."

★ ★ ★

Eastern Front HQ Saurimo

On 5 February 1994 the senior EO staff boarded an AN-26 transport aircraft for Saurimo to inspect the eastern staging point for the planned offensive. After a bumpy two hour flight, they spilled out into the tropical heat and humidity and silently shook their heads.

The airfield complex was in total ruin. Rusting tanks, broken aircraft and sagging fuel bowsers lay among waist-high grass between dilapidated buildings. The tower held an empty control panel sprouting a tangled spaghetti of snipped wires. Propped on empty ammunition crates were portable radios powered by truck batteries, and sitting on a rusty folding chair was the controller, a binocular with one working lens hanging from his neck. Split and flattened oil drums had replaced the former roof, and more covered the rotting floor. It was hard to believe that none of the damage was the result of combat.

They were introduced to General Sukissa, the youthful commander, who briefed them on known enemy strengths and positions in the Lunda provinces. They were immediately taken with the towering Sukissa, a Chokwe prince and womaniser of great renown.

"When the governor general arrived, we were treated to *hors d'oeuvres* and very civilized small talk," Carlos said, "before being shown into the dining room for a long and leisurely lunch on starched linen. It was somewhat surreal. Here we were, surrounded by a determined enemy, while smiling and attentive waiters dished up gourmet courses on fine china and filled our glasses with very respectable Portuguese and South African wines. And all the while we were chatting pleasantly with the generals about subjects that had nothing to do with the war. You'd never have thought there was a war.

"The next morning we inspected our proposed quarters, a complex of buildings and hangars inside the Saurimo base, all built around a soccer pitch and previously occupied by the Cuban air force. We had more discussions with General Sukissa and his staff, who promised their complete co-operation. Shaking hands all round, we boarded our AN-26 for the flight to Luanda. Late that afternoon, Ricardo and I were back in Cabo Ledo and already planning the move."

★

As the time drew nearer for their departure, the helicopter pilots set out to militarise their three civilian Mi-17s. Flying down to the Rio Longa base, they talked their heavy weapons expert out of a Russian AGS-17 automatic grenade launcher, then headed for Luanda's international airport, where the Angolan air force had its bone yard of derelict aircraft.

"What we needed was a ball joint that would allow the gunner to swivel it about and shoot at people we didn't like," Carl Alberts said. "We were stripping parts off a weathered Mi-25, when a FAA security officer arrived and in machine-gun Portuguese told us that what we were doing was a big *problema*. Absolutely forbidden. Nodding in rhythm to his waving arms, we smiled and continued, growling that the wrecks were treated like they were sacred, whereas the few serviceable ones were treated in a way as to make them sacred as quickly as possible."

They were called in to explain everything to General Afonso, who gave them *carte blanche* to continue their depredations and even conceded to a request for four 23 mm cannon pods and another two AGS-17s. Their fertile imaginations also came up with a requirement for a few 100-kilogram bombs. They were going to turn the Mi-17 into a bomber, they explained, by rolling them out the back. Laughing uproariously, the general agreed, but begged them to be very careful. A few years earlier one of his helicopters had been turned into confetti trying to deliver one.

★

"Everything had been well planned, so setting up our Saurimo HQ and getting the people there was not that big a job,"Ricardo said. "First to arrive were the headquarters personnel, with me as operations officer and Carlos on the intelligence side, as well as a small protection unit and two Chevrolet

78

pickup trucks. We immediately began setting up the comms centre, ops room, sick bay, kitchen and stores."

Rolf's BMPs were ferried two at a time in the cargo holds of Russian Il-76 heavy transport aircraft. Forbidden to drive them in or out of the Ilyushins, the South Africans were finally asked to take over after two of the aircraft were damaged by FAA drivers. The newly-arrived armour was deployed on the western side of the town as a deterrent against an anticipated Unita attack from Mona Quimbundo thirty-six kilometres away. They were ready to receive the air wing.

"With two ferry tanks installed in each aircraft," Alberts said, "we climbed into our steeds at 2 a. m. on 22 February for the 815 kilometre flight. Mine was so heavily loaded with steel cupboards, bombs, guns, ammunition, beer, ration packs, beds and the weight of the extra fuel, that it was impossible to get the wheel chocks out in order to taxi. It was only after pulling a handful of collective to lift the squashed tyres a bit that the chocks could be removed. After a long take-off run using virtually all available power to get airborne, we inched our way to altitude in a black, moonless night and checked our new Magellan 5000 GPS. Our two Mi-17s and one PC-7 headed for Saurimo.

"With a separation between the helicopters of ten minutes and 500 feet, we routed direct, Arthur and I chain-smoking Chesterfields all the way. Acutely aware that our lives depended on the mechanical integrity of our Russian helicopters, our eyes kept flitting nervously over the aircraft instruments. Dodging thunderstorms, we reached Saurimo without incident, but JC and Juba lost their GPS fix making a rapid descent under the weather and were sucking fumes by the time they found the airfield. We were all relieved to feel solid ground under our feet.

"We moved into an open plan building previously used by the Cubans as a political indoctrination and lecture room. Although more spacious than our accommodation at Cabo Ledo, the piles of 'human landmines' deposited by the more recent FAA inhabitants imparted an aroma that lots of scooping and scrubbing failed to entirely eliminate. Not in the habit of doing 'it' around our beds, we dug a long-drop topped with a pair of truck springs and an ammunition case with a suitably shaped hole. For a shower, we suspended a two hundred-litre drum from a tree and filled it with buckets of river water which, surprisingly enough, was very clean and drinkable."

★

As the chopper pilots settled into their homes, Ricardo and Carlos were putting the final touches to the tactical HQ. The ops room was soon covered in maps of various scales, as well as graphs and statistical charts for monitoring reserves, personnel strengths and status and, most importantly, a flow chart to couple plan to execution.

Each snippet of intelligence that came in was added to the map and a picture of the enemy's locations and strengths slowly began to develop. The positions and strengths of FAA units were also plotted. Having the first accurate regional order of battle in the hands of their former South African enemies initially caused the Angolans some discomfort and anxiety. Old habits die hard. The intelligence section, where Carlos had his computer and extra maps, was divided from the ops room by a low wall and adjoined the communications centre. This was permanently manned by two signallers who had comms with forces in the field and then backwards to Luanda, Cabo Ledo and, when necessary, Pretoria. Ricardo and Carlos slept next to the signals room in case of an emergency and to monitor the duty signallers.

Under Carlos, the comm centre also had the responsibility of conducting signals intelligence in conjunction with the Angolans. Despite Unita's attempts at communications security their codes were soon broken and sigint became a major source of intelligence. Still, what was intercepted had to be treated cautiously, as the South Africans had previously tutored Unita in the art of deception.

To further ensure their own communications security, EO used state of the art frequency-hopping HF base stations as well as backpack HF hoppers. They also employed data encrypted transmissions compressed into data bursts, giving them three counter-measures against interception. From interrogations of prisoners and intercepts, they learned that Unita was unable to read or DF their transmissions. On the other hand, EO's latest generation HF scanner meant no amount of frequency changes by Unita could conceal new ones, while equally sophisticated DF equipment was able to pinpoint Unita positions.

"FAA was enormously impressed by all of this," Carlos said, "and were soon using our net, much to the dismay of Unita, who had previously gleaned much information from their own intercepts of FAA radio traffic."

Knowing that casualties were inevitable, Ricardo selected the room closest to the soccer field-cum-helicopter pad as the sick bay. With an adequate operating theatre, six beds and modern resuscitation equipment, it was manned by a qualified medical doctor and experienced ops medics capable of treating everything from serious trauma to malaria. When the injured were flown in by helicopter, they would be stabilized, then flown directly to Lanseria on "Tango Romeo," the dedicated casevac King Air 200B, and transferred to the nearby Olivedale Clinic.

"As soon as the sick bay became operational it was swamped by local troops and their families asking for treatment they couldn't get from their own doctors," said Carlos. "The demand was so overwhelming that our medical supplies were rapidly depleted and we had to request more from Pretoria. Ricardo and I suggested to the governor that he make a formal request to the United Nations or Médecins Sans Frontières for a clinic. Neither was able to supply the personnel, however, so we opened a bi-weekly clinic for the very appreciative *povos.*[27]"

Supply stores are part of any military establishment, and it was no different for Executive Outcomes. Locked away behind steel mesh were reserves of fresh food, field ration packs, webbing, freshly-charged nicad batteries for the radios, and canteen items such as cigarettes, beer and toiletries. Storemen who had learned their trade in the SADF kept strict control and demanded signatures for everything before grudgingly handing it across. They were particularly humourless about accounting for ammunition, weapons and other equipment supplied by the client, which was a bit rich, given FAA's own extremely lax system. After work the area doubled as EO's pub, signposted by the non-combatant admin and support personnel as *Gang Goggas* Corner, Afrikaans for "Corridor Insects." Between deployments to the field, the men could unwind with a few beers and listen to a ghetto blaster playing the latest hits.

"On the liaison side, things were a little complicated," Carlos admitted. "General Sukissa was the local commander, and anything that dealt with Saurimo came under his thumb. Barely thirty years old, he was African royalty, being a hereditary prince of the Lunda Chokwe tribe, very switched on with a network of powerful friends that stretched back to Luanda. On the operational side, however, we dealt with General Mendez, a thin, light-skinned mulatto whose behaviour towards us bordered on the

[27] Povo – Portuguese-Angolan slang for the local population or peasants.

hostile. He was soon supplanted by the quieter and more helpful General Marques as overall operational commander. Eventually General McKenzie[28] arrived and, much to our relief, reorganized the command structure so that everything went through him. The air wing suffered the same problems, only worse. They took their operational orders from Luanda, but had to go through Colonel Gino, the airfield commander, for access to the helicopters and PC-7s, then another senior officer for fuel and a third for ordnance. It could get very frustrating for them.

"There were other political cliques that frustrated us as well. Brigadier Pepe de Castro, whom some of us had met when he was the FAA commander during the Soyo contract, had been named as the ground commander for the advance on Cafunfo. He had highly placed friends whom he consulted privately and regularly and General Marques was often powerless to overrule him. It was a system that seemed designed for inefficiency."

★

"Charlie Tait and I shared a veranda in the ex-political conference centre," said Alberts, "and soon had it fronted with a metre-high wall of sandbags topped with a couple of PKM machine guns and plenty of ammunition. Our living quarters looked like a mechanical workshop, with welding machines, cutting torches, grinders and compressors, as well as piles of PC-7 rockets and all sorts of big guns we hoped to use against the enemy.

"We were still unsure about Unita's anti-aircraft capability, but it was likely that they were using their diamonds to purchase things more threatening than stock options. They definitely had plenty of 14.5 mm AA weapons and the deadly two- and four-barrelled 23 mm cannon. We also knew they had stocks of SAM-7 surface-to-air missiles. More disturbing, however, were unverified reports that they had bought SAM-16s from China, which gave any operator who got the hang of the technology a virtually guaranteed hole in one.

"To make our helicopter a less conspicuous target, Mike and I spent two

---

[28] General McKenzie, a black Angolan despite the Scottish *nom de guerre* (which even his wife used in public), had been a senior Unita officer prior to the 1992 national elections. When Savimbi rejected the results and returned to the war, a disillusioned McKenzie remained in Luanda and joined FAA as Deputy Chief of Staff of the Army and right hand man to General Luís Faceira.

days covering the blue and white Aeroflot colours with olive drab and Desert Storm brown in a SAAF camo pattern. We really liked the paint job, but some of the FAA pilots said that it looked so much like a SAAF Puma that we were likely to take fire from friendly forces thinking Savimbi was getting South African help again."

They had finally mounted the AGS-17 grenade launcher on Albert's helicopter but firing trials were quickly abandoned when the 30 mm weapon bucked so wildly that it threatened to hit the main rotor blades. Sighing, they chucked it back in the storeroom and addressed themselves to the 23 mm cannon pods. Although the Mi-17s weren't wired for them, Peet reckoned he could run a cable from the pylon-mounted pod into the cockpit and wire it to a simple push-button switch that would activate the firing solenoid. But without a technical manual, they were unable to get them to fire more than one round. Hauling around single-shot, breech-loading cannons seemed a waste of fuel and time, so these went back in the crates, too.

They'd by-passed the idea of rolling 100-kilogram bombs out the back for mounting a 250-kilogram bomb on each of the six pylons. Although the muscular Mi-17 wouldn't complain about hauling the load, there were one or two minor drawbacks. The optimum altitude they'd chosen for accurate bombing – from a hover, no less, for pinpoint accuracy – was 8,000 feet. This might place them out of range of small arms fire, but 14.5 mm and 23 mm anti-aircraft guns would have no *problema* making very big holes in their helicopters. It was also the optimum altitude for a SAM-7, and in a hover they'd be pushing out an infra-red signature no self-respecting surface-to-air missile was likely to miss. A SAM – never mind a lucky large-calibre bullet – was sure to deliver lots of Mi-17 spare parts over a very big piece of Angola.

After much effort and long technical discussions over a few beers, they finally ended their efforts to convert the helicopters to bombers and gunships. It was a sad day.

★

"Unita was operating quite brazenly all around Saurimo," Ricardo said, "and, in fact, there was a contingent near the bridge over the Tchicapa River, just five kilometres outside the town. One of our first jobs, therefore, was to secure the immediate area by pushing them thirty to forty kilometres back. Carlos and I spent long hours wrestling with the int/ops plan and decided that once we'd chased them away from the town, we'd begin to attack bases within their areas of control. While we were working on this, most of our personnel busied themselves with camouflaging equipment, doing rehearsals, zeroing their weapons on the range and plenty of marksmanship training. The rest of the ruff and scruff were lying around and talking about how they were going to fuck up the enemy. I knew from the beginning that I'd have to keep my eye on this second lot."

"Ricardo had taken a few days' leave and Christo was filling in for him," Carlos said, "when General Sukissa dropped in and asked if one of our choppers could fly him out to the Lauchimo River to check a couple of FAA positions. The area seemed safe enough for a single ship flight so I rousted out some of the guys for a security detail and we took off for Catoca, one of Angola's largest Kimberlite pipes.[29] It was the site of a huge mining complex built by the Endiama Corporation, which wanted to know if the area was secure enough to resume operations.

"We landed and Sukissa was immediately mobbed by admiring *povos* and soldiers, all wanting to shake the prince's hand. A tour of the complex revealed that the troops and local peasants were putting their time to good use by panning for diamonds. The young general explained that they were *garampinos,* the term for illegal diamond diggers, and were only doing what anyone would do in their circumstances. On the flight back Sukissa asked Juba to take us a little higher for a better view of the area.

"We were thudding south along the river, when he saw a rock outcropping and said he'd like a closer look. Inasmuch as we were practically still within sight of Catoca, I gave my approval. Juba descended across the river, with Sukissa, Christo and me hanging over the back. Getting closer, we saw a lot of people running and assumed they were more *garampinos.* Suddenly, Sukissa was shouting and gesturing to break off and get away. In his haste to relay the message to Juba, Christo's parachute battalion beret was dislodged and sailed out the open tail. As we turned away and started climbing, I asked the boy general what was wrong. They were Unita running for their weapons, he said, laughing uproariously.

"Later that day, radio intercepts confirmed that we had surprised a group

---

[29] A Kimberlite pipe is a geological phenomenon of volcanic origin containing diamonds.

of rebels who were very upset by a 'FAA' helicopter flying over 'their' side of the river. We teased Christo unmercifully about the fact that there was now a Unita troopie wearing a very nice Parabat souvenir. If there had been any doubt in the rebels' minds that the South Africans were back and allied with FAA, that beret had dispelled it.

"Although we weren't exactly under Sukissa's command, except for matters dealing with Saurimo, he took full advantage of our helicopters to keep his presence known to the *povos*. But he was such an engaging and enthusiastic chap, that we were usually happy to oblige. One morning he came into the ops room and told Ricardo that the governor wanted us to pay a confidence-building visit to Saidi Mingas. Straddling a strategic bridge on the road to the diamond areas of Lucapa and Dundo, its FAA detachment had been attacked at first light.

"Landing in an open area near the town hall, we were somewhat perplexed that the waiting crowd didn't come rushing towards us. I kept everyone on board until the rotor blades wound to a stop. When the dust settled, we were greeted by wildly waving arms and worried faces from twenty metres away. Eventually a FAA troopie walked very gingerly towards the choppers and explained that we had landed in the middle of a minefield! Cautiously tiptoeing to a safe area, General Sukissa and I had discussions with the mayor and a traditional chief, who demanded that our South Africans be available for follow-ups after any future attacks. Sukissa consented in principle and we lifted off with the dead and wounded from the morning's fight.

"A few days later the locals at Dundo on the Zairean border insisted that we pay them a visit as well. Ricardo and Sukissa flew up in the King Air and were treated to a traditional gourmet meal that included worms and various other creepy-crawlies that I was pleased to have missed. The important thing about these visits were that they sent the word to Unita that we were prepared to support outlying areas and these town were not attacked again."

Meanwhile, Hennie and his team had been busy assembling their forces for the western front attack.

★

Western Front Spearhead

"On 18 February we were again summoned to Cabo Ledo for a planning session," said Oom Hennie. "There we met General Marques, who would control the operation from Saurimo. The stocky, pipe-smoking general confirmed that part of the overall plan would be the advance of our armoured combat group from Luanda to Dondo and from there to Malanje. The plan was to shuttle the tanks in stages on seven available low-loaders to an assembly area outside Dondo. Mickey, a very experienced South African armour officer, plus his staff of instructors from Rio Longa, would join the last shuttle to ensure that the combat group arrived complete.

"On 2 March I flew to Dondo, from where General Marques and I departed for the combat group's headquarters at Dange-ia-menha. We were met by Brigadiers Sachimo and Mandinu of the 16th and 45th Brigades whom General Marques briefed on the battle plan. Mandinu would secure the Lucala River bridge, then allow 16 Brigade to cross on its advance towards Malanje. Protection forces from 45 Brigade would then follow to protect Sachimo's logistics and rear elements.

"Until 9 March 45 Brigade was busy deploying three platoons of nine newly-arrived T-62 main battle tanks to reinforce elements clearing the road up to the crossing. At the same time I was involved with the detail planning of 16 Brigade's movement across the Lucala, and then the advance towards Malanje. Everyday I joined Brigadier Sachimo and his staff officers in planning, preparation of maps, lectures on mobile warfare techniques and general contingency planning. The latter included defile drills, immediate counter-ambush drills, laager techniques at night with the whole combat group setting up a temporary base, protection of the laager and joint infantry-armour operations in general.

"The terrain between Dondo and Dange-ia-Menha was covered in thick bush and forest and ideally suited to Unita's small-unit guerrilla tactics, and over the first two weeks FAA logistical convoys were regularly hit. Ambushing at short range with anti-tank weapons and then disappearing into the bush made pursuit by the armour-heavy FAA almost impossible.

"On the morning of 10 March Mickey and his staff of fourteen EO armour officers and instructors arrived with the remaining elements of 16 Brigade. I brought them up to date with a detailed briefing on the situation, and the next morning they began organizing the tank battalion, allocating drivers, crew members and support personnel and prepared to start training the armour crews. This led to a major disagreement between us and Brigadier Sachimo. He and his officers believed their crews were already fully combat capable and saw no need for further training. We finally persuaded him to allow Mickey to make his point by organizing a little shooting competition. Mickey selected a large granite outcropping on a mountain slope a kilometre away and invited the tank gunners to hit it. There was a lot of very satisfying smoke and noise, but none of the shells landed anywhere near the target.

"Fortunately, two officers from the Directorate of Army Inspection were there to evaluate the standard of battle readiness and agreed with our assessment. Their report, which Sachimo refused to believe, caused a bit of friction between us, but in the end he was persuaded to hand over the training to Mickey and his instructors. Time was running out and they made every effort to upgrade the standards of gunnery and battle drills and maintenance, and after about ten days we began to see a remarkable improvement.

"On 14 March two Dauphin helicopters arrived at Dange-ia-menha with Chief of the Army General Luís Faceira, General Nando, General Marques, General Nindo and their senior staffs. The aim of the visit was to confirm the detailed plan of action for 16 Brigade's advance towards Malanje. The brass departed a few hours later, happy with the plan and wishing us good luck."

The ever-present problem of small scale guerrilla attacks against 16 Brigade's logistics tail was overshadowed by the possibility of either a full scale battalion-strength night attack (a favourite tactic Unita had learned from the SADF in years past) or, more likely, penetration teams of section to platoon strength slipping through Dange-ia-Menha's defensive perimeter. What made it even more probable was that this position had changed hands so many times over the years that Unita knew the ground very well, to include the locations of FAA's mine fields.

"We had a couple of false alarms," Hennie said, "with troops swearing they saw something and cutting loose. Most of the time it was their imagination, but resulted in the entire perimeter, to include tanks, anti-aircraft guns, and even D-30 artillery guns lighting up the sky with a lot of fireworks. Of course, the Angolan troops had every reason to be nervous. Not long after 45 Brigade moved up to the Lucala, a daring Unita penetration team slipped through the perimeter and cut the throats of eight soldiers in their sleeping bags.

"Unita succeeded in penetrating 16 Brigade's defences on two occasions while I was there. My black EO interpreter and I were the only South Africans present when the first attack came, but it was fairly insignificant, with one Unita soldier found dead the next morning inside the perimeter. The next one was more serious. We were sleeping in Brigadier Sachimo's quarters when, at 0400 on 15 March, I woke to the sounds of gunfire. It was sporadic, a few bursts, a pause, a few more shots – then suddenly it escalated into a massive volume of fire from every available weapon around the defensive perimeter.

"My first thought was that it was a typical over-reaction by the Angolan troops. Then I heard in-coming mortar bombs exploding along the north-western part of the perimeter. I didn't know enough Portuguese to understand what Brigadier Sachimo was saying over his radio, but the expression on his face and the speed he was dressing told me it wasn't a false alarm. He snapped at my interpreter, 'There's a problem outside,' and headed out the door, with me right behind him. Tanks were firing, DAF-mounted 23 mm guns, machine guns – just an earth-shaking roar of heavy and light weapons. It went on for about ten minutes, before gradually dying down. Only the mortars continued, then they also finally stopped. The first reports coming over Sachimo's radio confirmed that we had definitely been the target of a Unita penetration attack.

"About an hour later everything was back to normal and I went around checking on Mickey and his guys, who with good foresight had dug themselves holes soon after arriving a few days before. To my relief, none of them had been injured. At daybreak three dead Unita guerrillas were found inside the base on the north-western side. Next to the bodies were disposable light anti-tank weapons, as well as a new generation M-72 LAW complete with its missile. Scattered across the area of the attack were AK-47s, a couple of PKM machine guns, ammunition belts and dozens of white phosphorus grenades. A number of blood trails were also discovered.

"A little later two wounded rebels were captured and brought into the base. Brigadier Sachimo asked Mickey if our ops medic would tend to them. After their wounds were cleaned, stitched up and bandaged, they revealed they had been part of a company-strength group split into a penetration unit of about forty, a back-up reserve and a fire support group with 82 mm mortars. They told us where the fire support group had been positioned and Sachimo sent out a heavily armed force to investigate. Alongside the depressions made by the base plates were large piles of mortar bombs. This had been quite a determined effort to destroy the armour.

"The next day another of the attackers was captured. During interrogation he said that they believed Dange-ia-Menha's defences had been denuded when 45 Brigade deployed to the Lucala River. When they crossed the defensive positions, they were staggered by the massive fire from 16 Brigade and forced to withdraw. He also confirmed that a number of wounded who escaped had died of their injuries."

On 16 March Brigadier Sachimo received a change in the battle plan. While 45 Brigade would continue to hold the Lucala River crossing, 16 Brigade would now take an easterly detour along the northern side of the Kwanza River before swinging north again to the main Dondo-Malanje road, before swinging east to Malanje. "To me, this was a safer option," Hennie said, "in that 16 Brigade would now be on a secondary road approximately fifty kilometres south of the main road, minimizing the possibility of Unita harassing its rear echelon logistics elements. But it required a complete change in plans, preparations and briefings."

★

By the last week in March everything was ready. Final briefings had been conducted, tank crews upgraded, logistics elements were in place and the troops had been paid and issued new uniforms, boots and rucksacks. Hennie and 16 Brigade waited for the green light from Cabo Ledo to launch the operation. Nothing happened, however, and they continued to fine-hone the training and preparations.

"At the end of the month we received a signal that the EO contingent and all its equipment were to be airlifted back to Cabo Ledo the following day and take leave prior to the operation. I couldn't believe it. A three-week delay would mean new intelligence assessments, new briefings, getting the troops psyched up and ready again. For the sake of operational security alone we should complete the operation now. Our anticipated time frame for taking and consolidating Malanje and the surrounding area was fourteen to twenty-one days; surely it was better to go now and then take leave. But the decision had come from General de Matos himself, and my objections fell on stony ground. Even worse, on our arrival at Cabo Ledo I was informed that we were no longer part of the western front combat group and that when we returned from leave we would once more take up our former training duties. I was sick with disappointment."

★

Unknown to Hennie or any of the EO senior management, General de Matos had delayed the advance on Malanje in favour of an attack on N'Dalatando, without the South Africans' involvement.

"I happened to fly into Luanda the morning of the election in South Africa," said Eeben Barlow, "and was sitting in General de Matos' office with someone whom I will not mention.[30] [Because] of the media coverage we were getting in South Africa he wanted to see what we were doing in Angola and I had invited him to fly up with me. He asked General de Matos how satisfied they were with the training we were giving them. Now bear in mind that this ANC guy came there with his own frame of reference: we'd fought them, after all. General de Matos said he was extremely satisfied with the training, and we would soon know just how satisfied.

"That was the morning that the first [EO-trained] combat team took the large Unita base at N'Dalatando, with four men killed. Then, about two days later Lieutenant Antonio Lopes, the liaison between Executive Outcomes in Luanda and the Angolan high command, told [Dolphin],

---

[30] Tokyo Sexwale, a senior member of *Umkhonto weSizwe*, the armed wing of the ANC

'The first combat team have done bloody well, and the generals are very chuffed.' No one yet knew what the result of our training would be. Would we be the same as the Cubans? – who did not teach them much. Would we be the same as the Russians? – who really weren't bothered about them. Or would we be pro-Unita and train them in the wrong things? That was a major concern to them. But the results of this spread like wild fire throughout the Angolan army."

"After their meetings in Luanda," Carlos said, "Eeben flew Sexwale down to Cabo Ledo, where he was given a first-class guided tour of the project, and he was openly astonished at the number of blacks in Executive Outcomes. All his questions were answered within the security strictures established by General de Matos, and Sexwale took home a glowing report on us. The rumour-mongers at Defence Force Headquarters were furious."

*

By the time Hennie and his staff were ordered back to Cabo Ledo, a dramatic string of events had already taken place on the eastern front. If there had been any doubt that they were facing an extremely dangerous foe, that doubt had been dispelled.

★ ★ ★

Midnight Extraction

"With the arrival of Papa Whiskey, aerial reconnaissance became a daily event," Carlos said. "Though these flights inevitably compromised the operation, it wouldn't have taken a brain surgeon to realize that our presence at Saurimo meant an attack on Cafunfo. What we didn't want them to know was our route. Ricardo and I had priority in tasking the recce bird, and were soon making good use of it over the intended route of advance and locating potential targets. It was of immense value in testing the viability of our planning. Later on, when feedback was urgently required, the King Air would land at Saurimo so Ricardo and I could run through the tapes on the aircraft or, if something of immediate tactical significance was spotted, it could be transmitted in real time to our Tac HQ. This was an enormous advantage and the Angolans were astonished by the technology. Papa Whiskey was kept very busy throughout our time there."

Although they suspected that Unita had become somewhat complacent, there was little doubt the rebels would react quickly and robustly to the threat of an armoured advance. In the past they'd done well against FAA's annual offensives aimed at Mavinga, though much of their success had been the result of direct SADF support. But one thing Unita had never been threatened by was a competent and aggressive air force. As soon as aerial reconnaissance had identified a few suitable targets, Ricardo and Carlos decided it was time to start shaking their confidence with air strikes.

*

"We didn't arrive at Saurimo until 10 March 1994," Pine said "and on the same day flew our first combat sortie against a Unita command element at

Muhango, the Unita area headquarters a few kilometres south of Xingi.

"Taking front and back seats, Louwrens and Goose, and Lenny and I did the strike. We hit the headquarters at last light with rockets and took a few of the buildings out, with no return fire or any other resistance. Louwrens followed me along the road towards Saurimo and I fired my remaining rockets into a small group of troops. They were ready when Louwrens passed them and he took a hit through the wing."

"When I heard Louwrens say on the radio that he had been hit," Carlos remembered, "I grabbed our King Air pilot and we bolted from the comm centre, jumped in our Chevvie pickup and raced for the runway. We were airborne in no time at all and as soon as we had Louwrens visual I could see a trail of Jet A1 streaming from the wing tank. We followed him back and he put the airplane down safely. I met him as he was climbing out the cockpit with a huge grin on his face. His first remark was that he had plotted the spot from where the fire had come and wanted to go back and take it out.

"Louwrens and Pine were typical jet jocks in the sense that they loved flying and nagged us incessantly for sorties. Their enthusiasm was infectious and they would spend hours in the ops room looking for any excuse to fly. If anyone was in trouble on the ground, these two guys would do everything, break any rule, to help. Both were slightly-built, good-looking and so energetic and determined that Ricardo and I had our hands full keeping them occupied. Daniel 'Skeeries' Scheurkogel, our non-combatant personnel officer, would wander in and listen spellbound to their debriefs and practically beg to be allowed to get a ride in the PC-7's back seat, but they'd catch Ricardo's warning eye and politely refuse.

"Saurimo had been surrounded for over a year and a half, surviving only through air resupply. The nearest Unita element was north-west of Saurimo at Daru, five kilometres to the east at the Luachimo River bridge and another approximately fifteen kilometres south on the Dala road. Most of these withdrew when they became aware that the town had been heavily reinforced by 16 Brigade and Executive Outcomes. When Unita's withdrawal from the immediate area became known, the atmosphere in Saurimo became far more relaxed.

"Among our first priorities was dealing with the sizeable enemy force at Mono Quimbundo, which we decided would be a conventional, joint EO and 16 Brigade operation. Concurrent with that would be a ground reconnaissance of Cafunfo and the nearby enemy base at Cuango, to determine how well they were defended. Using all of EO's manpower, we also decided to hit at least one Unita base along the route to Cafunfo with a large Special Forces attack. All four operations would take place over a 72-hour period, starting with the recce missions."

"I told Meno to select the recce teams," Ricardo said, "and gave him ample time to work out the ops plan. My basic guidelines were that they picked their landing zones properly, moved only at night, and if they were compromised then they aborted the mission and followed the time-tested rendezvous system of emergency, main and alternate RVs. If for any reason they couldn't make any of the pickup points, they were to escape and evade to the south and then east along the Cuango River.

"Meno picked two experienced small team operators from our days in the Recces, gave them their orders and maps and a free hand to work out their own operations. We attended the briefings they gave their teams, before Meno personally checked the forty-five to sixty kilos of equipment that went into each of their rucksacks."

In anticipation of these missions, the helicopter crews had already been practicing night formation flying and establishing routes that avoided Unita bases with known concentrations of anti-aircraft weapons. The biggest problem was weather. It was the middle of the rainy season, when clouds often came down to the ground, making navigation difficult. But it would also cover the landings. When everyone was satisfied, the teams blackened up and boarded the choppers.

Flying 300 kilometres in cloud and rain, the helicopters dropped Renier, Steyn and Handsome at their pre-selected landing zone some twenty kilometres from Cuango at last light on 18 March. After making dummy insertions, they headed north at low altitude to insert Simon and his team on their pre-selected LZ some distance from Cafunfo. Each team of one black and two white South Africans would carry out a four-day reconnaissance of its assigned area before being uplifted. But only two nights later an emergency call came from Simon. They were in trouble and needed to be extracted immediately.

It was approaching midnight when JC and Juba ran for their helicopter and took off in heavy rain, followed by Charlie and Sonny. In the back of each aircraft rode an eight-man protection element. Soon afterwards, the

PC-7 Telstar broke ground and flew ahead to establish comms and relay the team's GPS position. After ninety minutes of low-level instrument flying, Juba began calling. The response was immediate. Simon, Rich and Willie were on the run, a group of very determined Unita hard on their heels. The helicopters turned towards his position.

"We were about 300 feet above ground and it was very dark," Juba remembered. "Thick mist lay in the valley but as we flew over Simon's position we could see his strobe light flashing. As we came around I told Tattie [Charlie Tait] in the other helicopter to maintain his altitude and talk us in to the pick-up point. This wasn't going to be easy, but as Puma commanders in the SAAF, JC and I had flown together in similar conditions in the Drakensberg Mountains and had no doubts about each other's ability or what tasks each of us had to perform. Behind us, Percy was equally experienced and aware of his job as flight engineer. As soon as we were settling into the LZ, he would be our eyes.

"We set up our approach from about half a kilometre and as we descended into the mist visibility immediately deteriorated. Instead of looking straight down through a hundred feet of misty cloud, we were now looking obliquely and everything was solid. Not only did Simon's strobe disappear, but we couldn't see the terrain ahead of us."

Inside the darkened cockpit Charlie's reassuring voice came through their earphones. They were on course for the waiting team. Trees loomed directly under them and JC eased the descent, windscreen wipers beating back and forth. Rain ran in streams along the side windows.

"We saw the strobe just off to our left," Juba said. "As JC turned I was giving him the instrument read-outs and Percy keeping us aware of what was below. We were wrapped inside a cloud, everything closed around us, especially in front, where the landing light made a white wall as we air-taxied towards Simon. The next moment the landing light penetrated the mist and we saw trees and a rock face rising vertically in front of us.

"*Pull up!*"

"JC was already lifting the helicopter over the escarpment, taking us just above the layer. We looked back and saw our path clearly marked where the downwash of the blades had blown the mist aside. There was the strobe. JC brought us around again, keeping to the right of the first approach. It was hard not wondering how close Unita were. We heard the steady voices of Charlie above and Simon below giving us minor corrections."

Then the LZ appeared in the harsh glare of the landing light. Hacked out of the trees and undergrowth by the *povos* for planting their cassava, it lay on a thirty-degree slope. Hemmed in by the cliff face and trees writhing under the rotor wash, JC tried to squeeze the bulky Mi-17 closer to the ground. There was a slight bump as the nose wheel touched, but the three Recces couldn't reach high enough to pull themselves in. With the light and noise telling the approaching Unita exactly where they were, Juba glanced to the right and saw that if they shifted over slightly they could get lower. But first, he told JC, they'd have to prune that dead tree.

Okay.

JC eased to the right and started a slow descent. A blizzard of rain-soaked branches exploded against the fuselage. Behind the cockpit machine guns and assault rifles pointed into the rain and swirling mist.

Percy talked him down, ignoring the hammer blows as the middle of the rotor disk hit the trunk and began to eat down it. Trim tabs were ripped from the 34-foot blades. The tree trunk grew thicker and increasingly heavy vibrations slammed through the helicopter. Lower trees started losing branches. The collective control in JC's right hand shuddered alarmingly, instruments a blur in the dancing panel.

There was no way of knowing how badly the blades had been damaged or how much more they would take. If the helicopter started to go down, they'd try to land under power, join the recce team and, with luck, escape and evade to where Charlie and Sonny might pick them up. But the Unita force were running towards them, RPGs shouldered and ready as soon as they had a clear shot. If that happened everyone on board was dead or on the way to agonizing torture and execution. The only other option was to say fuck it, haul the team on board, pull power and hope the helicopter didn't come apart in mid-air. Then …

"Okay, okay! Hold it!" Percy shouted into his mike. The protection element started pulling the team in. Willie. Rich. And finally Simon. *"We've got them! Go!"*

With the aircraft shaking wildly, JC drew up on the collective, praying everything would hold together. The trees fell away in the opaque mist – a quick jab to switch off the landing light, everyone holding his breath – and they were flying – but towards the torches of the approaching enemy. Muzzle flashes sparkled in the rain. Then they were past them, tracers in their wake. As the chopper picked up speed the missing trim tabs sent the blades flexing uncontrollably, making the shaking even more violent.

They nursed the damaged helicopter ten kilometres before finding a marshy clearing big enough for both helicopters. Shutting down but leaving the auxiliary power unit running, they hurriedly inspected the damage as the recce team and protection element transferred to Charlie's helicopter. Percy's voice suddenly came through the earphones.

"*Start up, start up! We're sinking!*"

The wheels had already disappeared into the swamp and water was lapping over the tailgate. Hands were a blur over the switches, there was the muffled, blow-torch roar of the two turbines lighting off, eyes watching the power come up, and as the blades started turning Percy was already shouting, "*Pull power! Pull power!*"

"I looked back to see what was happening," Juba said, "and the tail rotor was like a boat's propeller in the water."

Swamp grass clinging to the undercarriage, they dragged their way out of the muck and turned for Saurimo, a waterfall cascading from the back. The tension burst and the two pilots were suddenly doubled over with laughter. For the next 300 kilometres the blades flapped away on their individual tracks, threatening to wrench the aircraft apart. Between bouts of hilarity, the crew gave silent thanks to the Russian designers.

During Simon's debrief he said that after the drop-off they had made their way through heavy bush to within sight of Cuango the first night and found a hiding place. Unfortunately, the next day some locals literally walked into Willie and escaped to raise the alarm. Soon afterwards, a Unita follow-up operation began. In the shoulder-high elephant grass, any attempt at anti-tracking was out of the question. They were chased all day and into the evening, with Unita using torches to follow their spoor and occasionally closing to within 200 metres. They had been very close indeed when the helicopter arrived. But even while being chased, Simon was able to see that Unita were definitely preparing to defend the source of their most strategic asset.

★

"On the same morning our three helicopters were tasked with moving FAA troops for the attack on Mono Quimbundo," Alberts said, "but the other two helicopters had just returned from pulling Simon and his team out of the shit so only mine was available. Arthur and I landed at first light on the outskirts of Saurimo, where General Sukissa had set up his tactical headquarters. The first problem was the ninety troops expecting three choppers to load thirty troops each. Shouting over the roar of blades and engines, I gave a FAA colonel the new plan. We would load as many as we could for the first lift and then come back for the rest.

"A line of troops shuffled towards the aircraft. They appeared to be about sixteen years old, each laden with his AK-47, some RPG rockets, a couple of 82 mm mortar bombs, a plastic bag full of AK-47 rounds and an opened Portuguese ration pack spilling sausage and bean tins along the road and into the helicopter. Some shuffled in new boots, some in flip-flops, some barefoot and some with only one boot, with his buddy behind wearing the other one. Mike was trying to count the ragtag combatants climbing in and finally put up the 'bus full' sign when the first one on was being pressed into the cockpit. I couldn't believe it when this little guy calmly reached out to the centre console and helped himself to my lighter and one of my Camel filter cigarettes!

"In a storm of empty rat pack boxes, we got airborne with half of Angola's defence force on board for the ten-minute hop to the first landing zone. The first drop was to coincide with a rocket attack by the PC-7s, followed by Rolf's bombardment with his BM-21 multiple rocket launcher. Ahead of us I saw rockets from the first airstrike exploding. We were rudely reminded of the artillery strike by a salvo of 122 mm rockets exploding not too far from us. We politely mentioned this to Rolf, who thanked us for the accurate corrections and placed the next lot in the town.

"Once Rolf had used up all his rockets, the EO contingent withdrew and left FAA in place. Because we had been briefed by General Sukissa that any vehicles outside specific grid references would be enemy, FAA received clear orders not to move until after the attack. But then, figuring orders were what they made of them, they decided to shift a few kilometres closer to the town and shot off some of their own rockets."

"I was overhead in the Telstar, with Ricardo in the back seat providing fire control corrections for the artillery," said Pine. "We were orbiting about ten klicks from the target when I saw a big cloud of dust and smoke on the ground, and then the flare of what looked like a surface-to-air missile heading for us. At 8,000 feet, we were right in the heart of the SAM envelope and I broke into it, pulling hard into a six or seven G turn, then climbed like hell to 15,000 feet to get us out of range.

"By this time I'm on the radio, yelling for our guys to get their pods reloaded and come back and give us a hand. We're within sight of the airfield, where Lenny and Goose are scrambling and the docs are preparing the operating theatre, so at least I know we're close enough to make it back if we take any damage. We're up there feeling edgy and I'm explaining what had happened to Ricardo, who's just lost his breakfast from all our violent manoeuvres. Suddenly, there's another cloud of dust and smoke and the bright trail of another rocket. I was absolutely furious at whoever it was that had the bloody cheek to shoot a *second* missile at me. This time we locked eyes on where it had come from and spotted vehicles. Lots of vehicles. All outside 16 Brigade's assigned area.

"When Lenny pulled alongside, I explained exactly where the launch site was and he went in for the attack, rippling all four rocket pods. Tragically, what I had thought were SAMs had been BM-21 rockets fired by FAA. Their initial trajectories had been directly towards us. It was a classic case of the Angolans ignoring battle plans – in this case moving their forces and using the rockets when they'd specifically been told not to – and six of their people were killed in our attack."

"We were offloading the third and last group one kilometre out of town," Alberts said, "and amidst all the bangs and smoke, we got a call for casevacs. We landed a short distance away from the BM-21 and filled up with broken and moaning wounded, some of whom we'd brought in only thirty minutes earlier."

"The debrief that followed was somewhat tense," Ricardo said with typical understatement.

★

"A few days earlier I had given Braam the task of putting together the large Special Forces attack and selecting a target," Ricardo said. "He'd picked Xingi, a Unita logistics base. His Plan A was to ambush the general who was reported to operate out of the town, and if that failed, Plan B was to hit the base with mortars and withdraw. I gave it my approval and they began their preparations."

"Mono Quimbundo was still smoking from the morning's attack, when we loaded Braam's guys and took off at last light," Alberts said. "We low-levelled the 140 kilometres and made two dummy insertions before dropping them about five kilometres west of the town. Night had fallen and as they piled out I could see cooking fires in the enemy base up on the escarpment. If we could see them, chances were that they could hear the choppers and I figured our guys were in for a good punch-up. When we returned to Saurimo, Carlos had already intercepted Unita radio messages that they had seen and fired at our helicopters, which came as a surprise as none of had been aware of any ground fire."

The ops room lost contact with Braam and just before sending up a Telstar to re-establish comms he came through on the HF radio to say that the locals told him Unita had poured out of Xingi when they heard the helicopters and were now searching for him. The team was still making its way through heavy bush towards the road, but it didn't seem likely that any Unita general was going to be using it any time soon. The next morning the inevitable contact occurred and Polly went down with a bullet through the thigh. Braam called for an uplift and two helicopters were scrambled in bad weather. From about ten kilometres out, Alberts started calling.

"'Braam, Braam, this is Carl.' I waited. Nothing. 'Braam, Braam – Carl, do you read me?' Silence. I continued the run-in at tree-top height and tried again. Still no answer. We passed over the LZ without seeing him and still nothing on the radio. After repeated attempts on the VHF radio, I switched to the Saurimo HF frequency. Bingo! I could hear Ricardo talking to him, but could not hear Braam answering. I broke in to ask what the hell was happening.

"'Braam is heading for the secondary landing zone,' Ricardo said. 'The enemy is in hot pursuit.'

"All of a sudden, a breathless Braam came through on the air-ground frequency, saying they couldn't make the primary landing zone. Unita were right behind them and they were heading for the alternate LZ. He gave me a bearing and rough distance from Xingi, which put them almost within small arms range of the town. We turned towards them, praying Unita had no anti-aircraft weapons deployed on the escarpment. Even if they didn't, I could imagine mortar crews following our progress, waiting until we landed before stonking us. Tension in the cockpit was ratcheting up as we flew closer.

"Then we spotted them crouched in low bush. The LZ was a bitch, lying on a slope surrounded by large trees only one kilometre from the town. I landed as far forward as possible, main rotor blades clipping the leaves of the nearest tree as Charlie Tait dropped in behind me. Seconds ticked by with agonizing slowness as Polly and the mortars were lifted on board. *Come on, for fuck's sake!* Unita had to be closing fast. With visibility barely five metres in thick bush, we wouldn't see them until it was too late and just one RPG would ruin our whole party.

"It's difficult to describe the feeling of impending doom while on the ground. It felt like an eternity waiting for the guys to board. With every second that ticked by, everyone in the helicopters held his breath. This is where we were most vulnerable, sitting on the ground with thudding rotor blades and screaming turbines telling the enemy exactly where we were. You didn't want to be here. You wanted to suck the collective up and get the hell away, but you couldn't leave your friends. You were their only hope of seeing tomorrow.

"Then the last man was in, everyone accounted for, and there was a voice in my earphones telling me to *Go!* I rolled in power and drew the collective up, bush shaking under the rotor wash, then eased forward and we were over the trees, staying low and heading for home. The relief in getting airborne unscathed was always enormous and invariably led to a very happy and 'wet' debrief back at base. Another respite, another party with much joviality. Until next time."

★ ★ ★

Searching for the Recce Team

Nothing had been heard from the second team of Renier, Steyn and Handsome Ndlovu.

Reconnaissance teams have strict radio schedules. If they fail to make comms at specified times, it could be for a host of reasons. They might be too close to the enemy to risk being overheard, they might be on the run, and there's always the possibility that their radio is malfunctioning or the batteries dead. But with one sched after another producing only static, more faces gathered round the radio for the next, checking watches and brows furrowing deeper. Something was clearly wrong. Everything else was put on hold and a search and rescue operation launched. The first day they found tracks that had probably been made by the team. They returned to Saurimo to refuel and set off again. And again. The search took them south and then east along the Cuango River, the predetermined escape and evasion route. Nothing. Landing after last light, the air wing gathered in the ops room to trace their search patterns on the wall map and discuss possibilities and options, before grabbing something to eat and a few hours' sleep.

They lifted off at 0430 the second morning, with Alberts and Arthur carrying Shaun's team, and Meno's team riding with Charlie and Sonny. Two armed PC-7s had Goose and Lenny in the front seats, with Pine in the Telstar.

Arriving at sunrise, they started at the primary pick-up point and a nearby position where tracks had been seen the previous day. Lenny and Goose circled overhead, trying to raise Renier on the HF radio. The two helicopters, with the teams hanging over the sides, flew at tree-top height. Any hint of tracks saw them land, investigate and take off again. With a substantial enemy presence situated on high ground to the west, the helicopters were certainly visible to the enemy garrison. A well-maintained road led out of Cuango to the south-east, where there were additional enemy camps, the closest just six kilometres from the team's primary extraction point. Four days of helicopters and PC-7s criss-crossing the same area had already told Unita that the South Africans were conducting a search and rescue operation. It seemed inevitable that the rebels would deploy teams to shoot them down.

The helicopters again flew out to the primary pick-up, where they located two spoor heading towards the emergency pick-up point, and a third paralleling them some distance away. From the air they couldn't tell if it had been made by man or animal, but at least it gave some indication of life and raised hopes. An hour later they'd seen nothing more and with fuel gauges telling them it was time to go, headed for home. On the way back they drew fire from a village near Lubalo, but low gauges held them on course.

"Emotions were running high on our return," Alberts said. "After a short debrief, the aircraft were refuelled and with a group of our rapid deployment force, we set out for the village where we'd taken fire. The PC-7s put a strike in and our teams were dropped on the outskirts. Within half an hour, not a single hut was left standing. The message was very clear. If Unita fired on our aircraft from a village, we would destroy it."

They returned, refuelled again and set out for the long flight back to Renier's pick-up point. After locating the spoor seen the previous day, they dropped Shaun and his team with Koevoet trackers, who quickly established that the tracks belonged to Renier, Steyn and Handsome and that at that stage, they were still carrying their full kit. After following the spoor for a while, they came across Unita tracks criss-crossing it, and later more enemy tracks on top and going in the opposite direction. Fearing an ambush in the dense undergrowth, the team was uplifted to continue the search from the air.

Although the terrain was operationally friendly for the most part, there were large areas of shoulder-high elephant grass where both man and animal left clearly defined trails. But they found nothing that hadn't been seen on previous searches. The search was extended to the very outskirts of Cuango, where the PC-7s and helicopters drew 23 mm anti-aircraft fire. After a lengthy debrief back at Saurimo, it was decided that if Renier's team were still in the area, they would have made some attempt to signal the searching helicopters. They had a HF radio for communications to Saurimo and three VHF radios for ground-to-air comms. Even if all their radios had broken, they had strobe-lights, flares, heliographs and day-glo panels to attract attention from the air. There was no doubt that Unita were tracking them, but if they had been shot or captured, surely something would have been heard through radio intercepts. Another possibility was that the team had walked into a booby trap and were lying dead in the jungle. But it was all guesses, what if's and maybes.

"We started taking our searches closer and closer to Unita lines," Carlos said, "staying at branch-trimming height. I was sitting on the jump seat between the pilots as we flew precariously close to Cuango two days after their last pre-planned pick-up. We passed over a cluster of huts and, having drawn no ground fire, I impulsively keyed the mike and asked the pilots if they were willing to land so I could speak with the *povos*. Our protection team was out the back as soon as the wheels touched and I hopped out to face the astonished locals.

"Before anyone could react we had bundled one of them onboard and lifted off, fully appreciating that we'd pushed our luck far more than was prudent. When I looked at our new passenger, I was surprised to see a willing and grinning passenger giving us a double thumbs-up. Back at Saurimo he told us that he'd been press-ganged by Unita and was to be sent to a training camp, when he escaped and hid in the village. Our 'abduction' had actually been a rescue! When questioned about the missing recce team, he said that everyone had heard about one black and two white foreigners who had been captured and taken to Unita's Jamba headquarters in the south.

"He also happily volunteered Unita positions around Cuango, adding that the day after we went to look for Renier the first time, a Unita platoon arrived at his village and shot three of the *povos* for not informing them about the helicopter movements. Because his abduction would probably mean more retribution, he had no desire to go home and ended up working for us as a labourer."

General de Matos flew to Saurimo to discuss the missing men with Ricardo. He said that Unita were claiming to have captured twelve foreign mercenaries, including two whites. There was no explanation for Unita's exaggerated claims, but few of the South Africans believed that, given talk of the barbaric 'pockets' torture, their colleagues would have been captured without a fierce fight.[31] Nonetheless, EO's Padre Thinus accompanied Brigadier Dolphin and Lafras to South Africa to inform the next-of-kin, then issued a press release stating that the men had been unlawfully kidnapped while on a training exercise. It was unlikely that anyone believed it, but President dos Santos, who still didn't want to advertise that he was employing South Africans to fight his war, insisted on the cover story.

"Despite all this fairly convincing intelligence," Carlos said, "the choppers and PC-7s were in the air 24 hours a day for a week, calling on the HF frequency, checking the primary and alternate rendezvous points. We flew dozens of missions until we were sure in our own minds that there was no chance of them making an appearance. Ricardo admitted that calling off the search was the hardest decision of his military career. They were declared missing in action."

★ ★ ★

---

[31] Savimbi had gone on record as saying any mercenaries captured by Unita would be summarily executed. This was somewhat hypocritical, inasmuch as Unita had a long history of employing Moroccan, Zairean and South African mercenaries. Additionally, his entire logistical air support was flown by an international melange of freelance soldiers of fortune flying out of Kinshasa, Lubumbashi and Point Noire in Zaire, N'dola in Zambia, and Entebbe in Uganda.

Camaxillo

"The generals were pressing us to attack Camaxillo, another Unita logistics and transit point," Ricardo said. "We agreed and I selected two mortar teams and protection groups, each totalling twenty-three men, and sent them to ranges for a lot of retraining whilst we waited for a deployment date. Rather than an early morning attack, which both FAA and Unita usually favoured, we decided to hit them at siesta time, when the heat made everyone lethargic.

"On the afternoon of 2 April they were preparing to board the helicopters, when the Boeing came in from Pretoria. Some of guys returning from leave came running over to ask if they could join the operation. One was Padre Thinus, who, even if he was unarmed, felt he should be supporting the men with his presence. I appreciated his concern, but told him that his place was in the church and not on a dangerous op like this. Willy, an experienced team leader, asked if he could accompany us and I gave him the nod. Then Kallie, our camera man, also pleaded to go. I wasn't happy with it but he was so insistent that I finally said he could come along if he really wanted to."

The heavily armed teams boarded the helicopters and lifted away from the soccer field. Ninety minutes later, escorted by two PC-7s acting as top cover and a third with Pine in the Telstar, they were approaching Camaxillo.

"As mission leader for this attack I decided that I'd land first and Charlie to follow," Juba said. "One of the PC-7s flew ahead and confirmed that the chosen LZ was suitable, but when I saw it I wasn't impressed. Barely 600 metres east of the town, the only natural obstacle between it and Camaxillo was a small stream. But there wasn't another suitable LZ within range of the mortars. It was so close that after dropping the team I had to make an immediate left bank to avoid overflying the town.

"As Charlie came in behind us, JC and I made two decoy landings some distance to the south, then our gunners opened up to keep the enemy in their trenches. Charlie and Sonny dropped their team and lifted off to the north-east to stay clear of the rocket attacks and the mortars. Because the Mi-17's Russian radio can only monitor one frequency at a time, we stayed on the air-to-air frequency so that the Telstar could keep us informed about the ground situation. What none of us in the air knew was that an enemy force was very close to the LZ."

At this point some of the men on the ground later said they heard voices from the nearby bush, but the message was not passed on and no one in the circling PC-7s saw anything. Because of the difficulty in spotting the fall of the mortars and relaying the information, the attack took almost forty minutes to complete.

"I heard the ground force commander telling the mortar teams to finish the last bombs and get ready for the pick-up," Juba said. "We were setting up our approach, when Sonny asked if they could go in first.

"'Negative, I'm on final approach already,' I told him. It was one of the most fateful decisions of my life. I went in, picked up my team and lifted off to the south to wait for Charlie and Sonny to join us."

"I waited until JC and Juba had taken off," Charlie said, "and as soon as they were clear I brought us around on a nice, easy approach and settled in. The guys were getting on, when, not five seconds after touchdown, we heard and felt small arms rounds slamming into us. Everyone was diving for the helo while the port and starboard PKMs opened up to try to keep the Unitas' heads down, anything to give us time."

"I was sitting on the jump seat between the pilots," Carlos said. "The elephant grass around us was flattened by the rotor wash and beyond it was thick bush concealing Unita. I was just about to light a cigarette, when they opened up. They were close enough that I could clearly hear their gunfire over the sound of engines and blades. The two PKMs blazing away must have suppressed them somewhat, but there was still an incredible amount of fire punching through the aluminium skin, most of it concentrated on the back of the helicopter. I saw Willy take a hit and then saw four guys still outside go down. Suddenly jet fuel was spewing everywhere. I was sure we were going to be incinerated when it ignited, or stranded and cut to pieces by the incoming fire. My combat webbing got snagged on something, and as I was struggling to move, Mike unceremoniously yanked me out of the seat."

"I was overhead," Pine said, "when the radio went crazy, everyone screaming about taking fire not from the town, but from behind them. I heard Tatti say he was taking hits, someone else was shouting that they were taking fire from the town *and* from behind them as well. The other two PC-7s rolled in. Not having any target indication, they rippled their rocket pods into Camaxillo and as close to the Mi-17 as possible."

Three men had been hit inside the helicopter. Medics scrambled to help as the door gunners swept their PKM muzzles across the bush. Others inside were emptying magazines out the open tail in long continuous bursts of suppressive fire. Holes were opening up everywhere in the fuselage, bullets leaving little clouds of insulation in their wakes. Entire sections of the insulation panelling were hanging down and fuel was pouring from the ferry tanks and overhead tanks. Bullets passed through backpacks stuffed with RPG-7 rockets. If one of those took a direct hit, the helicopter and everyone on board would go up in a fireball. In the cockpit, Charlie was wondering if all the team were inside yet. The idea of leaving anyone behind was unthinkable, but it was decision time.

"Not knowing how many of our people were still on the ground, I was trying to decide whether to flee or not to fly. In the middle of the tremendous roar of both in-coming and out-going fire and the sound of the blades and engines the flight engineer's voice came over the intercom system.

"'The guys inside are taking hits!'

"Natasha, the Russian audio warning for emergencies was screeching and the No 2 engine oil pressure warning light was illuminated. If we didn't go now, we were going to be stuck and everyone was going to die. There was no choice. I pulled collective and we got airborne, firing still going on full blast from us and the Unitas on the ground. Our transition wasn't very graceful, but we were out of that hellhole and I was just trying to fly the beast. Keep her airborne! The co-pilot and flight engineer were assessing the damage and we were all wondering if we were going to make it home. We had three wounded guys in the back, one of whom was going to die if he didn't get treatment soon. Fuel was everywhere, a haze of Avtur being blown through the back. Visibility inside the cockpit and through the windscreen was not good and fuel was streaming down on us from above. I turned south, shouting for someone to switch on the wipers.

"Fuel is on the inside of the windscreen!" Mike shouted back.

Oh, shit.

A fine mist started to fill the helicopter. Rusty was leaning outside, spraying the countryside and sending hot shell casings from the PKM blowing back inside the helicopter to land in Charlie's flying overall. Realizing the consequences if the fuel ignited, everyone stopped shooting.

Juba and JC had cleared the area to wait for Charlie and were out of range of the VHF ground-to-air radio. In the heat of the moment the airborne commander in the back of the Telstar failed to relay what was happening.

"It took longer than it should have for Charlie to appear," Juba said. "When I saw him, there was vapour streaming from their chopper. JC and I had heard nothing on the radio about a fight and thought they must have punctured the tanks on a tree stump. When I told them that they were pissing fuel, Sonny replied that they'd had a contact. He was so matter-of-fact about it, that we didn't appreciate how serious the situation was. One of the PC-7s had gone ahead to locate an emergency landing zone and JC confirmed that we'd pick them up there."

Charlie still had hopes of getting the helicopter back to Saurimo, but first he wanted to get some of his passengers out of what had become a flying bomb.

"By now we were two kilometres from the LZ," Charlie said. "It still wasn't a safe distance but we had to land in order to transfer the wounded to the other helo. The only choice I saw was an LZ littered with short tree stumps. Keeping our fingers crossed that we weren't going to land in another nest of Unitas, we set her down and the wounded and a number of the others transferred as quickly as possible. We got airborne again and my satisfaction at not landing on a tree stump was cut short by Sonny's voice.

"'Main gearbox pressure zero! Main gearbox temp is against the stop! Fuel 800 litres. We've lost 1,000 litres in five minutes. We've got a serious fire hazard!'

"I didn't know how close the Unitas were, but if we stopped then we didn't have the firepower to defend ourselves. I decided to push on past the next big river coming up just to give the bad guys a bit of an obstacle. As soon as we were past it I picked an LZ big enough that JC and Juba could also get in to pick us up. We landed and lost little time shutting down and unbuckling. I grabbed my survival gear and maps and headed for the door, wondering where the other helo was, when someone shouted, 'Rotor brake!'

"'Fuck the rotor brake!'

"We scrambled out of the helo and there was Juba coming in, the defensive guns ready to give us covering fire if the bad guys suddenly pitched up. We sprinted for it, leaping on board in a tangle of weapons and kit. There was a quick, final check to make sure we were all there, and the helo lifted off. As she made the transition and picked up speed, there was an audible sigh of relief in the back. We were the lucky ones. The four friends we'd had to leave behind were probably dead."

"Even with 42 on board – twenty more than recommended – I got airborne without having to pull emergency power," the imperturbable Juba said. "The PC-7s stayed in low-level formation with us until the sun disappeared about half-way home, then climbed higher while we maintained low level on the radio altimeter. I glanced into the back and thought about the confusion right after we'd landed to take the wounded from Charlie's helo. As we'd gotten airborne, Percy started shouting that we must go back to pick up the people who'd been left behind. Thinking he meant the LZ we'd just come out of, I banked sharply to get myself on downwind, when Percy said, no, no, the original LZ. That required a quick, hard decision. It was obvious that we were going to have to abandon Charlie's helicopter. That left just mine. Unita were waiting for us. If we went back and were shot down, then we were all behind enemy lines, with no chance of rescue. So I'd shaken my head and followed Charlie."

"The cigarette I'd just started to light when everything went to shit had gone," Carlos remembered. "I can tell you that by the time we'd gotten out of there, landed once to transfer the wounded and then a second time for the rest of us, I definitely needed one. But I had to get a smoke from someone else because mine tasted like jet fuel."

They headed for Saurimo, the ops medics working on Quinton. The other two wounded were Willy, who'd been shot through the arm, and cameraman Kallie, who had picked up shrapnel in one arm. They landed on the soccer pitch and Quinton was rushed to the sick bay and then to the King Air with a doctor and medic. He was unconscious, still barely alive and hung on until reaching South Africa. He died as they were transferring him to the ambulance.

"As soon as they got back I called in both teams, the chopper pilots, PC-7 pilots and Sarel the airborne commander for a debrief," Ricardo said. "We went through the sequence of events from landing to uplift. The conclusion I came to in the end was that some of the people on Team One heard voices or movement to their southern side but did not advise the team leader. Clearly, it had been a Unita patrol operating on familiar ground very close to its home base.

"Everybody was very emotional that night and a number of our guys demanded we launch an immediate search and rescue mission. It was one of the hardest decisions of my life, but I refused. Unita knew how we felt about losing guys and would be waiting for us. I wanted them back as much as anyone, but we didn't need to lose more of our people. They even appealed directly to the pilots, but the chopper guys understood how slim the chances were of a successful rescue and not one of them agreed to fly.

"It is still unbelievable that Unita didn't use RPGs while the aircraft were on the ground or while they were getting airborne. When they had the opportunity to kill a chopper and everyone on board, they blew it. Unita kept very quiet about the contact and no radio intercepts were picked up that would shed any light on the fate of our colleagues."

"It was a huge propaganda success for Unita," said Carlos. "They took the bodies to Cafunfo and journalists were flown in from as far afield as Portugal to have a look. Unita eventually released a photo of three dead whites to the international media. Under the title 'Not a pretty picture,' it was of poor quality and the bodies were somewhat disfigured, preventing positive identification. Everyone was hit really hard by their deaths."

*

"The helicopter side of the air wing had taken quite a hammering," Alberts said. "My aircraft, which Charlie and Sonny had borrowed, was lying in the bush near Camaxillo, and JC and Juba's aircraft, despite a complete blade replacement, still had a pronounced 'gallop' feel after their tree chopping episode. With the deaths of some of our men, the fate of the others uncertain and the loss of our helicopter, Unita's morale and confidence was probably at an all-time high. Given our reduced air assets, we were somewhat limited in altering that confidence any time soon. The South African newspapers were full of fanciful talk about a peaceful settlement between the MPLA and Unita. Nothing could have been farther from the truth."

* * *

Airstrikes and Rumours

Much to their satisfaction, Ricardo's determination to take the war to the enemy saw the fixed wing pilots spending more and more time in the air. "With full fuel and four pods, the PC-7 had about three hours' endurance, plus a fifteen minute reserve at 240 knots, which gave us a reasonable radius of action in searching out targets of opportunity," Pine said. "Though the aircraft wasn't set up for them, night sorties were much more effective than day missions. Because there were no civvie vehicles in the area, anything that moved was Unita and with our NVGs we could pick up their headlights from quite a distance. On our first night mission we destroyed three trucks and from the intercepts Carlos started getting, Unita were extremely worried by this new development.

"We were using third generation night vision goggles that we had acquired privately, but the problem we ran into was that the amplitude of the instrument lights interfered with them, so we had to switch the lights off entirely. Fortunately, chemical illumination sticks didn't bother the NVGs so we'd tape one inside the cockpit and then just peek under the goggles when we wanted to check the panel.

"On 28 March Carlos told us that the Unita commander at Muriege was getting married and maybe we should pay him a visit. It was an excellent example of the quality of the intelligence he was getting that he knew not only what time the wedding party would be, but the specific building where it was to be held. We arrived overhead at 2200, saw lights blazing on the ground and rolled in. We went through some 12.7 mm ground fire and put our rockets right into the reception party. Carlos picked up intercepts that the bride and groom escaped, but a number of guests were less fortunate. Unita was learning that they were no longer safe in their rear areas.

"We soon started having problems with the pods. The North Korean rockets dirtied them quickly, leaving a residue that interfered with the electrical connections, so quite often the rockets simply refused to fire. The Angolans just shrugged and couldn't be bothered to clean the tubes, so we had to take on the job ourselves. But even then, they were never one hundred percent reliable.

"While all this was going on, we were still pestering the Angolans to let us fly their SU-22M4s, which is really a fantastic aircraft in the ground attack rôle. You could call it the Russian version of the Buccaneer, and the only operational mud-mover they had. From a distance they appeared to be quite new, or at least extremely well maintained, and were the pride and joy of the Angolan Air Force. Our requests went right to the top and eventually came back approved, but in the end General Afonso - who was a SU-22 pilot himself - said no. So we were stuck flying top cover for the Mi-17s and doing reconnaissance and FAC work."

On 21 April the long-planned advance set off from Saurimo, the EO contingent commanded by Rolf. Aside from problems with BMPs throwing tracks and logistics vehicles getting stuck in the soft sand, they advanced without incident to Dala. After a sharp fire fight, the defenders retreated to the town's empty school. Rolf requested air support and Louwrens scrambled from Saurimo. When he arrived, Rolf described the building and located it relative to the road with the distance and bearing from his own position. Louwrens repeated the instructions, rogered that he had the target and rolled in. Strapped into the PC-7s backseat, Carlos watched the rockets blast away from under the wings and streak into the school. Rolf advanced and reported that they'd killed most of the rebels in the assembly hall and sent the rest running out of the town.

"Making a wide sweep of the area, we saw a dust trail and turned to investigate," Carlos said. "It was a military vehicle making a hell of a run for Cacolo. When the Unitas realized that there was an aircraft overhead, they swerved off the road in panic and we watched it roll over a couple of times before coming to a stop. The shaken drivers climbed out and bomb-shelled into the bush. The vehicle was pretty much totalled, so we didn't bother wasting any ordnance on it."

★

With Rolf's combat group heading for Cafunfo and many of EO's personnel on leave and the PC-7s undergoing maintenance in Luanda, Unita mounted a daylight attack on Mono Quimbundo. The town fell, but General Sukissa led a counter-attack that recovered it the next day. The following morning the South Africans were awakened by the distant sounds of artillery as a duel developed between the returning force and Unita. The "ruff and scruff" that Ricardo had been less than pleased with immediately demanded that an evacuation plan be readied.

"Although a few of the chaps were a little twitchy," said Carlos, "from the intelligence side it didn't appear that the threat to Saurimo was serious. Unita did manage a small infiltration under cover of darkness at control point Zorro, about eight kilometres north-west of the runway and our position. They pulled back and at first light began an artillery bombardment. FAA responded with everything they had, shooting off their big guns for hours – in fact long after Unita had withdrawn. When intercepts showed that the attackers had retreated, the artillery crews demanded to be uplifted, citing a shortage of ammunition. As an alternative, we suggested an immediate resupply, with which General Sukissa agreed. By Monday morning everything had returned to normal.

"It was about this time that the G6 rumour surfaced. Now, the G6 is a South African-designed, self-propelled version of the G5 155 mm howitzer, an extremely sophisticated and long range gun that's the envy of every artilleryman in the world. The rumour was, that Unita had got hold of one and it was already halfway across Angola with a South African crew, who were going to blow us to Kingdom Come. Ricardo and I were approached by a certain faction of our blokes, demanding that we withdraw before it got in range.

"I couldn't believe my ears. No one with half a brain could have believed so absurd a rumour. We calmly explained that, for starters, the technology was super-secret; secondly, that the SADF had very few in any case; and thirdly, in light of the UN arms embargo against Unita, it was highly improbable that the new South African Government would even consider selling one to Savimbi, whom they didn't like anyway. And on top of that, with so many bridges blown along any possible route to Saurimo it would be damn-near impossible for the weapon to even reach us.

"When the rumour persisted, Ricardo ordered me to investigate the source. I went to our old and loyal ex-32 Battalion troops, who pointed me in the direction of Sarel, who had been the airborne commander at Camaxillo. As it turned out, Sarel's daddy was a senior government official. We did the math and it had all the earmarks of a disinformation operation. Sarel's mediocre career with EO was quickly terminated and he was sent packing. To my immense frustration, however, mutterings amongst his none-too-bright friends about 'that G6 coming towards us' continued."

★

"To improve the working relations between us and the FAA pilots, General Afonso decided that their pilots and technicians should stay in the same building as our pilots," Ricardo said. "I instinctively knew that this would lead to problems and confrontations. Their chain of command was virtually non-existent, and our pilots were becoming increasingly frustrated and resentful at being tasked to support the operation and then often having to go though the awkward Colonel Gino to get permission to fly. They were also flying far more dangerous missions than the Angolans. One night a fight broke out between the Angolan pilots and some people visiting our pilots, causing a big problem. Luckily, I got there soon enough to sort it out, but it just led to further command and control problems."

"Not all of them were that bad," Alberts admitted, "but General Afonso thought that by allocating an Angolan crew to us, they would receive invaluable on-the-job training. He had given us João Ferreira and John Vierra, both of whom assisted with our conversions onto the Mi-17 and were damned good pilots, as well as Tino Nuñes, who often flew with me as a flight engineer.

"The problem wasn't that they couldn't fly the aircraft, but that they had no idea how to use a helicopter on operations. Their idea of close air support was dumping their ordnance on a pre-determined grid reference from a safe altitude and then shooting back to base. All their routing was done during the day with an outdated Doppler navigational system or a road map. Everyday tasks such as uplifting a casevac from a random grid reference, deployment of troops to a specific position, low level tactical navigation and routing in battle formation were all foreign to them.

"When it came to command and control from the air, artillery fire control, forward air control and general battlefield support, not to mention instrument and night flying, they drew a blank. What compounded the problem was that they couldn't speak English, let alone Afrikaans, which we used for ninety percent of our air-ground communication for security reasons. To be honest, including the Angolans in our crew was often more a hindrance than a help."

* * *

Mig-23 Conversion

Pine and Louwrens had finally proven themselves in the PC-7s and on 29 April flew back to Luanda for a MiG-23 conversion course. "Our instructor was Major Diaz," Pine said, "a Portuguese-Angolan who spoke Russian, but no English. He was a fine pilot and on a scale of one to ten, I'd have to give him a good eight. The only reason it wasn't a ten was because of his lack of tactical experience. He was a soft-spoken, well-educated man with whom we could discuss a wide range of subjects from history to international politics. We respected him and got along well. Given that he was earning the equivalent of $50 a month, he was never resentful of us.

"He would conscientiously translate the Russian flight manual into Portuguese, then our interpreter, who was not a pilot, would translate into English. As you can imagine, this caused a certain amount of confusion from time to time. When the translation made absolutely no sense, we'd get Diaz to explain what the instrument actually did and after that we'd equate it to what we knew. All the instruments were in metric – metres, kilometres and kilograms – rather than the feet, knots and pounds per square inch that we were used to. We did pick up enough technical knowledge during the two-week conversion course to get us through and give us background that helped later, though we pretty much taught ourselves.

"When the time arrived for our check ride, Diaz kept delaying it because he wanted it done in one of their two dual MiG-23s, but they were both unserviceable. We eventually cooked up a bit of a white lie and told him that in the SAAF we went straight into the Mirage because there were no dual models. What we didn't mention, of course, was all the hours of Mirage simulator time before getting into the cockpit.

"Probably the most impressive thing about the aircraft was it's acceleration. In the 1980s three of our Mirages cornered a MiG-23 over

Angola and the young Angolan pilot was screaming for help. A Cuban instructor came on the radio and very calmly told him to point the nose north and go to max afterburner. He did and left those three Mirages in the dust.

"Advancing the throttle through a first clip engages the first stage of the afterburner; push it the rest of the way forward through the second clip and it's like a rocket kicking you in the backside. Without a weapons load, it has an almost 1:1 thrust to weight ratio. Taking off on a 10,000-foot runway, you'd be doing almost 350 knots by the time you passed over the end of it. The variable sweep wings started at sixteen degrees, then the next indent on the control lever was forty-five degrees and at full sweep they folded back to seventy-two degrees. The most we ever used was forty-five degrees and would ease the lever forward to thirty degrees for our attack profile. There was also a 'stick-pusher' that took over if the aircraft decided it was too slow in any particular configuration. This would automatically push the stick forward to lower the nose to gain airspeed."

Pienaar's first flight in the MiG on 20 May 1994 was very nearly his last.

"I took off and after getting the feel of the aircraft starting doing circuits, touch and go's, making sure I knew how to land the thing. After five or six of them I was feeling reasonably comfortable with the aircraft and decided, what the hell, might as well give my guys a low-level, high-speed pass. I started accelerating from about two miles out. A quick look at the airspeed indicator showed 300 knots and at a hundred feet I put it into a three or four-G turn to line up on them and started sweeping the wings back. Suddenly the stick-pusher took over, trying to get the nose down. At first I didn't know what the hell was going on and started fighting it. At a hundred feet, the ground was definitely not the direction I wanted to go and this was all happening in split seconds. The stick jumped forward again and I pulled back again. My speed deteriorated a little more and I had lost a little more altitude. The situation was getting worse and worse. The airplane was telling me that we were too slow.

"Still in a bank, I fire-walled the throttle through the first and second clips, felt it kick in, but there still wasn't enough room between me and the ground to recover. Directly in front of me was a wide, deep *donga* – a ravine – and the guys back at the airfield watched me disappear into it, still in a ten to twenty-degree bank, and waited for the fireball. At almost the same moment, there was this huge cloud of dust and out of the cloud came me and the MiG-23 screaming for altitude. I'd read the air speed indicator wrong. Instead of 300 *knots,* I was doing 300 *kilometres* per hour – about half of what I thought. I never made that mistake again!"

Because their MiG-23MLs had figured as a serious threat in the old days when the SAAF was operating over Angola, they had studied every report available on its performance and trained extensively in anticipation of meeting it in the air. Now, sitting behind the controls of their former front-line adversary, they put the Mikoyan fighter through its paces.

"Although the aircraft is optimised for air combat manoeuvres," Pine said, "we decided that in the air-to-air rôle it's not as good as some people say. It's got a tremendous roll rate, but even when you bring it over it still wants to go straight; you really have to wolf it around the corner. The ergonomics of it are a total nightmare. Visibility is atrocious, with zero rearward vision except through a small periscope-cum-rear-view mirror. The side of the cockpit is at mouth level, so high it's like sitting in a bathtub. To look at your three o'clock, for example, you have to roll it. If I was engaging a Mirage in a MiG-23 and the Mirage tried to run away, I'd catch it up. But I'd prefer to be in the Mirage. If you break a lot of angle, the -23 can't turn with you. You can break him down and kill him, easy.

"The take-off run was about 4,000 feet. The manual said 150 knots for take-off and 140 knots for landing, but we always added a few knots for the wife and kids. It just felt better. The serviceability of the aircraft we flew was excellent. Extremely reliable and incredibly tough. I flew most of my sorties in the same one, No C461, and it just never broke, in spite of minimal maintenance. But here I'm really talking about the engine and airframe, which were great. The systems themselves hardly ever worked. Radar? It was there in the nose, but I think the Angolans thought it was used for ballast. It never worked. There was no active electronic counter-measures. The MiG-23 had a radar warning receiver, which is very crude; a Mk I eyeball is better. Even worse, we didn't have flares or chaff. This caused us some worry because Unita certainly had plenty of SAMs, so we did a lot of brainstorming on devising something to counter or neutralise the threat.

"For nav instruments there was an ARK, which is a military VOR or TACAN, but it was useless because no ground stations were working. There was an Infra-red Search and Tracking unit coupled with a Russian LAZUR system used in conjunction with a ground controller to provide discrete intercept courses, but again, it didn't work because there was not a single ground radar system in all of Angola still operating. After the Russians left, every radar system had turned into junk and was rusting away. There was a RSBN nav system that also didn't work. No instrument landing system, no nav aids of any kind to get us back on the ground. As a result we only flew VFR. We used a hand held GPS for all our navigation, which worked brilliantly. Best thing the Yanks ever came up with. The Angolan pilots didn't fly if there were clouds, and never, never flew at night. Later on, when we flew night operations, they thought we were completely crazy."

Their check-out in the MiG may have saved their lives. While they were in Luanda, Unita was preparing an all-out assault on EO at Saurimo.

★ ★ ★

"Just then Charlie's helicopter exploded"

"After Rolf's combat group departed, we had about forty EO guys still at Saurimo," Carlos said. "Our headquarters personnel slept in the building containing the ops room and comm centre some 200 metres east of the front gate, and the pilots in an open hall about a 150 metres away on the north side of the soccer pitch. The different teams of operators billeted directly across the pitch from the air wing, or in huge hangers just behind. Because we were essentially a base within a base, no one had dug defensive trenches or foxholes.

"On the Friday night our Angolan sentries spotted someone examining the generator. When challenged, the figure disappeared into the night and we put it down to one of the FAA soldiers looking for something to steal. We knew that our actions against Unita so far was seriously worrying to them and that they would do anything to kill us, but we were inside the Saurimo base protected by 16 Brigade and it really didn't occur to us that we had been the subject of an enemy recce."

"Every Friday afternoon," said Ricardo, "some of us would fly back to Cabo Ledo for a weekly co-ordinating conference. These usually finished up late Saturday morning and we would then fly straight back to Saurimo for a 1700 hours conference. This time, however, it carried on a little bit longer than usual and the KingAir didn't get us back until just after last light on 18 May. There was nothing pressing to discuss so I told everyone that we'd have our meeting the following day, and we all headed over to *Gang Goggas* Corner for a braai and a few beers.

"As usual, Skeeries, our personnel officer, cornered me and asked to go for a ride in the PC-7. Thin as a rail, with thick spectacles, Skeeries had been a SADF clerk assigned to Special Forces. Having no operational experience, he'd be a liability for the pilot if anything went wrong so as usual I said no. With a fairly strict limit on how much we drank, I set the example by wishing everyone *lekker slaap* and most of us headed for bed around 2330 hours."

★

As the full moon was sinking towards a black horizon Unita were setting up mortars along the airfield's southern perimeter. Just after midnight at least fifty enemy special forces soldiers wearing FAA uniforms and South African webbing walked brazenly past the gate guard and into the EO complex, splitting into two groups. The first of about twenty approached an empty barracks, shouting, 'Come out and die, come out and die!' following it with a burst of gunfire. Those EO employees still awake thought it was drunken FAA soldiers, until the enemy group walked around the corner and stopped outside a room where a handful of the rapid reaction force were finishing off their braai. One of the ex-32 Bn operators calmly asked in Portuguese what they wanted.

A chilling order came out of the darkness. "All you whites come outside. We won't shoot you."

In the few seconds of stunned silence the enemy spread out in front of the rooms. Blackie Swart, an ex-Special Forces operator, suddenly appeared in at his door and opened fire. In the exchange he was hit and the enemy turned and ran as everyone scrambled for a weapon. The helicopters and buildings where the air crew slept were the next targets.

★

"It had been a busy day," Juba remembered. "First there'd been a test flight on Charlie's chopper. Later I did a recce and comms flight west of Saurimo and then gave Arthur two hours of instruction in the PC-7. After the previous night in the air wing's pub, I was a little tired.

"Arthur and I shared a room that opened onto the open lecture hall where Sonny and Peet had their cots among all the spares, tools and equipment. Percy joined us for a quiet nightcap, when we heard some shots. We decided it was just FAA having one of their regular domestic disputes, and carried on talking. There was another long burst. Thinking that was little odd, I stepped through the door to see what was going on and found Sonny, Pete Peet, and João Ferreira, the senior FAA pilot, already outside. There was a bright moon dropping towards the horizon and we could clearly see a group of soldiers shooting at the generator and chopping the supply cable leading to us. All the lights went out. Someone came on the radio to say that it was a FAA group investigating something so I didn't bother to get my gun.

"Then I saw a group come from the HQ side, run up to my chopper and start shooting at it. They saw us and turned their fire our way. We had one door and, being the smallest of the three, I was the last to get through it just as a bullet slammed into the wall above me. It was pitch black inside and I don't know how many things I stumbled over trying to get to my weapon. I found my beer, took a gulp, and moved to cover the back door, where there was another group of Unita. Arthur put on his webbing, grabbed his AK and dashed out to where Carl Alberts slept. Just then, Charlie's helicopter exploded."

★

"I came awake at the sound of automatic weapons fire very close and instantly knew that we were under attack," said Ricardo. "I rolled straight off my cot onto the concrete floor and looked squarely into the eyes of my roommate Carlos, who as a good soldier was on the floor as well. Rounds were coming through the window and slamming into the wall behind us. We grabbed our AKs, crawled forward to the window and returned fire. Unita had put a couple of armour piercing rounds through our generator, killing all the lights – which was fine, I didn't want anyone switching on lights anyway – but I couldn't see anything to shoot at.

"I shifted towards the door just as an ecstatic roar came from outside. When I looked out the entrance, I knew why: they had hit the nearest helicopter with a combination of RPGs and tracers and the resulting flames lit up the whole area. I heard their whistle signals to advance and in the glare of burning fuel and aluminium I saw about thirty of them attacking towards us over the soccer field. The Mi-17 burned out very quickly, plunging the area back into darkness. We were giving speculative fire into the night, when we ducked as a 60 mm mortar exploded about two metres in front of us."

★

"I snapped awake when the first mortar bomb landed and quickly realised that this was for real,"Alberts said. "I ripped open my mosquito net and fell out of bed onto the floor, stupidly groping in the darkness for something to wear while bullets were sparking and cracking through the room. Outside, tracers were going in all directions, RPGs and mortars were exploding, people were shouting and screaming. The lights went out just before a RPG rocket hit Charlie's chopper 200 metres away. H581 exploded into a ball of flame, illuminating a group of Unita jumping up and down and cheering so loudly that I could hear them clearly over the gunfire. With the bright magnesium fire from the burning helicopter, I could at least see what was going on.

"With Charlie away on leave, I was alone in the open front room and more Unita were coming through the long grass on the western side. Scrabbling frantically in the darkness, I found the two PKM machine guns that had been saved when our helicopter was abandoned at Camaxillo. I clipped a box magazine onto each and looked over the metre-high veranda wall. A lot of tracers were coming from the west side. They stopped momentarily while a BMP roared past ten metres away, then resumed with long bursts that hit it from behind and ricocheted all over the sky. Not wanting to open up in case the FAA gunner turned the 30 mm on me, I waited until it passed and let rip into the spot where the fire was coming from.

"Then someone wearing only underwear, flip-flops and combat webbing came tearing into my room. It was Arthur, clutching his AK in one hand and a half-full glass of Jack Daniels in the other. He took a long swallow, grabbed the other PKM and joined me behind the low wall. 'So who the fuck invited them?' he demanded, and we started firing at a sweep line of soldiers moving towards us."

"I was covering the back door and sky was lit up with tracers coming in and my own going out," Juba said. "Most of the concentrated enemy fire coming past me was from PKMs near the main gate. Then 60 mm mortars started falling all around us. I ducked when the first ones came in, then realised they were burying themselves before exploding, sending the shrapnel straight up. Noisy but not very affective. The problem started when the 82 mm mortars started hitting the roof overhead. Each time one exploded above me I wondered if the next one might come through the ceiling. The echoes in the open hall were something else.

"There were only four of us in the air wing returning fire and at one stage I went to the front to have a better view. With the burning chopper, the tracers and mortar bomb flashes it looked like something out of the movies, only it was for real. Pilots are trained for and understand fighting from the air, but this was a new and interesting experience."

"I ran into the comm centre to see if I could pick up any information on the radios," said Ricardo, "then climbed onto a table to look out a high window. Directly under it was a group of about ten crouching soldiers slipping towards the front entrance. It was impossible to tell if they were our people or the enemy, but I decided it was probably the latter and told everybody inside the ops/signal room to prepare for a house-clearing attack. But there were no grenades, no shots from them. They entered, went down a hall straight through to the rear exit and disappeared around the building."

"The situation was completely chaotic," Alberts said, "with tracers going in all directions. The burning helicopter was collapsing and the light was fading, when we saw more Unita shooting the shit out of the second chopper, which refused to burn. Then they started retreating across the soccer field, running left to right back towards the main gate. This took them diagonally past us fifty metres away and we blazed away at them. A blinding flash from a mortar sent us sprawling on empty cartridge shells. Groping around trying to find fresh magazines, we cautiously lifted our heads again. Across from the burning helicopter, we were treated to the spectacle of two Unita soldiers running after a BMP, firing their AKs up its backside."

"In the middle of all this," Carlos said, "a squad-size group of Unita was double timing towards the front gate in formation. They even kept formation while making way for a BMP that was screaming aimlessly around the soccer field. Their kit was so obviously FAA that no one even thought about challenging them as they headed through the gate."

"I saw one EO operator run from his barracks towards the air force barracks with an RPG, shouting his head off but not knowing what he really wanted to do," Ricardo said. "So far we'd been lucky, but with friend and foe impossible to distinguish in the dark, and indications that the enemy were withdrawing, I gave the command to cease fire."

★

Silence descended and they started checking for wounded. Incredibly, Blackie Swarts was the only serious casualty. He was carried into the sick bay and the doctor started working on him under the light of torches and got him stabilized. EO's new King Air pilot, who had just experienced his first night at Saurimo, was immediately sent with an escort to pre-flight Tango Romeo. Everyone held thumbs for Blackie as the King Air took off for the five-hour flight to Lanseria.

"The attack had lasted almost an hour and changed direction a few times," Juba said. "Some of the Special Forces guys said later that they'd considered coming to help the air wing, but thought better of it when they realised how much lead was flying around from every direction. The enemy had used the moon to infiltrate and initiate the attack and then towards the end of the fight the moon set and it became very dark. After everything calmed down we moved more weapons into position and got ready for another attack. I slipped out to my chopper at 0200 to asses the damage. Shining my torch over it made me feel like a sitting duck in the middle of that soccer field, but I had to see. It was badly ventilated, with holes all over the fuselage and the cockpit. When I got inside it, the dripping oil and fuel made me think of the Camaxillo episode. I then realised that we had no more chopper capability."

"FAA started up their BMPs and patrolled the streets until the first sign of dawn at around 0400," Ricardo said. "At first light a terrain inspection was done by General Sukissa and myself. I found out that my shooting was not so bad at all. I'd put two nicely double-tapped holes right through my own Chevvie pickup truck. Fortunately they weren't through the engine.

"One enemy, possibly the victim of our speculative fire, was found dead immediately in front of the HQ and two more bodies were found in the area of the burnt-out Mi-17, where lots of blood trails led back out of the base. The second helicopter was full of holes and after a thorough inspection it was judged to be beyond repair. While I was doing a damage report, our guys loaded up in the BMPs and headed out of the base for a follow-up. A few hours later the follow-up commander radioed a report that they'd discovered fifteen Unita bodies in one location a few kilometres from Saurimo. From the evidence, it appeared that they had been badly wounded during the attack but could not be carried any further. Rather than allow them to fall into FAA's hands, they were killed by their own people."

"I got airborne with the PC-7 at first light and stayed over the BMPs," Juba said. "When they got to the Luachimo River southeast of the base they had to stop. I continued past it and picked up a clear track through the elephant grass. Unita must have seen me approaching and set the grass alight. I followed the fire to were it started. Beyond was a large area of jungle, with no tracks coming out. With no more choppers, and with the difficulty of getting the ground forces across the river, it wasn't worthwhile to carry on with the follow-up operation."

"A message came through later that morning," Alberts recalled, "that on arrival at Lanseria Blackie's pulse rate was down to three beats per minute. He was admitted to Olivedale Clinic and taken straight into the operating theatre but, sadly, as strong as he was, he did not make it."

One experienced operator had been killed and two helicopters destroyed, but Unita's primary objective of killing EO's senior officers and air crew had failed. It was a failure they would live to regret.

★

"On our side the attack had revealed an EO element with a definite lack of enthusiasm for combat," said Carlos. "Some wanted out, others requested a transfer to the training section at Rio Longa. These were the same ones who were still convinced there was a G6 on the way. If there were a group that might be described as riff-raff, this was them, blokes who talked a good fight but didn't like the real thing. We decided that we didn't need baggage of that sort and gave those who wanted to depart our encouragement. This effectively combed our ranks of the loud-mouthed teddy bears, leaving only the quieter and more dangerous grizzly bears."

"I wanted them out of there as quickly as possible," Ricardo said grimly, "and arranged with HQ in Pretoria for one of the Boeing 727s to fly up. The next day they were all on their way home and we were digging trenches and fox holes. It may sound strange, but those who stayed seemed almost inspired by the event and were more determined than ever to complete the job. Needless to say, from that night onwards we couldn't trust FAA to protect the base and 'stand to' was implemented, with everyone pulling sentry duty."

"The blokes who remained were in for a pleasant surprise" Carlos said, "when the same gorgeous blonde reporter we'd met in Soyo arrived. We were still reeling from the attack and she was a very pleasant distraction. Ricardo gave up his bed for her and I, the only teetotaller, was appointed her chaperone. For the next few days I was the object of many envious looks from my colleagues, who speculated aloud as to what was going on after lights out.

"Shortly after the dust had settled, we were visited by some very belligerent political types from Luanda who wanted to find a scapegoat for FAA's failure to provide effective security. Ricardo and I were grilled separately for hours as they tried to find inconsistencies in our accounts. I explained repeatedly and with great patience that the attackers were wearing FAA uniforms; as a result, we had been concerned about killing their own people, which was a bit ironic, inasmuch as they never got out of their bunkers. This made no impression on our interrogators.

"We were getting very irritated when General Sukissa stormed into the ops room and demanded to know what was going on. When it was explained, he went ballistic, pointing out that we had offered the only resistance during the attack. Fortunately, Sukissa had considerable status within FAA because of his royal connections. He stomped out and reached General de Matos on his satellite phone. As it turned out, our visit had been a unilateral decision by a senior political commissar, who had left de Matos out of the loop. Shortly thereafter, some chastened and very contrite officers were waiting by the runway for their flight back to Luanda."

★

"A lot of chaps had chosen to resign," Alberts said. "Most were not spur of the moment resignations either, but rather the result of disillusionment with broken promises from the government. The guys who stayed behind were those prepared to do the job they had been contracted for. The bulk were black operators from the Reconnaissance Commandos, 32 Battalion and Koevoet, who, like all of us, had been accustomed to doing risky work for far less than we were being paid here.

"Due to the vulnerability of our building, we temporarily moved in with the rapid deployment force guys. It was closed all around and far easier to defend than ours in the air wing. We broke through the walls in all the rooms, giving us access to the trenches outside the building without running the risk of getting nailed en route. With a thousand-odd sandbags,

above: 'Liberated' 122 mm D-30 at Soyo being used for harassment and interdiction fire against Unita.

below: These new FAA troops are beginning their training under EO instructors at the Rio Longa base.

above: After eight weeks of 'vigorous' training by EO instructors, these FAA soldiers are being introduced to Camouflage and Concealment. Their standard of training was such that Unita grudgingly admitted that they were far better than the run-of-the-mill FAA troops they usually faced.

below: An EO medic gives medical ordnance training to FAA personnel at the Rio Longa base.

above: At Cabo Ledo BPM-2s were loaded into Ilyushin Il-76s for ferrying to Saurimo. Weighing 13 tons each, two of the armoured fighting vehicles could be carried on each flight.

below: Charlie Tait's Mi-17 just prior to take off for the attack on Camaxillo. The four men at the back armed with PKM machine guns were cut down during the exfiltration barely two hours later.

Former Koevoet members crew a BMP-2 en route to Cafunfo. Note the addition of a pintle-mounted ASG-17.

'Carlos' reassuring FAA contingent at Saidi Mingas that EO would respond to any future Unita attacks on the garrison.

above: Carl Alberts' Mi-17 with an AGS-17 30 mm automatic grenade launcher mounted in the door. The difficulty of controlling the weapon on automatic made the possibility of hitting the main rotor blades too great and the idea was discarded.

below: Mi-17 exchanging its Aeroflot colours for camouflage pattern at Saurimo.

above: 'Carlos' and a Unita prisoner at EO's Saurimo headquarters.

below: EO employees en route in a Mi-17 from Saurimo to Cacolo. Note ferry tank one man on the left is sitting on.

above: One of the regular Il-76 flights touches down at Saurimo.

below: One of DAF lorries mounted with 23 mm ZSU-23/2 anti-aircraft weapon that accompanied Colonel Nevis's combat group to Cafunfo. Used in the direct fire role, these weapons were extremely effective against ground targets.

above: 'Carlos' and others examine destroyed Mi-17 after the Unita attack against EO at Saurimo.

below: On of FAA's 122 mm BM-21 multiple-barrel-rocket-launcher's near Saurimo. The Soviet-designed weapon based on the original 'Stalin's Organ' has a range of 11,000 metres.

above: In goggles and scarf, Col Hennie Biaauw pauses on the advance to Cafunfo as Paul fills Nicks canteen.

below: Former Koevoet operators install a twin-GPMG pintle mount on a BMP-2. The additional firepower provided by extra machine guns or the AGS-17 automatic grenade launcher would later prove crucial in their battles with Unita.

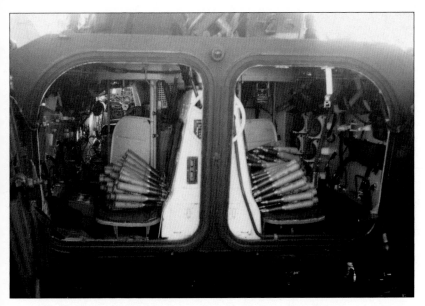

above: View through rear of BMP-2 where belts of linked 30 mm armour piercing and high explosive ammunition are ready to be loaded into magazine.

below: Final co-ordinating conference with FAA generals and EO staff at Cacolo prior to departure for Cafunfo.

above: Colonel Nevis (right) and a staff officer from Brigadier de Castro's HQ prior to departing Cacolo for Cafunfo.

below: Caterpillar front end loader ready to be towed to safety after it had slipped off the TMM mobile bridge at the Mucuegi River on 2 July 1994.

above: Fresh supplies are distributed following Russian air drop near Sassa. Note towed ZSU-23/2 in background.

below: Nic, wounded on 12 July near Firiquich, is readied for helicopter casevac.

above: Taken from Hennie's command vehicles one kilometre outside Cafunfo, this photograph shows the final drive towards the objective, the air thick with gunsmoke, ash and dirt.

below: To the victor's: EO brothers in arms raise beers soon after the capture of Cafunfo.

above: EO's administration and comms centre at Cafunfo after its capture.

below: Tattra being used in direct fire role during second assault on Cacolo.

above: Unita dead on road after contact on the way to Cacolo.

below: BMP-2 'bundu-bashing' during the second assault to retake Cacolo.

IN MEMORY OF:

W. ROSS-SMITH † 11. 11. 1993
C. I. NDLOVU † 29. 03. 1994
I. C. J. COETZER † 02. 04. 1994
J. LAUBSCHER † 02. 04. 1994
R. D. NITZCHE † 02. 04. 1994
L. A. SWART † 20. 05. 1994
N. H. HAYES † 25. 07. 1994
P. H. DITTRICH † 07. 09. 1994
H. NDISHISI † 13. 10. 1994
J. A. KELLERMAN † 05. 11. 1994
A. EFRAIM † 12. 06. 1995
E. A. TUSHUMBENI † 08. 02. 1996
S. P. KOEKEMOER † 08. 02. 1996
M. SHITANGO † 11. 03. 1996

EXECUTIVE
OUTCOMES

Memorial to those killed in Angola.

above:. EO Mi-17 in South African Air Force camouflage pattern.

below: Pine Pienaar (L) and Louwrens Bosch with one of the Pilatus PC-7s. A Swiss-built aircraft powered by a Canadian-built engine, with American pylons carrying Brazillian pods containing North Korean rockets and flown by South Africans under Angolan insignia, it was dubbed the 'United Nations Lorry'.

above: Juba Joubert in the cockpit of a Mi-17 after a mission to Cafunfo.

below: Pine Pienaar next to a MiG-23ML. In front of the cockpit are the three IFF Oddrod antennas they used to line up on a target during a bombing attack.

above: With 40 Kilogram napalm canisters under the wings, this MiG-23ML is being refuled prior to a sortie. (Pine Pienaar).

below: MiG-23MLs flown by EO pilots at Saurimo airfield (Pine Pienaar).

above: SU-25 ground attack aircraft flown by Angolan air force. One of these was subsequently lost in Zaire. (Pine Pienaar).

below: Unita Land Rover mounted with 106 mm recoilless rifle. Hennie's combat group came under fire by these weapons en route to Cafunfo. (1989, Jim Hooper).

above: Unita Land Rover mounted with KPV 14.5 mm heavy machine gun near the Benguela Railway Line in 1989. (Jim Hooper).

below: Mi-17 helicopter gunship destroyed by Unita mortar fire at Munhongo in 1988. (Jim Hooper).

above: Unita intelligence officer briefing assault forces prior to attacking an Angolan government garrison in 1989. (Jim Hooper).

below left: The author with Unita forces during an advance towards a major government garrison in Bie Province in 1989. (Jim Hooper).

below right: A Unita battalion commander surveys the perimeter of a Fapla garrison minutes after overrunning and scattering the defenders. (1989, Jim Hooper).

above: Unita General Ben-Ben Pena calls in mortar and rocket fire on Fapla positions near the Benguela Railway Line in 1988. (Jim Hooper).

below: Lt Col Ricardo as a young Special Forces officer during the Christmas 1986 operation.

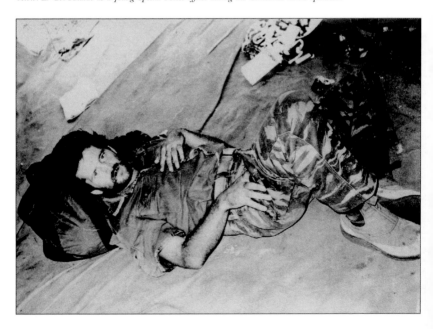

a few kilometres of razor wire and plenty of trip flares, we anticipated making a reasonable stand from our new Fort Apache when the time came.

"One unwelcome addition was the guard duty that we had to share with the rest of the guys. Although it was just an hour a night, it got pretty lonely staring out into the darkness with a pair of NVGs looking for Unita. We kept three-way radio communications with headquarters and a team of guys up in the watch tower. Ricardo instituted a lights out and general curfew from 9 p.m. and anyone seen moving around after then was considered to be hostile.

"In order to keep Rolf supplied and maintain a casevac capability, two more choppers were delivered. Besides being absolutely filthy, with floors caked with dried blood and everything stinking of fish, they were covered in dents and holes and many of the blades were patched with some sort of a bitumen mix. The FAA crews who flew them in acted like they were God's gift to aviation. To avoid any confrontation, we decided that we would fly the sorties supporting our guys, and they could fly all the sorties for their men."

★

"We were understandably pissed off by the attack and as soon as the new choppers arrived decided to show the flag with aggressive area operations," said Carlos. "The first target chosen was Lubalo on the route between Cacolo and Cafunfo. It was decided to do a hit-and-run mortar and rocket attack on a nice quiet Sunday afternoon. We split Deon's team between the two helicopters and headed for the target." Thunderstorms concealed their approach as they low-levelled to within two kilometres of Lubalo. The mortar team hopped out and the choppers orbited within sight of the town. Deon had the bearings and distances all previously sorted out on his GPS and after two or three minor corrections, he kept up a steady barrage with the balance of the eighty mortar bombs.

"As they started impacting Unita cut lose with a crescendo of small arms fire that came nowhere near the team. They were digging the mortar base plates out of the ground and carrying the steaming hot tubes to the awaiting helicopters, when Goose emptied two rocket pods into the centre of town, starting more fires. On the way home, they passed a village complex containing four vehicles, one of which Pine Pienaar was sure he had seen during another attack a few days earlier. The helicopters turned to investigate and immediately came under fire. They slipped out of range while Lenny and Goose rolled in and emptied their remaining pods, leaving most of the fifty-odd huts ablaze."

★

"The Angolans had been bugging us about the strategic Lui Bridge at Xa-Muteba, part of a crucial Unita logistics route from Malanje," Carlos said. "They insisted that it should be destroyed to prevent Unita moving men and supplies to Cafunfo. The first option Ricardo and I looked at was landing a heliborne force to destroy the bridge with explosives, but Pine and Louwrens, always looking for missions, insisted they could do it with the MiG-23. Pine gave it a couple of goes and managed to get his bombs close but not close enough. So we held that option in reserve and went back to the first plan."

Ex-Recces Shaun, Simon and Rich presented their own daring solution. First, to ensure enough of a bang to guarantee dropping the bridge, they proposed that two choppers, each carrying three 250-kilogram bombs and fifteen people, would drop Shaun and his team at either end of the target. Once it was secured, the helicopters would land one after the other on the bridge, the bombs rolled into position in specially built cradles and then all wired to a two-and-a-half minute timer. Everything would have to smoothly. Operating 360 kilometres from Saurimo, the Mi-17s had only thirty minutes of loiter time. If the fire force team didn't neutralize the Unita guards very quickly, then they'd have to withdraw. Ricardo gave them the thumbs up to begin detail planning and rehearsals.

To test the destructive capacity of the bombs, one was taken far outside Saurimo and detonated with a pound of Russian plastic explosive. The results were impressive enough that they ran a rehearsal using the Saurimo bridge as a dummy target.

"We were orbiting over the bridge with bombs and personnel, and I watched Charlie go in to drop off Shaun's team," Alberts said. "He had crossed the river and was going through transition at about thirty feet, when he lost an engine just short of the road. At an all-up weight off about thirteen tonnes, he planted the helicopter solidly in a cloud of dust. As the dust settled I heard him say that everyone was okay. With 750 kilograms of high explosive and all our guys on board, if that had happened over the bridge the result could have been quite spectacular. He taxied to the road, drained most of his fuel and after we had taken his bombs and passengers he lifted off on the one engine and flew back to Saurimo. It was decided that supporting Rolf's advance with the helicopters had to take priority, so the job of taking out the Lui bridge was handed back to Pine and Louwrens."

★ ★ ★

Hennie Assumes Command

"We were back in Longa, still training new recruits," a frustrated Oom Hennie grumbled. "Inasmuch as we had been looking forward to going into combat with 16 Brigade, we were already somewhat demoralized. Our feeling of being out of the action was magnified by the loss of our four blokes near Camaxillo, the disappearance of our three-man recce team near Cuango and the attack on Saurimo."

A month later a baby came to his rescue. Rolf had promised his wife that he would be there when she delivered. And that time had come.

"On 1 June I was flown to Saurimo," Hennie said. "Standing in while Ricardo was taking a few days' leave, Dolphin asked me to assume command of EO's mechanized combat group. I accepted immediately. Going to the wall map, he showed me the route, noting that the long-span steel bridge over the Alto Cuilo River had been blown by Unita,[32] forcing the combat group to move east across the Luachimo River, then head cross-country towards Dala on the Tchihumbe River. They'd had a bit of a punch up with Unita at Dala and were now heading for Alto Chicapa, a strategic Unita logistics base.

"I spent the rest of that day familiarizing myself with the situation and the next day was flown directly to Tchicuza, where the combat group was assembled. As we came in I could see the vehicles waiting in tactical formation and could hardly contain my satisfaction. Because of the threat of mortars, the Mi-17s dropped me and the needed supplies, then immediately lifted off again to orbit about a kilometre away. Rolf gave me his maps, said Jos would brief me, wished me luck and dashed for the chopper coming back in to lift him out.

---

[32] There had been a long-standing gentlemen's agreement between FAA and Unita that whoever held the bridge shouldn't destroy it. However, when Unita recognized the seriousness of the threat to Cafunfo, they took the sound military decision to blow it up.

"As soon as the dust settled, Jos was alongside to put me in the picture. We were under the command of Colonel Nevis, an above average, Russian-trained mechanized infantry officer, he explained. Our job was protecting Nevis's rear elements and making sure that logistical vehicles bogging down in the soft sand were pulled free. This immediately wound me up a bit. With all our experience, we should be part of the lead element, but that was something I'd take up with Colonel Nevis at the first opportunity. Jos was also favourably impressed with Captain Mundoreal, one of Nevis's young commanders, but warned that we needed to keep an eye on him. He was so aggressive – a rare enough quality amongst FAA – that sometimes the battle formation and teamwork suffered.

"Our crews, most of them ex-Koevoet operators like Jos, with a sprinkling of ex-Recces and 32 Battalion guys, were working well together and the BMPs were in good condition. The latter was helped by the daily maintenance he insisted on being carried out. He was so taken with these tough Russian vehicles, that if they could have cooked I think he'd have married one. (Even at that early stage Jos predicted that the Angolans would soon start suffering mechanical problems because of their unwillingness to do basic maintenance.) EO choppers were keeping us well supplied with essentials and morale was good, the guys confident and itching for more combat. He traced our projected advance on the map and finally showed me my command BMP. When Jos finished, I was in a positive frame of mind. Taking command of such a professional and highly motivated unit was nothing but a pleasure. By the time we got moving, I was a happy man.

"The terrain we were passing through was variable – from very thick bush to open savannah – and extremely dry and dusty, a condition made worse by the traditional slash and burn methods the local peasants used to clear the ground for planting. Between the dust and the ash from the fires, the white EO guys were as dark as their black South African comrades.

"We were now advancing towards Alto Chicapa, some 120 kilometres away. Because the area was so isolated, FAA forces had never before ventured into it. As a result of Unita's sensible hearts-and-minds, which saw large doses of anti-MPLA propaganda handed out with occasional distributions of foodstuffs and other supplies, the local population were understandably pro-Unita and deeply frightened of the government forces. Thus, the approach of our forward elements saw the *povos* abandoning their villages and escaping to the bush.

"Over my strongest protests, Nevis magnified the anti-government feelings by allowing his men to torch the empty villages. This not only turned a potential source of valuable intelligence against us, but the smoke from burning villages allowed Unita to plot our advance. Because of the many streams, we had to keep to the water shed of high ground. Unita could read a map and it wasn't difficult to get a bearing on the terrain features we were using and lay down accurate mortar fire. It took another fifty to sixty kilometres of constant nagging from me before Colonel Nevis finally accepted the logic of what I was saying and ordered his troops to leave the villages untouched.

"We were making good progress, when about forty kilometres from Alto Chicapa the engine of one of Nevis's BMPs seized through lack of oil. The central lubrication and cooling system is simplicity itself, needing only regular checking and topping up with oil or water as needed. Thus it was simply through a lackadaisical attitude towards the most basic preventative maintenance that this one had to be abandoned.

"Just as Jos had succumbed to its charms, I was soon a real convert to this vehicle. Like typical Russian equipment from the AK-47 to the MiG-23, the BMP-2 is a rugged and very functional piece of military kit. Its tracks make it ideal for cross country movement, without the worry of flat tyres through wear or combat. The armour was generally adequate, capable of deflecting 23 mm fire to the front and 7.62 mm armour-piercing to the sides. The 30 mm main gun is a joy – a stoppage-free, high-velocity cannon capable of delivering accurate, high volume fire until the last of its 500 rounds has left the muzzle. The high explosive shell has a kill radius of up to five metres and the fuse is very sensitive; even a small branch would detonate it. This made it extremely effective against troops in thick bush. The cannon is backed up by a PKT 7.62 mm machine gun with 2,000 rounds. The BMP's greatest weakness is its relatively thin belly, which is easily ripped open by any standard anti-tank mine. The results, as we would later see, were horrific for the crew and passengers.

"Our ex-Koevoet guys had replaced the standard Russian radios with South African sets and harnesses for two-way communication within and between vehicles,[33] and added ground-to-air VHF sets in the command vehicles. They also designed mounts for double GPMG and CPKM machine guns, or for a Russian AGS-17 belt-fed 30 mm grenade launcher for each crew commander. The latter was ideal for rapid target indication and additional fire power in general.

"We were never allocated a proper command BMP and I had to occupy the seat just behind the driver and directly in front of the 30 mm gunner. I could not convert the personnel compartment at the back to a proper control centre as we needed all available space for the accompanying infantry. All my planning and battle control had to be done out of my map case. The cannon traversed directly over my seat and, as I would soon learn, during a contact it was absolutely deafening. Wearing the padded Russian helmet with built-in ear phones was the only way of muffling it.

"I'm convinced that if I had do the same operation over the same distance and terrain with any other vehicle, especially any of the wheeled APCs used by the SADF, I'd not have completed it. So I was sorry to see that BMP abandoned. It was a waste of a fine piece of military equipment.

"Ahead of us lay Cacolo, where in the original plan the east and west pincers were to have met and consolidated before advancing to Cafunfo. It would be our next important staging point. We'd remain there until Brigadier de Castro, en route from Saurimo, caught up with us."

★ ★ ★

---

[33] The foundation of Soviet military doctrine was a strict hierarchal system that precluded individual initiative or any questioning of orders; this was reflected in the BMP's downward, one-way communications system from company commander, to platoon commander, to vehicle commander to crew.

Cacolo Taken

"Because our route had not been anticipated by Unita," Hennie said, "most of their troops in the area were from logistical units, which meant we met little serious resistance. This made the initial 250-kilometre advance relatively uneventful, though on 10 June another of Nevis's BMPs suffered a seized engine for precisely the same reason as the first.

"The next day at 1200 hours we received information that a FAA special forces company was already engaged in a fire fight in Cacolo. Nevis and I stopped some two kilometres outside the town and agreed that I should swing towards the northeast to take the airstrip, then lay a stop line to cut off and destroy any Unita vehicles or personnel trying to escape. He would drive straight in to support the special forces company, after which we would consolidate on the northern side.

"With only a bit of speculative fire from Unita, we soon had the airstrip, then roared down the road, established our stop line and waited. To our disappointment, they had already withdrawn. With dusk approaching, I established my tactical HQ at the end of the airstrip to protect it for resupply by air. On 12 June Nevis sent a recovery team for the second abandoned BMP and, despite my warnings, another BMP was lost when it detonated an anti-tank mine. There were some broken bones, but fortunately none of the crew was killed. Nevis had now lost three of his twelve BMPs, a twenty-five percent reduction in his armour force, which I considered a serious setback.

"Inasmuch as we would remain in Cacolo until joined by Brigadier de Castro, my immediate priorities were to consolidate the area and extend our defensive positions. At Nevis's request, I detached two BMPs and crews to a patrol led by Mundoreal. They hit a contact in Muhango on 14 June, cleared the town and sent back a report that the four Unita troops who had been killed were armed only with AK-47s and seemed in poor physical condition. A recce to the Alto Cuilo bridge confirmed that it had been destroyed, which meant that our advance was halted until de Castro's combat group arrived with the TMM mobile bridge and engineering equipment.

"With a couple of days' respite, Jos turned to pulling maintenance on our BMPs. One of them, which we'd nicknamed 'Puffing Willy', had a broken piston ring and was chucking oil and smoke. Impossible to repair under field conditions, by keeping it topped up with oil the tough armoured vehicle refused to die. Nevis received unverified reports of strong Unita elements preparing to hit us with mortars or even an assault, but I suspected that it was Unita disinformation to keep us off balance. Just to play it safe, however, I used the BM-21 for predawn and early dusk harassment and interdiction fire.

"On 15 June Nevis requested that one of our BMPs accompany a patrol to Xingi, from where Unita were reported to be withdrawing. Because all of our vehicles had been working hard, I declined; we were reaching a critical phase of the operation and I didn't want to start suffering mechanical problems that would reduce our effectiveness.

"Though we had our disagreements, the working and personal relationship between me and Nevis improved by the day. About 35 years old, Nevis had been trained as a mechanized infantry officer in Russia. Despite the fact that he was nowhere nearly as experienced as a Western battalion commander would have been, you could immediately see the difference between him and most of the other Angolan officers. He had a firm grasp of command and control and was very professional in his briefings and the deployment of his combat group. Even under the strain of intense combat, he remained calm, issuing clear, concise and intelligent orders. Mutual cooperation and support developed to the point of us establishing a joint tactical HQ. We each had our own line of communication back to Saurimo, his to General Marques, the theatre commander, and mine to Ricardo in the EO ops centre. This kept both HQs up to date on the current situation and our future intentions.

"The local population, which was sympathetic to Unita, cautiously began returning to Cacolo. I set up a clinic to treat those who had been wounded in the crossfire, along with the standard cases of malaria and intestinal parasites. The relations between us began improving, the small markets started operating again and something approaching normal life returned. However satisfying it was to see Cacolo returning to a semblance of normality, it also presented us with a security problem. Unita had treated the locals well and it stood to reason that some were reporting on our strengths and dispositions. We had no way of knowing who were still loyal to the rebels, or even who might be soldiers disguised as civilians. Because of our efforts to provide medical care and clean water, as well as repairing the town's infrastructure, the local mayor was soon on our side and set up a network to screen those passing in and out. It was a help, but still no guarantee that we weren't being spied on.

"Proud father Rolf had returned from South Africa and been flown out to join Brigadier de Castro's combat group that was heading for us from Saurimo. I suggested that he stay with him as his senior advisor and liaison officer. Inasmuch as Rolf and I had a radio link but Colonel Nevis and Brigadier de Castro's combat group did not, he could keep de Castro advised of our tactical situation and keep me updated on their progress towards Alto Cuilo.

"By 20 June, Ricardo was back in Saurimo. He confirmed that accompanying de Castro's group were new Ural logistics vehicles for my group. I was also getting twenty new EO personnel, while Mickey with a mixed group of twenty South African and FAA instructors would arrive to train a Cacolo home guard. The next morning Deputy Chief of Staff General McKenzie, Chief of Special Forces General Antonio Faceira, Brigadier de Castro, and EO's Lafras Luitingh, Ricardo and Carlos arrived by helicopter for a final co-ordinating conference. General Faceira went over the operational plan in detail. Deception was at its core.

"Terrain and infrastructure are crucial to any military campaign, and never more so than in the situation we now faced. Because of numerous rivers and small streams, deep ravines, very dense bush and virtually only one reasonable road, we could not advance on more than one route to our final objective. The situation was aggravated by limited supplies and barely adequate artillery and air support for ground forces on a wide front. Our best hope, therefore, was for our combat group to advance along the main road to convince Unita that it was our main axis of attack. At the same time Brigadier de Castro's reserve combat group would move independently, and hopefully undiscovered, along an old Portuguese laterite track direct from Cacolo to Lubalo.

"With Nevis providing reconnaissance ahead of him, it was anticipated de Castro would reach us by June 25. If he were unsuccessful in crossing the Alto Cuilo River he would proceed another 100 kilometres and cross at Lubalo. This seemed a shaky proposition, given that we had no idea if the bridge could be taken intact.

"General McKenzie confirmed that a Russian air resupply would be dropped into Sassa, two-thirds of the way to Cafunfo. FAA Special Forces would secure the drop zone and infiltrate the area around Firiquich, ready to link up with the mechanized column for the drive towards Cafunfo. Lafras promised to expedite needed spares and tactical equipment and confirmed that Rolf would stay with Brigadier de Castro. Although I had opposed the original concept of approaching Cafunfo from the east, it was now up to me to assist in executing this plan. D-Day was set for 6 July, two weeks away."

★ ★ ★

Fixed Wing Ops

"When I returned to Saurimo from Luanda on 26 May I'd had another orientation flight in the MiG," Pine said, "and then the MiGs were grounded for almost a month because of very limited fuel supplies and we went back to the PC-7s."

Three hundred kilometres away, the airstrip at Cafunfo continued to serve Unita as an entry point for arms and other supplies. Lured by the sparkle of Savimbi's diamonds, mercenaries from South Africa, England, France and Russia were landing heavily loaded transports to keep the rebels well stocked.

"The Angolan high command had a fixation about shooting down one of the aircraft," Carlos said, "and we devised a couple of plans to accomplish just that. The first was to deploy a Special Forces team with surface-to-air missiles under the northern approach path to the runway. Given the loss of the recce team near Camaxillo, we saw it as fairly high risk, but the guys were confident they could pull it off. And all we needed to do was hit one aircraft to convince the others that it was too dangerous. The team was infiltrated but, unfortunately, most of them contracted malaria and we had to extract them before they could accomplish the mission.

"The other option was for the PC-7 to destroy one on the ground with a rocket attack. For a while we had a PC-7 on standby at night, but just couldn't get an early enough warning of an in-coming flight to launch in time. When Pine and Louwrens came back from their MiG conversion course, the word got out and the supply flights suddenly stopped. Their intelligence wasn't too bad, because when we then suffered a fuel shortage that kept the MiGs grounded for almost a month, the flights started again. So we put the PC-7s on standby again."

"I was the night duty pilot," Pine said, "when Carlos got an intercept about an incoming flight and told me to scramble. The idea was to catch them on the ground and I immediately launched. It was an hour and twenty minute flight in the PC-7 and I was only about fifteen minutes away from Cafunfo in really bad visibility, when Carlos radioed to say that it had just taken off and I should come back. I thought I'd try to catch it, relying on my NVGs to pick it up, but he just outran me. With just enough fuel to get back, I turned around for Saurimo. After I had left EO I ran into someone who was doing the Cafunfo flight, and he said we had them plenty worried."

★

"We eventually got round the fuel problem by filling our bowser directly from the wing tanks of arriving Il-76s," Pine said, "but it wasn't until 23 June that I got into the MiG's cockpit again." With three familiarisation flights now recorded in his logbook, he was soon in the air with his bomb-laden MiG-23 and hoping that all the brainstorming on anti-missile tactics was going to work.

"We'd finally decided that the best way to minimise the Stinger, SAM-7 and SAM-14 threat was by transiting high and maybe thirty kilometres from the target backing right off on the throttle. This reduced our noise to almost nothing on the ground, but more importantly reduced the infra-red signature. We'd roll in at idle power from about 25,000 feet and let the aircraft accelerate to about 400 knots in a thirty degree dive, release our bombs at about 6,500 feet, pull out at 4,500 feet and hit max afterburner, betting on the slow reaction time of any SAM operator. Because the aircraft was so quiet at idle power, even if the operator already had the SAM on his shoulder he wouldn't know we were there until we'd already pulled out of the dive and gone to afterburner. With an advertised climb rate of 45,000 feet per minute, our defence was to simply out-climb a missile if it was fired. In no time at all we'd be between 20,000 and 30,000 feet again, well out of range. If they ever did launch a missile at us, we never knew about it.

"The MiG-23's acceleration is just amazing. At 28,000 pounds of thrust the engine is very powerful, but it's unbelievably thirsty, which gives it a very short endurance. We never had the fuel to check the burn rate, but I would guess at low level in max afterburner it's drinking around 1,000 litres per minute. As result, the farther Hennie got from Saurimo, the less time on target we had when we got to him.

"The other threat, of course, was ground fire, and when we were down and dirty we regularly had everything from small arms to 23 mm coming up at us, but except for that one hit Louwrens had on 10 March and another when a spent bullet ended up on the cockpit floor next to Lenny, none of us took any further damage.

"As a mud-mover, on a scale of one-to-ten the MiG-23 is about a two. It has four weapons stations, two on the belly and two on the wings inboard of the sweep. There is a centre-line station for a fuel tank only. You can't load the aircraft asymmetrically and you have to release both bombs from the belly stations or the wing stations at the same time. If we were carrying missiles – we never mixed our weapons load – the same goes for them. If you want to fire a missile, you have to fire two. If you're carrying a fuel tank, the two belly hard points are useless, and if you're carrying anything on the belly at all you can't use the cannon because of the shell casings hitting it. The sight seldom worked and even when it did a piece of chewing gum stuck on the windscreen would be about as good. Fortunately, just ahead of the cockpit there are three *Oddrod*[34] IFF antennas in line with each other. We'd line them up and with any decent aiming picture it worked like a charm. Louwrens Bosch took out a bridge on his first try with dumb bombs. You only have to ask people in the same business to realise what a bloody impressive effort that was.

"A real problem was getting the Angolans to understand that different targets required different weapons loads. When we'd come back from a mission, the aircraft would be armed almost before we walked away from it. The problem was, they'd load it with whatever was handy or what they felt like at the time. Usually it was what was easiest. They didn't have any hoists, and it took about ten men to lift a 500-kilogram bomb over their heads and attach it to the shackles on the hard points. I was once tasked to hit a bridge, but when I got to the aircraft, it was loaded with forty-kilogram napalm canisters. On another mission to hit a bridge, I found it had been loaded with rockets.

"The Angolans who gave us our missions were often neither pilots nor even trained in target assessment. They'd give us targets without

---

[34] NATO designation for the Identification Friend or Foe system used in the MiG-23.

understanding anything about them, and then got very touchy when we said we wouldn't fly unless we had the correct weapons loads. The job was dangerous enough; there was no point in attacking something that wasn't going to be damaged by the weapons package we were using, something they had great difficulty understanding.

"Another problem was a very awkward chain of command. All the fixed wing aircraft were under the control of Colonel Gino, the base commander, an extremely arrogant officer whom we had to ask for permission before being allowed to climb into 'his' aircraft. Then there was a lieutenant colonel in charge of the ground crews, another for ordnance and a third for fuel – until we started taking Jet A1 directly from the Il-76 wing tanks. Their lack of co-ordination was appalling. Fortunately, Major Diaz followed us to Saurimo and he regularly interceded for us, but even then it was a struggle.

"As far as armament, the MiG's twin-barrelled 23 mm cannon is an excellent piece of kit. Very accurate, very effective against ground targets. The only problem here was that it was time-consuming and difficult to reload, and the ground crews often couldn't be bothered, so we seldom had the opportunity to use it. Our most common weapons loads were 250 or 500-kilogram bombs, but we occasionally carried napalm and rockets. Interestingly enough, we also had some US Air Force Mk82 500-pound bombs kindly provided by the Israelis, who had modified the American ordnance to fit the hard points on Soviet aircraft. The most effective area weapon we used, however, was the Russian RBK SWAB, an 500-kilogram cluster bomb. Once we'd pulled off and looked back at the target you could see hundreds of explosions going off over at least a 300-metre radius. It was beautiful weapon for trenches.

"Of my twenty-five operational sorties in the MiG, four were at night using NVGs. The reason we didn't fly a greater proportion of night missions was due to the infrastructure problem at Saurimo. The runway had no lighting and we had to resort to filling tins of various sizes with sand and Jet A1 fuel. These were positioned along the sides of the runway and lit approximately fifteen minutes before our return to the airfield. This worked well enough, but the locals stole the tins at such a rate that we eventually had to give up! Just before I left EO, we were seriously considering a mobile runway lighting system that could be laid out before landing and recovered again once we had finished flying for the night.

"The Saurimo airfield was terrible because of the pot holes and amount of debris," Pine said. "There had been a lot of Il-76 traffic and the sheer weight of the four-engined Ilyushins was breaking up the runway. When the debris became too bad, we just refused to fly. One time I taxied out and came right back, thinking if I tried it I'd find myself farming with this thing. We'd make the Angolans get a truck and we'd go along the runway clearing it by hand. Fortunately, while we had lots of cut tyres, we never had a blow-out."

★ ★ ★

River Crossing

Early on 23 June Hennie led a patrol to Muachimba, some twenty kilometres to the north-east, where they discovered fresh enemy tracks and a BMP damaged its steering box on an anti-personnel mine. Reaching the outskirts of a small village, they braked to a halt at the sight of twelve bodies lying in the middle of the road. According to the surviving villagers, they had been executed by Unita two days earlier, along with twenty three children burned alive by the rebels. Hennie was unable to confirm the latter claim, as FAA insisted the hut in which they had died was surrounded by mines, but the bodies coincided with intelligence reports from Carlos that much of the local population had fled the area because of Unita atrocities.[35]

Making his way back to Cacolo, Hennie received a call from Micky that another fifteen-hundred civilians – mostly children – had returned to the town. They now had over 5,000 hungry and injured civilians and the food and medical situation was critical. EO's medics were treating the worst cases, but were short of supplies. Hennie asked Saurimo for an emergency shipment of food and a mobile clinic. Ricardo acknowledged the request and, to Hennie's considerable relief, reported that the logistics convoy with Brigadier de Castro's combat group should reach the Alto Cuilo bridge by that evening.

A late afternoon reconnaissance by a SU-25 reported a heavy concentration of Unita about four kilometres north of Muachimba, where Hennie had turned around that morning. The pilot had strafed the area, but could give no details of damage.

---

[35] The apparent paradox of treating some of the local population well, while brutalizing others, rested primarily on tribal affiliation. Those who were naturally sympathetic, or whose chiefs had struck an alliance with Savimbi, found favour with the rebel movement, while those who were not were treated less well.

The next morning two Mi-17s landed with Generals Marques, McKenzie and Antonio Faceira accompanied by Ricardo and Carlos. There to assess battle readiness and tie up any loose ends on the logistical side, Faceira confirmed that two FAA Special Forces groups of company strength were being deployed, one to link up with them at Lubalo and the other at Sassa after the scheduled airdrop. Unfortunately, a message had just been received that de Castro was unable to cross the Alto Cuilo River and was heading for Lubalo. This meant that the original D-Day schedule would have to be pushed back.

Early on 30 June General Marques flew in again, ordering that they continue without de Castro's combat group. Hennie would be Nevis's tactical reserve and provide security for the logistics vehicles up to Xingi, then link up with de Castro at Lubalo.

"Marques departed and we were moving, when it was suddenly realized that Nevis's troops hadn't been issued rations or told in which vehicles they were to travel," Hennie said. "Two hours of chaos ensued, before we said goodbye to Mickey again and set off, but, due to mines, advanced barely twenty kilometres before dusk.

"After a cold, windy night in the deserted village of Tchiuhua, we set off, FAA deploying skirmish lines to either side of the road as defence against ambushes and others sweeping it for mines. We replenished our water supply at the Tchisimbo River, passed through a deserted village and reached Canhenque at midday, where we were joined by a company of Katangese.[36] We stopped two kilometres south of Xingi to wait for them to sweep forward, when we came under accurate B-12 and 60 mm mortar fire from our right. My EO guys and the remaining Katangese formed a second assault line and advanced towards the ambush. A fierce fire fight developed before Unita withdrew, abandoning a light anti-tank weapon and a couple of PKM ammunition belts. Fortunately, we took no injuries.

"The leading elements of Nevis's combat group entered Xingi and engaged a Unita platoon, which retreated up the tar road. The direction of their withdrawal strongly suggested that this was the route they now believed we would take to Cafunfo. Our deception plan appeared to be

---

[36] From Katanga Province in Zaire, they had supported Moise Tshombe in the 1960s and then fled to Angola when Mobutu Sese Sekou took power. Being anti-Mobutu meant they were anti-Unita, and in exchange for being allowed to remain they had to do military service. Aggressive, disciplined fighters under good leadership, their arrival was recognized as a stroke of luck.

working. Nevis wanted to leave a holding force, but I persuaded him that this would weaken us and affect the overall plan. We reached Muhango at 1600 only to have him order the Katangese back to Cacolo. A fierce argument developed between him and Colonel André, the Katangese commander. I interceded by reminding him that the Katangese had cleared Xingi on their own, and it would be unfair to send them back without armour support. Also, quite selfishly, I wanted these tough soldiers with my combat group all the way to Cafunfo. Nevis reluctantly agreed.

"Brigadier de Castro didn't link up with us until late that afternoon and we established a temporary base ten kilometres north of Munhango. Just before setting off the next day Nevis came over and began arguing with the Katangese officers again. It was obvious that there was a personal problem between him and Colonel André, or that he simply didn't like the Katangese as a group. I repeated very firmly that I wanted them under my command all the way to the final objective. When Nevis argued that there were insufficient rations to support them, I promised to have additional supplies flown out and we set off with some very grateful Katangese troops.

"The next fifty kilometres were extremely dusty and completely devoid of any sign of Unita. By the time we reached the Mucuegi River Mundoreal's combat team was already crossing. We were well back in the queue, when word was passed that the makeshift wooden bridge had collapsed. I walked down to the river and to my surprise found that, instead of standing aside and allowing the engineers get on with the job, Brigadier de Castro had taken personal charge and was down in the mud with them. I watched as his Caterpillar front-end loader smoothed the approach on our side and the TMM mobile bridge was manoeuvred into position. It began unfolding but when the end settled on the higher and uneven far bank, the steel tracks were canted precariously sideways.

"We recommended levelling the bank by hand, but an impatient de Castro ordered the first vehicles across. The balance of Mundoreal's group reached the other side successfully and de Castro ordered one of his BMPs to tow the Caterpillar across. Rolf and Jos advised against it, but de Castro ignored them. The Caterpillar was just short of the far side, when it slid sideways off the bridge and ended up almost on its side. Its position made recovery extremely difficult, if not impossible. This was a potential disaster, as we needed that Caterpillar for the advance. Rather than taking time to assess the situation and begin a recovery attempt, de Castro ordered the next vehicle across. To my immense frustration, a DAF truck towing a twin-barrelled 23 mm anti-aircraft gun got stuck as it tried to edge past the Caterpillar. A second DAF got stuck when one wheel slipped between the TMM's steel planking. Our advance had been halted.

"When night fell we were still stalled south of the river and de Castro had decided to destroy the Caterpillar. We managed to dissuade him, arguing that it would be crucial for bridging water obstacles once we'd left the main road and headed cross-country. Late that night de Castro asked us to take over the recovery operation. By 0800 the next morning we were in full swing. Pressing the blade down to lift the front, we jammed logs under the low side, then attached steel cables to two BMPs in tandem. Two hours after taking over we had it levelling the same bank that had tipped it over. We freed the two DAFs and at 1200 the first Ural truck towing a D-30 gun was crossing when the driver accelerated and slipped off the far end.

"This was absolutely unbelievable. We unhooked the gun, off-loaded the ammunition and, worried that it might topple over, gingerly towed it out with the Caterpillar and two BMPs. A furious de Castro ordered all the Angolan drivers out of the following vehicles and replaced them with our guys, who soon had them safely on the other side. At 1500 the TMM was recovered and an hour later was bridging the Luagi River, where yet another truck was driven over the side. It, too, was eventually recovered.

"De Castro's group passed me to join Mundoreal at the head of the column. They were just south of Lubalo, when they drove into a Unita ambush. The BMPs' 30 mm guns decimated the enemy, killing fourteen. With the light fading, we established a temporary base and at 2000 hours a single mortar bomb landed next to my command vehicle. It was obviously meant to draw counter fire to determine our strength. Although all guns were immediately manned, I ordered that no one fire unless he had a target. I could hear a heavy exchange of gunfire and Rolf radioed to say all hell had broken loose on the FAA side of the TB, with Mundoreal in the thick of it. The fight gradually ceased as Unita made a tactical withdrawal.

"The lean and wiry Mundoreal continued to impress us. Of medium height, he was very black and I used to counter his shy jokes about my red hair and sunburnt nose by telling him he was perfectly camouflaged for night operations. He was battle scarred, with a slight limp from previous operational injuries, passionate about BMPs and an absolutely fearless commander. Brave to the point of recklessness, yet extremely modest, I never saw him closing his commander's hatch in the heat of battle, no matter how intense the incoming fire might be.

"When his driver or 30 mm gunner was not performing to his liking, he would simply order the individual out of his seat and take over. The negative result of this was that the remainder of his combat team would lose contact with him. Nevertheless, to his men he was an absolute hero. We made an effort to advise him on all aspects of leadership and command, for which he was always grateful and I made a point of debriefing him after every contact, reinforcing his successes and offering specific suggestions on how to prevent a repetition of mistakes. His gradual but steady development into a competent commander was remarkable."

★

"On 3 July the Angolan pilots came to me in tears," Pine said, "pleading for help in locating one of their friends, a SU-25 pilot. It seemed he was returning from a mission and because of the terrible visibility had gotten lost. (As a result of the smoke from the burning of the fields, you could actually lose sight of the ground from above 1500 feet.) They had been talking to him on the radio and then lost comms. Could I help, please? I agreed, and in record time the MiG-23 was fitted with three drop tanks, which just showed they could get things done in a hurry when it suited them. The wing tanks prevented any rear sweep and limited me to 440 knots, but I didn't figure I'd need any real speed.

"A half hour before sunset I took off and headed for his last known position, staying at a hundred feet because of the really terrible visibility and looking for the smoke of a crash site. I searched for about an hour and a half, but found nothing. The next day Papa Whiskey, our recce bird, found the SU-25 sitting on the main street of a town just over the border in Zaire. We never discovered if the pilot got lost or had defected. There was some talk by the Angolans of attacking and destroying it on the ground, but nothing ever came of it."

★

Through all of this, the anti-EO campaign was alive and well in Pretoria. Every arrival and departure of a Capricorn Systems Boeing 727 at Lanseria airport was under surveillance by SADF counter-intelligence agents who photographed departing and arriving employees. Whether it was families laughing with relief as their men came down the steps, or tearful last hugs before boarding, all was recorded on film.

"Possibly the most unpleasant and intrusive of the watchers was their boss, Colonel Jap Swart," said Carlos. "Short and stocky with a broom handle moustache, he had made it his personal crusade to harass our employees and make life as difficult as possible for them. The nickname 'Pink Panther'—an allusion to the bumbling Inspector Clouseau in the film—had apparently been applied by his own colleagues at MI. It was not, we'd heard, a term of endearment.

"As farewells were being made prior to one Saurimo departure, Swart and his beer belly marched in with a squad of embarrassed military policemen. Shouting and standing on tiptoes to get everyone's attention, he barked in guttural English, 'You're all under arrest!' By this time everyone knew that we were operating well within the law, so as far as we were concerned Jap Swart could go fuck his budgie. There were a few smirks in the departure lounge, before everyone studiously ignored him. A perplexed Jappie looked completely lost. It was said that even one or two of the MPs had a giggle behind his back. The little man then turned to bullying one of EO's female clerical staff who was there to see the men off. This was just too much and airport police were summoned to chase him off the premises.

"Although never proved, we also suspected that he was behind the anonymous phone calls to our families. Some brave chap who refused to give his name rang my wife to say that I would be arrested on my return to South Africa, adding that Savimbi had many powerful friends in the country who would 'get' us.

"Then the legendary founder of both the Reconnaissance Commandos and 32 Battalion stepped into the controversy. I always held Jan Breytenbach in high regard. Affectionately known as the *Bruinman* [Brown Man] or Carpenter by those of us who had served under him, he was worth his reputation many times over, and were it not for his dislike of bureaucratic bullshit and military politics, he would have retired a general rather than a colonel. But to our dismay, he began making anti-EO statements to the press. This was not only disappointing, but surprising, given his past criticism of Savimbi for slaughtering elephants to fund his war with the sale of ivory.[37]

"I was home on leave, when I got a message to ring him. After a few pleasantries, he abruptly asked what I was doing by supporting the MPLA. When I said it was business, he told me that Savimbi was going to floor us all. I said that we were confident that we could put what we'd learned from him to good use and take care of ourselves. When I declined to give him the names of other ex-Recces in EO, he said that Hennie – whom I hadn't mentioned – and I were 'tickling the lion's balls', without specifying which lion he was talking about. When he used the word 'traitor', I asked him if having the new ANC government meant that everyone in the SADF would be resigning: the ANC, after all, had been our enemy for far longer than the MPLA. He chuckled uncomfortably and after I promised to resign from EO if he could match my salary, we said goodbye for the last time."

★ ★ ★

---

[37] Unita's three major sources of cash came through the sale of diamonds, ivory and teak. During one of the author's three trips with Unita to cover the war in 1988–89, he was shown a warehouse of elephant tusks in Jamba, and regularly saw large herds between Jamba and Likuwa en route to the Benguela railway line. Elephant carcasses were also not uncommon.

Casevacs and Choppers

"At 0600 on 4 July I briefed my crews to expect increased enemy activity and to be ready to execute counter-ambush drills," Hennie said. "We could also anticipate finding more mines on the road. We moved out and less than 500 metres up the road found two dead Unitas from Mundoreal's contact the night before. By the time we entered Lubalo at 0945, Rolf radioed that Colonel Nevis and Brigadier de Castro were twenty kilometres ahead of us. I contacted Saurimo to request an air reconnaissance of the roads to the north, but not to give our game away by being too obvious. I was sure that our deception plan was working and that Unita was still unaware that we were planning to turn west at Camaxillo. I radioed de Castro to advise him of the intended air reconnaissance, only to hear him arrogantly say he wanted to be in Cafunfo by the next day. I could only shake my head.

"We passed through a village twelve kilometres north of Lubalo, where the locals complained that the FAA troops ahead of us had raped some of the women, shot one man, burned huts and stolen money, blankets, food and some diamonds they had mined. I was deeply disturbed by this. These sorts of atrocities would only encourage the *povos* to support Unita against us. I promised that I would discuss their complaints with the FAA commander. That night I raised the issue with de Castro, emphasising the negative consequences. Though he ordered his political commissar to investigate, I never heard the outcome.

"At 1700 we made a TB near a river and the guys had the opportunity to wash off the layers of dust and ash. Convincing de Castro that we needed regular evening coordinating conferences, I brought all the team leaders together to confirm the next day's time of departure and the route, hoping to make eighty kilometres. Although the plan called for us to refuel before moving out, de Castro, with typical unpredictability, suddenly insisted that we would not refuel until the next evening.

"At dawn the next morning de Castro changed his mind and decided to refuel the entire convoy now, which cranked up my frustration yet again. We'd had the previous evening to prepare for refuelling so as to move out with full tanks. This was especially important in this kind of terrain, where I wanted to clear the TB before first light to avoid an early morning attack.

"Though I made every effort to get along with him, in the final analysis Brigadier Pepe de Castro was an incompetent brigade commander, lacking knowledge of command and control, deployment drills and basic combat control. Very arrogant, he blamed all his mistakes on subordinates and regularly assaulted them in front of us if they questioned his decisions. But we were together in this operation and it was essential that I kept the peace between us. But there were times it required all my patience.

"We were still at the LZ at 0700 when the choppers arrived with Ricardo and our supplies. My blokes took advantage of the delay by enjoying the very welcome two beers they'd each been allocated in the resupply. After briefing Ricardo and seeing him lift off in the helicopter, we were finally on our way at 1200, the clean faces soon caked with dust and ash again. Three hours later we were just south of Sassa, when a DAF and its 23 mm gun were destroyed by a landmine. Almost immediately the lead elements came under fire from a large Unita ambush that eventually withdrew under heavy return fire. We were waiting for a report on the action when, at 1700, I was told by Saurimo that another flight of choppers was en route to pick up fifty FAA commandos and fly them farther north on our route of advance. The Mi-17s orbited for fifteen minutes as we collected the wounded and prepared them to be casevacked."

★

"I had just stepped off the Boeing after two weeks' leave in South Africa," Alberts said, "and found Arthur, Sonny and Charlie awaiting my arrival to make up a second crew to fly out to Hennie. We were needed to shift some FAA troops and pick up some casevacs.

"The replacement aircraft which Arthur and I were to fly looked in a very sorry state. The front windshields were so opaque and dirty that even flying during the day required a fair amount of instrument reference. I hurriedly put on my flying suit over jeans and T-shirt and we set out into the sunset to resupply Hennie. Our straight line track of 200 kilometres, with deviations to avoid village concentrations, was covered in forty-five minutes under virtual instrument flight conditions due to a glowing sun on the horizon and the very milky windscreen. We made comms with him about five kilometres out and were informed that he'd had a contact with Unita less than an hour ago and killed a number of rebels. Locating his position was made a lot easier by the bush that had been set alight by the fighting.

"Charlie and Sonny landed while Arthur and I orbited to give what cover we could with our PKM gunners. The supplies were offloaded and Charlie agreed to uplift a few FAA casevacs who had been wounded and were, as Hennie put it, 'getting a little puffy'. After an uncomfortable delay a packed Ural truck slid to a stop in a cloud of dust. Without hesitating, the uninjured occupants abandoned the wounded and stormed the helicopter, attempting to get through the side door four at a time. After much shouting and screaming, Charlie eventually managed to get the casevacs aboard. When he got airborne there were more than twenty healthy FAA troops along for the ride as well.

"Arthur and I landed as soon as Charlie lifted off and experienced an action replay of the first uplift. Two of our guys were standing at my side cockpit window, punching and kicking the troops attempting to squeeze through the side door. This was a bit dicey as they had had a contact less than an hour earlier and each was still carrying a loaded and cocked weapon. All in all, Charlie and I uplifted about forty fully serviceable troops with a real possibility of the little shits shooting us out of the sky from inside the helicopter. Charlie's aircraft only had one grease-covered formation light working on top of the tail-boom and trying to keep it in view through the semi-opaque windscreen was impossible. Because we wanted to stay close in case one of us went down, we maintained separation by using our GPSs in the very black sky."

★

"Not only did we made little progress that day," Hennie said, "but had taken casualties and lost an important asset with the destruction of the DAF and its 23 mm gun. At our evening conference de Castro asked me to clear the road up to Muengue, which was about three kilometres past the point where we were planning to turn off to the west. As soon as the rest of the combat group had swung off, we would backtrack and follow them. The purpose was twofold: to add to Unita's confusion about the line of our advance, and to ensure that our rear was clear. He also said he preferred to keep us in the rear as a reserve and to give close protection to the logistics vehicles. This made sense to some degree, but he had five BMPs to fill this rôle. We would be better deployed alongside Mundoreal's combat team, which would simplify command and control and alleviate the need for Mundoreal to switch back and forth across the road. De Castro refused my suggestion.

"At 0600 on 6 July I told my group that the landmine threat was now serious and no one was to walk or drive on the road. We reached Muengue at about 1300 and I questioned the village chief, who was aware that a helicopter had been shot down north of his village and three whites killed. This was when Charlie had been forced to abandon his chopper. He said that one white had been captured, interrogated at Camaxillo and then taken to Cafunfo. It was just one more variation on the fate of our men.

"In the meantime, de Castro and the rest of the force had swung west towards the main objective, when they hit a large L-shaped ambush ten kilometres east of the Chifa River bridge. According to reports from Rolf, some thirty of the 150-man ambush force were killed. Much of the success was due to Mundoreal, who impatiently pulled his driver out of the seat, took over and drove straight into the enemy position, throwing the BMP around like a sports car and crushing some of the enemy under his tracks.

"Approaching the spot where the ambush had taken place, we debussed and swept through it, counting fourteen bodies and picking up two AK-47s. I was struck by how emaciated and poorly equipped they were. Rucksacks had been improvised out of mealie bags, while the rifle slings were made from flexible bark. On one of the bodies we found a Zairean military ID card, evidence that some of Mobutu's soldiers were fighting alongside Unita as mercenaries.

"It was late afternoon when de Castro reported that the bridge over the Chifa River had been blown. The amphibious BMPs could get across, but not the wheeled logistical vehicles. With Rusty handling the Caterpillar, he and his crew worked all night to span the gap. Trees were cut and placed in the river, then tons of sand and gravel scooped up and dumped on top. At about 0300 hours the job was completed and the exhausted crew retired for a few hours' rest. If Rolf and I had not talked de Castro out of destroying the front end loader we would have been halted right here, unable to advance or retreat.

"The next morning the forward elements began crossing. While awaiting our turn, a Katangese patrol came back with two terrified Unita deserters. They were delivered to my command vehicle, where we calmed them with assurances that they would not be harmed. I had just started to interrogate them when a group of FAA soldiers arrived and demanded the prisoners be handed over. Knowing the outcome would be torture and execution, I refused, which resulted in a scuffle breaking out between them and my group. The Angolan soldiers literally tried to break through the cordon to hack at the prisoners with axes. It was a tense few minutes and I was concerned that an actual fire fight might start at any moment. They were furious, accusing us of being pro-Unita. Fortunately, the Katangese commander, Colonel André, persuaded them to withdraw.

"Once the situation was under control I returned to questioning the two. They admitted being part of the 12th Unita Regular Battalion involved in the previous day's ambush. Some two hundred of them had departed Cafunfo by vehicle four days earlier and crossed the Chifa River with orders to intercept us at Lubalo and fight a delaying action. A two hundred-man commando unit had departed the same day in another four vehicles to overrun Cacolo and, because the Unita high command was unsure of the route we were taking, a third battalion had been deployed on the Camaxillo-Cafunfo road. This was literally life-saving information and I quickly sent a report to Mickey that a large Unita force was heading in his direction.

"Another valuable piece of intelligence was their description of the eleven ZSU-23 two and four-barrelled anti-aircraft guns deployed around Cafunfo. They also revealed that the 'Unita Cabinet' had been virtually wiped out by Pine's MiG-23 air strike a couple of days before their departure.

"Their admission that they had seen three white bodies brought in from the Camaxillo area and buried near Cafunfo was sad confirmation of our men's fate. They had also seen two white prisoners, one of whom had been wounded. My conclusion was that the latter had to be Renier and Steyn from the small recce patrol that disappeared near Cafunfo in March. They knew nothing of Handsome Ndlovu, the black ex-Recce who had been with them. It gave us hope that all three were still alive. Needless to say, we kept the two closely guarded to prevent our allies getting hold of them. I also decided to keep them with me all the way to Cafunfo."

★ ★ ★

Mines and Casevacs

"We crossed the Chifa River on the morning of 8 July and proceeded towards the west behind de Castro. As confirmation of what we'd learned from the prisoners, Nevis reported a force of some two hundred Unita and at least three vehicles, one towing an anti-aircraft gun, moving ahead of his column. Soon thereafter another of de Castro's DAFs was destroyed by a landmine, but the ZSU-23 was recovered. A few kilometres farther a wheel on the TMM had to be changed after hitting an anti-personnel mine.

"The forward elements had just started moving again when they made contact with the Unita force ahead of them. There was a brief fire fight before the enemy broke off. One FAA soldier was dead and three wounded as the result of one of their own mortar bombs hitting a tree near them. With Unita showing increasing determination to stop us, I again asked de Castro to let us move forward to Mundoreal's left. But again he disapproved my request.

"I contacted Saurimo to put the chopper crews on standby for casevacs and also requested that armed reconnaissance flights locate and pin down enemy concentrations ahead of us. If they could be fixed or at least slowed, it might allow us to close with and encircle them. We were starting to receive 106 mm and B-12 recoilless fire and it would be particularly helpful if these weapons could be destroyed by air strikes.

"Just before last light we laagered outside a fairly large village. Because the leading elements had already passed, we figured it was secure but a few minutes before midnight we heard the sounds of vehicles and went on high alert. Just after that, Unita opened up on us. Huge 23 mm tracers hurtled out of the night from high ground to the south-west, passing just over our heads with a deep-throated sound of ripping cloth. This roar was mingled with exploding mortar bombs and the sharper cracks of machine gun rounds. Tracers were all around us, ricocheting off trees and climbing into the sky like an incredible fireworks display. It was a terrifying experience. Nevis responded with his own 23 mm guns and after about twenty minutes Unita ceased fire and withdrew. Jos immediately went around checking the guys. Miraculously, we had no casualties and none of the vehicles had been damaged.

"At 0615 on 9 July we came under fire from two 82 mm mortars, most of the bombs landing just north of our position. De Castro suddenly radioed me to move my combat group forward to join Mundoreal. Such an order while we were under fairly accurate mortar fire was highly questionable, but I did a quick reorganization and sent my logistical element to slot in with the four BMPs de Castro had despatched to cover them. I was moving forward with my offensive element, when the enemy mortars were joined by accurate B-12 recoilless fire from directly ahead, the shells passing between the vehicles in the forward columns. Things were happening too fast to talk to de Castro through my interpreter, making our move an extremely difficult and dangerous undertaking.

"When I reached Mundoreal's position, he and I leapt out of our BMPs and dashed from the cover of one tree to another to confer. We quickly decided on our formation and counter-ambush drills, with him to the right of the road and my group to the left. We had just started moving again, when the enemy hit the rear echelons with 60 mm mortars, RPG-7s and heavy small arms fire. My logistical group returned fire, but two of the guys were wounded and the tyres on one of my Ural trucks were punctured by shrapnel.

"At this point one of de Castro's BMPs passed through the village where we had camped the night before. As it rounded a hut it detonated an anti-tank mine virtually centimetres from where one of my BMPs had passed earlier. The explosion ripped open the belly, killing the three-man crew instantly. The twisted chassis prevented the doors opening and the six infantrymen in the rear compartment were burnt to death. Another two FAA soldiers were killed by mortar fire and more logistical vehicles suffered flat tyres. I immediately radioed Saurimo for the casevac choppers and asked them to include ten sets each of Ural and DAF wheels.

"It was essential that we moved out of this hot spot as quickly as possible and I pushed Mundoreal to leave at best speed. At 1025 we reached a small village that had been used by Unita as a temporary base. Empty ammunition boxes lay everywhere, indicating a recent resupply. For the next four hours we were harassed by stand-off delaying attacks. It was precisely the situation I had predicted in the early planning discussions: as we advanced closer to Cafunfo Unita was throwing everything they had at us.

"We were passing through another kraal complex littered with empty ammunition crates when we hit a contact on our left flank. We killed a few of the enemy and the rest retreated. I swung back through the complex and noticed the body of a Unita soldier whose remains had been partially cremated in a burning hut. Unknown to me, one of my guys with a hidden video camera took some footage of the body and made comments about it and 'others to come' on the tape. The tape was later sold to the South African Broadcasting Corporation in Johannesburg and Channel Four in England, causing considerable controversy both at home and abroad.

"At 1500 Pine Pienaar rolled in with his MiG-23 and bombed the village of Sassa. Then, spotting a yellow Mercedes Benz truck, he came in again with cannon fire and set it alight. An hour later I was talking to Carl Alberts and Arthur Walker coming in with the tyres and other supplies."

*

"Because the other chopper was broken, we were breaking our own rules by flying a single ship mission," Alberts said, "but there were casevacs that needed uplifting and Hennie needed crucial supplies to continue advancing. Given how close Unita were, I decided that for the last ten kilometres we'd stay extra low. If the nose wheel clipped a tree or two, that was fine by me. While Arthur managed the GPS and the maps, I made comms with Hennie and informed him that we were five kilometres out, but when we got to the grid reference, we couldn't see him. Even worse, Hennie couldn't hear the helicopter.

"We eventually located him eight kilometres further north. He had chosen fairly open ground as a landing zone and had parked two BMPs facing outwards on the northern side. He wanted me to land between them, which would offer some protection for the short time we'd be on the ground. With the aircraft still close to its maximum weight, I turned final and was at about sixty feet and forty knots when we suddenly lost power.

As Natasha was screeching in Russian and Tino shouting in Portuguese that something was wrong, I saw the left-hand engine failure light illuminated on the panel between my knees.

"'Fucking engine's gone. We've lost an engine!'

"'Ja. Fuck it,' confirmed Arthur in his inimitable way.

"Using all available power and pulling off a few rotor revs, we made a 'positive' landing 500 metres short of our BMP protection. Hennie was on the radio immediately.

"'*Carl, no, no, no! Don't land there! You'll get fucked up! Come to where the BMPs are! Get the fuck out of there!*'

"Imagining Unita mortar bombs already in the air, we didn't need further encouragement, but when we attempted to get airborne on one engine, we merely extended the undercarriage shock-absorbers before the rotor revs started decaying. A BMP raced towards us in a cloud of black exhaust smoke and started firing its 30 mm cannon into the bush behind us. More BMPs moved to surround us and the two casevacs were carried to the helicopter in a groundsheet. I called Hennie to the window and hurriedly explained to him that as soon as the supplies were unloaded we'd attempt to get airborne on one engine.

"A crowd of troops gathered and after much punching and shouting by their officers they were persuaded to shift their own food and supplies. We had always flown with the rear clamshell doors removed to speed up the loading and unloading in a hot LZ. Thinking the doors gave them more protection, the FAA pilots always insisted on putting them back on, which made off-loading two tons of rat packs and tyres through the single side door a lengthy process. When the aircraft had been emptied, the casevacs, one burnt white from the chest down, started to board, but the rest of the crowd stormed it, bowling them over and trampling them underfoot. The burn victim screamed so loudly that I heard him through my headset over the engine noise. Simon and Rich punched and kicked to get the mound of soldiers off the wounded.

"An officer ran to my window and yelled to get airborne. As I explained that it was impossible on one engine with that load, fighting continued at the door and the aircraft continued to fill. In desperation, we attempted to start the dead engine. With Unita likely to start dropping mortars at any moment, we were sitting inside a potential bomb anchored to the ground by more than forty cowering troops. We had no other option but to shut down the good engine. Even after I applied the rotor brake and climbed out, they refused to budge. Simon and I went to the back and after some difficulty managed to unlatch the clamshell doors. They burst open, dropping troops into a heap on the ground. Emptying the aircraft was entrusted to Simon and Rich, while Arthur, Tino and I tried to establish what had gone wrong with the engine.

"Hennie informed Saurimo of our predicament and Pine was scrambled in the MiG-23 to give us close air support. Arriving twenty minutes later, he sent rockets into Unita positions ahead of us. I spoke to him on the radio and he told us that, with no other choppers available, there was nothing that Saurimo could do about our predicament. This was very depressing, as I wasn't enchanted with the idea of going to Cafunfo in the back of a BMP.

"As Tino scratched around in the engine bay, Arthur and I thumbed through our home-made emergency manual and decided that the engine cut was probably due to a governor overspeed shutdown. After much searching and switcheology, Tino found the governor reset and on the first attempted startup the auxiliary power unit cut out, but on the second, we managed to light the failed engine. We immediately fired up number two engine, pulled power and got the hell out of there.

"Heading back at high level in case we picked up problems with the engine again, I asked Tino to check what was going on in the back. Our two casevacs were on board along with the FAA casualties and two bodies. There were great sighs of relief from everyone when we finally arrived back at Saurimo with our broken cargo. Our doctor was on hand with two stretchers to handle our wounded. About twenty curious Angolan troops were standing around when the burnt and bleeding FAA casevacs got themselves out of the aircraft. None of their fellow countrymen lifted a hand, even as one of them started crawling towards the sickbay truck.

"We lent the wounded a hand, much to the amusement of the spectators, and then departed for a much sought-after beer, the two bodies still lying sprawled in the back of the helicopter."

★ ★ ★

Russian Resupply

"Minutes after Carl and Arthur lifted off, Pine returned at low level and made strafing runs on Sassa," Hennie said, "raising cheers from our madly waving guys. With dusk approaching, we decided to set up a TB right where we were and immediately turned our hands to vehicle maintenance. Our Ural's turbo-charger had given out and the truck was towed into the laager area. I still had a number of logistical vehicles with flat tyres and other problems at the rear of the column and put Jan Kellerman in charge of sorting them out.

"In our earlier planning sessions we had jokingly dubbed this stretch of road the Savimbi Trail. We could no longer see anything funny about it. Before breaking out into open ground, mines had kept us off the road and weaving through the trees, where incoming mortar bombs detonated like air bursts in the branches. And the day had cost us dear: eleven FAA soldiers dead, others wounded, a BMP burnt to cinders and the TMM destroyed by an anti-tank mine as it crossed a shallow stream. Additionally, two Chevrolet pickup trucks used by the FAA commandos were written off. The really frustrating thing was that the enemy had remained two to three kilometres ahead, preventing us from encircling and cutting off the heavy crew-served weapons.

"That night I told de Castro that we needed the next day to do proper maintenance on all the vehicles still requiring it. I also suggested that the air drop be made on our present position. Plenty big enough, it was out of range of the 23 mm in case the Il-76s had to come in low. De Castro refused on all counts.

"On 10 July at 0600 we started on our trucks that were still unserviceable, our guys working frantically to get them ready. Pine came over in the PC-7, reporting that he had hit a white vehicle inside Sassa, but missed a BM-21. Thirty minutes later the Ural was ready to go and we set off in the lead, heading for the drop zone, when Pine hit an IFA three-tonne vehicle just to our west, then flew off to recce the area between us and Firiquich.

"We'd stopped ten kilometres west of the DZ and established a temporary base, when two of my guys came to me and said they were resigning from EO and wanted to go out on the next helicopter flight. I couldn't blame them. They were fairly inexperienced soldiers and the stress of the last couple of days in particular might have unnerved anyone. But because their return to South Africa might jeopardize our operational security, or set an example for others, I couldn't let them go until we'd reached Cafunfo. I did remove them from the forward fighting echelon and reassigned them to the rear logistical element, where they could still be put to good use.

"By mid-morning on 11 July we were waiting near the orange DZ marker panels. A fuming Brigadier de Castro roared up and demanded to know the contents of the air supply. I listed the main components of ammunition, lubricants, food, spares and tyres. To my utter bewilderment, he demanded that it all be replaced with ration packs. Holding my temper, I patiently explained that the cargo was packed and prepared in Luanda and that it was impossible to alter the contents at such short notice. Still furious, he roared off. The two Il-76s arrived overhead and the Russian crews rolled the supplies off the tailgates at 20,000 feet. We could see the drogue-stabilized pallets in freefall down to about 1,000 feet, where KAP-3 automatic openers released the parachutes, everything landing right in the middle of the drop zone. It was an impressive display.[38] Immediately afterwards Pine passed over in a MiG-23 and reported taking fire north of us.

"Unita was now fully aware of our main axis of advance and that the next town we'd hit was Firiquich. Sitting on a crossroads that branched north-east to Camaxillo, south-west to Cuango, west to Cafunfo and directly east to where we were poised, it was a strategic stronghold and there was little doubt that the Unita commander would initially hit us with everything he had to prevent us taking it. Putting myself in his shoes, I was sure that after a tough first stand his only option would be a series of delaying actions as

---

[38] A few weeks later the Russian pilots explained to Hennie over a bottle of chilled vodka that it was a technique they'd perfected in Afghanistan to avoid the Stinger missiles supplied to the mujahedin by the US.

he fell back under the weight of our armour. For us Firiquich was a crucial intermediate objective that had to be taken at all costs.

"I gave Ricardo a sitrep and requested an airstrike for 1000 hours the next day. Ricardo acknowledged the request, then told me to stand by for an important operations order to be delivered to Brigadier de Castro without delay. The order, from General Marques, was received in Portuguese for de Castro and an English version for myself. My eyes widened as I read it. It stated that as soon as we captured Firiquich, de Castro was to split his force, with an independent combat group proceeding south to capture the town of Cuango, while the balance of his force continued the advance to Cafunfo.

"My immediate reaction was one of sheer disbelief. The order was contrary to the basic principles of modern mobile warfare. With FAA having lost four BMPs, we were already under strength. Not only would our artillery support be inadequate, but the two MiG-23s and PC-7s were already stretched to the limit supporting our advancing column. By splitting our forces – thus weakening the weight of our momentum – we'd be playing into the enemy's hands. I stomped over to de Castro's HQ and angrily raised my concerns with Rolf while de Castro studied the order. Without looking up from it, he said through my interpreter, 'I do not agree with the idea. We stay as we are. We have come a long way together, we go together till the end,' adding that he would discuss the matter with General Marques. Later that night, Ricardo radioed to say that the order had been cancelled."

★

"Our air wing defences were bolstered with another thousand sandbags around and inside our building," said Alberts, "as well as twelve newly recruited black ex-Koevoet guys who moved in with us to boost our internal defences. This eased the load of doing guard duties and we only had to do a beat every fourth evening. The lights-out curfew had been moved forward to 7 p.m., so one should be able to get in a good night's sleep for a change. Theoretically, at least.

"At about eight o'clock the previous night, the odd burst of gunfire from the main gate intensified into something more serious. After a brief fire fight, with us observing from behind our sandbags, the gunfire gave way to much shouting and arguing that carried on well into the night. We established that the cause was the untimely arrival of two semi-inebriated commandos who didn't know the password. They'd been having a party in town and were on their way home when they walked into the same guards who had run away when fifty Unita hadn't know the password either. The result of this password problem was lots of exciting fireworks.

"We went to bed, only to be awakened at first light by renewed gunfire. The cause of this contact was retribution from the commandos. Not particularly brave at night, they waited until dawn, then set off past our room to take on the gate guards. This fire fight lasted a bit longer than the previous one, with commandos and guards running all over the camp. It was only when the 23 mm cannon at the gate was swung around to face into the camp, that we decided that even from behind our sandbags, this was not a healthy spectator sport. Once this shit came to an end, the camp returned to its normal routine as if nothing had happened.

"Later that afternoon the sickbay erupted, when one of the patients had an accidental discharge and wounded someone. The mate of the injured man grabbed his AK and started swinging it around. With only one participant in this potential gunfight, we keenly observed the proceedings and, with about ten guns trained on the cowboy, waited in anticipation for any hint of him starting to shoot in our direction.

"All in all, the entire bunch were the most trigger-happy and undisciplined rabble that one could hope to meet. Exceptionally gung ho when it came to shooting at each other, they were worthless at fighting the opposing side, as was demonstrated the night Unita attacked, when I doubt that a single shot was fired by our local gun-toting heroes.

"As for us, our aircraft situation was looking a bit sad right when we needed them the most to support Hennie, who was now within eighty kilometres of Cafunfo and possibly on the threshold of a major punch-up."

★ ★ ★

Gunfight at Firiquich

"At dawn on 12 July I established comms with Ricardo," Hennie said, "who advised me that Cacolo had been hit the night before at 2300 hours. They had come under heavy 82 mm mortar fire, followed by a penetration attack against the north-west corner where Mickey and his team slept. When the bombardment began it was extremely accurate, which had to be the result of Unita spies pacing off the distances to their quarters. One mortar bomb penetrated the roof of the house where Mickey and some of his guys slept. Had they been there, it is unlikely any would have survived. Fortunately, they had been on high alert since I'd passed on the information from the two Unita deserters six days earlier. At last light each day the team left their sleeping quarters for prepared ambush positions along the route Mickey anticipated Unita using to enter the town.

"As the bombardment was underway, the Unita assault group moved down the road to the forming up place from where they would launch their attack. They were entering the killing zone of Mickey's ambush, when a nervous FAA soldier opened fire prematurely. The rest of the team then opened fire, catching the enemy completely by surprise and killing seven. Very early the next morning they did a follow up and found the fresh graves of another four enemy, as well as numerous blood trails. I thanked my lucky stars that we'd saved those Unita prisoners from the axes.[39]

"Dawn was just breaking as I signed off and heard the in-bound Mi-17. Inside were replacements for my two guys who had been wounded on the 9th, as well as replacements for the two who had asked to be reassigned. I was a bit concerned about these four arriving at this stage of the game,

---

[39] Some weeks later I visited Cacolo and Mickey showed me the house where, had it not been for the intelligence from the two Unita prisoners, he would have been sleeping that night. A favourite souvenir from his days with EO is his attaché case with a large piece of mortar shrapnel embedded in the lid."

because today definitely promised to be a serious baptism of fire.

"One of my black ex-32 Bn troops came over and told me another FAA BMP had broken down due to the cooling system having run dry. To prevent it falling into Unita's hands de Castro ordered a hole dug with the Caterpillar, pushed the BMP into it and covered it up. This was the fifth one they'd lost, three through sheer negligence.

"I called everyone together for a briefing to orientate the new guys. The area was quite open, I pointed out, with low, rolling hills. We had good lines of sight, but so did the enemy. We would approach Firiquich over a wide front, with Nevis's combat group to our left, then swing right and bypass the town to take up positions on the road leading north to Cafunfo. Hopefully, we'd get there in time to cut off escaping Unita support vehicles and weapons. As soon as we were in position Nevis would enter the town.

"At 0700 we moved out of our TB, took our place and began advancing in a wide formation, my BMP leading between the first two combat teams and the third combat team following in reserve. The dust and black ash rising behind us made our advance visible for miles. Two kilometres from Firiquich, we started receiving accurate mortar, B-12 and 106 fire. As we got closer a twin-barrelled 23 mm opened up and we watched the huge tracers ripping towards us. It was moments like this that I gave thanks to the BMP's designers for the effective armour we had in front. I gave the order to return fire and the 30 mms began delivering speculative fire.

"Nevis and Mundoreal drove towards the centre of Firiquich, where the thatched huts were already burning from the high explosive incendiary rounds. We made a right hook, crested a small hill and started down, coming under extremely intense and accurate mortar fire. Keeping the infantry in the vehicles, I ordered the gunners to engage any position that looked like it might hide the enemy.

"Jos had just ordered Harry to traverse left and open fire on a low, wooded ridge at my ten o'clock, when suddenly we pitched nose down and I was hurled against the bulkhead. We had driven into a camouflaged tank trap and were tilted down at about a forty-five degree angle. Paul immediately tried to reverse out, but the tracks just spun on the edge. We were stuck, a perfect target for an anti-armour weapon.

"Jos ordered the two cars to my left to open fire on the ridge. As they were putting down suppressive fire, Riaan raced back with his BMP and stopped behind me. With in-coming small arms fire and mortars exploding all around us, the crew jumped out, hooked a tow cable to the rear of my vehicle and dived back into their BMP. The air was thick with dust and ash from the explosions and the BMPs' tracks churning up the ground. Even with our hatches closed, we clearly heard the mortar bombs. As Riaan's driver took up tension on the cable, Paul started reversing, and with the other car pulling we backed out of the tank trap. It was an incredibly courageous effort on their part.

"Mortar shrapnel was ricocheting off the sides, but so far none of our vehicles had taken a hit on top. In the rear compartments the infantry were ready, with the PKM gunners prepared to be the first out. Clear of the trap, we moved to join Dino's combat team on the left and advanced slowly, all of our guns concentrated on the ridge where most of the enemy fire seemed to be coming from. As we closed on it the mortar fire seemed to slacken and the Katangese infantry debussed and swept forward into the tree line. On the right Chris's combat team was already heading for the road to cut off escaping enemy forces.

"Our guys joined the Katangese and it was fantastic to see my black and white South Africans moving forward in pairs as the BMPs gave supporting fire. The mortars stopped and my guys, using fire and movement, swept through the wooded area with the Katangese. Ahead of them we could see the enemy running through the bush in the direction of Cafunfo. They were engaged with the 30 mms and PKMs. The infantry came out the other side of the wooded area to link up with us and the section commanders estimated that between fifty and a hundred enemy had been killed there. It had been sheer luck on our part, as we hadn't actually observed any movement when Jos ordered Harry to put down speculative fire. The effect of the 30 mm guns and AGS-17 grenades had devastated a well camouflaged enemy. We later concluded that they thought we'd come up the road and that once we had passed their position they would launch an infantry attack against the soft-skinned logistical vehicles following.

"As soon as all our infantry were back in the BMPs and accounted for, we moved forward to link up with Chris's combat team and by 1500 hours the entire group was complete again. Incredibly, not one of us had received the slightest wound.

"We didn't stop to consolidate the position or collect enemy weapons, leaving that for the rear elements to handle. Rolf radioed to say that Nevis's combat group were making good progress through Firiquich, had met little resistance and had captured the 23 mm gun that had given us problems earlier. At about the same time Louwrens called from his MiG to say that he'd hit a blue truck near the town of Muvuca, about ten kilometres north of us.

"An hour later Mundoreal joined us. After a quick planning session we decided to move down the shallow valley to the next village of Muana-Cagi, some two kilometres farther. This would get us out of Firiquich, which Unita was sure to hit with mortar fire come nightfall. We would then consolidate and set up a temporary base, where we could do our maintenance before last light and be resupplied with ammunition and water. I wanted to finish early and allow the guys to get their heads down for a well deserved rest. It had been another hard day and tomorrow was probably going to be just as tough. We could expect Unita to plot our advance by the dust trails and bring down indirect fire on every little village we passed through.

"Ready for an ambush, we moved cautiously up to Muana-Cagi, then another 500 metres or so past it to set up a laager area with Mundoreal. The guys began their daily maintenance while sentries established listening posts outside our perimeter. Rolf radioed to say that Nevis's combat group would laager in Firiquich, and that a sweep through our contact area had confirmed seventy three enemy dead and a large number of PKM machine guns. Most significantly, a well known senior Unita general by the name of Antonio Nevis was among the dead. According to FAA, he had been a real thorn in their side for years."

★ ★ ★

Point 1032

"Just before first light on 13 July everybody was packed, sleeping kit rolled up, crews manning the vehicles. I was having a final chat with the crew commanders, when we heard the faint but distinctive *thunk*s of mortar tubes. Seconds later de Castro's HQ and the rear elements were under a barrage of 120 mm mortars, B-12s and 106s. Rolf radioed that the mortar fire was accurate and they were moving into an open harbour area to lessen the possibility of casualties and damage to equipment.

"Suddenly, from 300 metres directly in front of us, more mortars started firing. This Unita group obviously didn't know we were there and the mortar bombs were sailing over us to land among de Castro's rear elements in Firiquich. I made a quick assessment. Here was a golden opportunity to capture some of their indirect weapons. Not wanting to reveal my position by starting the BMPs, I sent two seven-man infantry teams forward and placed my BMP crews on immediate standby.

"Thinking that the forward elements were only in Firiquich, Unita had placed no infantry protection in front of their mortar line. Moving cautiously, the teams closed to within thirty metres of the enemy position. As soon as I heard them open fire, I gave the *Go!* and Chris and Dino reacted immediately with their BMPs. The shock effect of the BMPs racing forward with their 30 mm guns and AGS-17s blazing was devastating. Exploding shells scythed through the Unita line, raising clouds of dust and setting the dry bush on fire. Within seconds, at least thirty enemy were dead or dying. There was only desultory return fire, before the survivors broke and fled.

"As the infantry teams advanced, Nick stopped to remove a weapon from a dead Unita. Just as he bent down, a wounded rebel opened fire, hitting him in the chest. The rebel was killed seconds later and Nick was immediately attended to by an ops medic, who sealed the sucking chest wound and got a drip in before loading him into a BMP and radioing a report back to me. By now the whole area was ablaze and all of them withdrew.

"Nick was brought back to my HQ as a Priority 1 casevac and I called for a chopper to take him out, along with the FAA wounded. The chopper crews responded quickly and were landing at Firiquich by 1000 hours, having drawn fire from the west on their way in. They picked up the FAA casevacs at Brigadier de Castro's position, then he and I had a blazing row over the radio when he refused permission for them to fly the additional four kilometres for Nick. I told Rolf that if I had to send Nick by BMP over the rough terrain he could very well be dead by the time he got there. De Castro eventually agreed and a chopper flew up to collect Nick and rush him back to Saurimo.

"At about that time Louwrens was on his way back from Cafunfo in a MiG-23, when he reported taking 23 mm AA fire from a position north of the town. I remember thinking it odd that a Unita gunner would give away his position by firing at a target too high to hit – unless he was nervous about protecting something.

"De Castro's group was still under heavy 120 mm mortar, recoilless and anti-aircraft fire from the northwest. I took a magnetic bearing on the sounds of the firing, converted it to a grid bearing and checked it against the map. The bearing led directly to a prominent contour feature noted on the map as Point 1032 and intersected a hairpin bend on the road crossing the feature. This made perfect sense. By knowing their own exact position, it was easy for them to get an accurate bearing and distance for de Castro's group in Firiquich. My guys were hurrying to assist FAA in setting up their own mortars, but I told them to forget it. Point 1032 was beyond the 82's effective range. When I contacted Saurimo to ask for air support, Ricardo advised that Pine was already airborne towards Cafunfo and would be diverted to me."

"I made comms with Hennie, who'd been complaining for days about a B-12 that had been hitting them," Pine said. "I flew directly over his position at about fifty feet and he gave me a bearing to the target. I picked up the road and began following it, looking for the hairpin where he was sure the Unita heavy weapons were firing from. As soon as I identified it I banked over it and continued another couple of klicks without seeing anything. I brought the airplane over to head back and just then heard the canvas-ripping sounds of 23 mm shells passing very close on my blind side. I couldn't spot the source and was heading back towards Hennie, when I caught a glimpse of a truck hidden in the bush about five metres off the road.

Gotcha.

"I firewalled the throttle in a climbing left tear-drop back towards the hairpin, setting my two rocket pods on ripple, and lowered the nose, centring on the camouflaged vehicle. At a slant range of about 600 metres I squeezed the trigger and both pods emptied in a second. They hit and before I could even blink there was a massive explosion, sending a white shock wave racing outwards and then giving the airplane a huge jolt just as I was pulling out above an enormous fireball. This was followed by a quickly expanding cloud of black smoke and the sound of the explosion penetrating the cockpit. Looking back over my shoulder, my first impression was that it had to be a petrol or diesel bowser. There was no point in hanging around. Out of rockets and already low on fuel, I gave Hennie a quick report and turned for home."

"We saw Pine roll in," said Hennie, "saw the rockets go and then a huge flash, followed by a mushroom cloud of black smoke. We felt the shock wave under our feet, and then the sound reached us, followed by the sounds of secondary explosions, one after the other, that lasted for a good ten minutes. Pine, already heading back to Saurimo, was jubilant in describing the fireworks display.

"Even as the explosions continued, we prepared to advance to take advantage of the enemy's confusion. At approximately 1300 we reached Point 1032 and stared in amazement. It hadn't been a fuel bowser he hit, but ammunition. Thick smoke hung over a carpet of exploded and unexploded ordnance. Mortar bombs, 106 shells, B-12 warheads and 23 mm ammo lay scattered everywhere – over the road and far into the surrounding bush. Pine had hit at least one of three trucks loaded with ammunition and the others had gone up in huge sympathetic explosions. From the human remains we could identify, it was apparent that the crews had dived under the trucks when they saw Pine roll in.

"There was also a Unimog mounted with a B-12 and towing a ZSU-23/2 that had been totally destroyed. Because the unexploded ammunition was extremely unstable from the shock and heat of the detonations I ordered everyone to stay in the vehicles. Some of my guys started coughing and gagging from the acrid smoke and I ordered the group to evacuate the area immediately. We made a wide detour around the area, taking great care not to drive over unexploded ordnance that had been hurled a hundred or more metres from the centre of the blast.

"Our fixed-wing pilots had traded aircraft again and Louwrens came over, looking for the 23 mm position that Pine had reported earlier. He drew fire also and rolled in for an attack, during which he spotted a partially camouflaged blue truck. As Louwrens headed back to Saurimo to swap aircraft again, he gave me an in-flight report and I made a note to investigate the village of Muvuca. It was now late afternoon. Mundoreal's group was on our left, both of us in line-abreast as we approached the village. Gunners were poised behind the 30 mm cannon, ready to open fire. But nothing. As we passed through the village, Jos noticed vehicle tracks branching off to the right.

"Jos, take the tracks and order the others to follow," I said, switching radios to tell Rolf that we were investigating and that they should sit tight. About 500 metres down the track we spotted the blue truck Louwrens had reported. I ordered the infantry to debus and, covered by the BMPs, we advanced cautiously. Then, for the second time that afternoon, we stopped and stared. We could not believe our eyes. What loomed in front of us could have been out of a film. Hidden from the air by trees lay a massive supply dump. Huge stockpiles of neatly stacked two hundred-litre fuel drums rested under grass roofs alongside row upon row of grass huts about thirty metres long. It had to be one of Unita's major supply depots.

"Cautioning them about the possibility of booby traps, I asked Jos to order the infantry to investigate. The huts were stacked to the roof with boxes of tinned food stuffs – corned beef from France, sardines from Argentina, pork from Holland. At a quick estimate there were over 500 drums of diesel and a hundred tonnes of food. The next day the FAA rear elements conducted a thorough search and discovered underground bunkers containing large quantities of landmines, B-10, B-12 and 106 mm anti-tank shells, 82 mm and 81 mm mortars as well as hundreds of thousands of rounds of AK-47 and PKM ammo. What was most amazing was that there was not a single Unita soldier to be found. Of course, after Pine's bombing earlier, that wasn't too surprising."

The air wing wasn't finished for the day.

The Angolans were still after us to take out the Lui Bridge," said Carlos back in Saurimo, "and as an added incentive, General McKenzie promised a very nice diamond to whoever managed to hit it. A couple of hours after Pine had taken out the ammunition vehicles, Louwrens headed for Xa-Muteba."

"I was monitoring the radios at Saurimo," Ricardo said, "when I heard Louwrens shouting, 'Yes, yes, yes!' I asked him what was wrong, and he said in Afrikaans, *'Hy is af!'* It is down! Everyone in the ops room cheered."

"Louwrens came over in a MiG-23," Hennie said, "and excitedly reported that he'd put a 250-kilogram bomb right on the middle of the Lui bridge and sent it collapsing into the gorge. That was going to really hamper Unita moving reinforcements and supplies to block our advance. As the light faded we hastily established a temporary base 500 metres outside the depot and I informed Rolf of our discovery, suggesting that we stay in the area for a day to check it out properly. Unita's strategy was emerging. They now knew that the route we were taking to Cafunfo. Should we succeed in taking it, they were planning a protracted war of attrition from the eastern region where they'd draw on supplies from central stockpiles such as this one.

"This day belonged to us: our success in knocking out the first mortar group, the destruction of indirect weapons and their ammunition train on 1032 and now this. To add icing to the cake, Rolf radioed to say that they had swept our first contact area where Nick had been hit and picked up two 82 mm and two 60 mm mortar tubes, 17 AK-47s, three LAWs and a total of thirty six enemy KIAs. Though tired, the guys were in fantastic spirits. They'd come through another day of hard fighting and done magnificently. We drank a toast to the excellent job by EO's air wing and wondered what the next day would bring."

★ ★ ★

ROUTE OF JOINT EO/FAA ADVANCE TO CAFUNFO

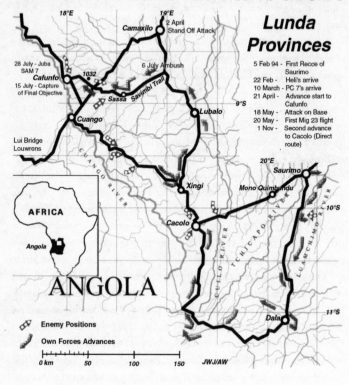

Lunda Provinces

5 Feb 94 - First Recce of Saurimo
22 Feb - Heli's arrive
10 March - PC 7's arrive
21 April - Advance start to Cafunfo
18 May - Attack on Base
20 May - First Mig 23 flight
1 Nov - Second advance to Cacolo (Direct route)

28 July - Juba SAM 7
15 July - Capture of Final Objective

2 April Stand Off Attack

6 July Ambush

Camaxilo
Cafunfo
1032
Sassa
Savimbi Trail
Cuango
Lubalo
Lui Bridge Louwrens
CUANGO RIVER
Xingi
Saurimo
Mono Quimbundu
Cacolo
CUILO RIVER
TCHICAPO RIVER
LUAMCHIMO RIVER
Dala

AFRICA
Angola
ANGOLA

Enemy Positions
Own Forces Advances

0 km   50   100   150

JWJ/AW

18°E   19°E   20°E
9°S   10°S   11°S

Heavy Fighting

14 July

"I'd just told my people to be ready to move at 0700, when B-12 and 82 mm mortar fire began landing about 500 metres due east of us. Unita had obviously expected us to make our TB farther away from the supply dump. Ignoring the in-coming fire, we jumped off at 0720, determined to fight our way through the next fourteen kilometres to the town of Fernandes by that afternoon. That would place us only ten kilometres east of Cafunfo, which meant we would probably face even more desperate Unita defences. At 0830 we came under heavy enemy fire from directly ahead. Mortars were hitting around us and small arms fire cut through the bush, but the thickness of the undergrowth prevented us from locating the source. Mundoreal was somewhere to the left front and we could hear him engaged in a fierce fire fight.

"At 0840 I scrambled two MiG-23s. At this critical moment one of my BMPs turned too sharply and threw a track. Dino and his crew were on the ground in seconds to sort it out, set the correct tension and scramble back into the vehicle. At 0900 Ricardo confirmed the MiGs were wheels up and heading in our direction. Ten minutes later very intense 14.5 mm and 23 mm fire began passing just over our heads.

"We advance slowly behind short bursts of speculative fire from the 30 mm guns. Approaching the village of Valodia, we halt for a quick planning session. It's to be a fast attack. Moving again at 1015. There's a steep escarpment to our left, making it difficult to encircle the town from that direction, forcing us into a frontal attack. 1145. Contact. Close range to our left. Infantry spill out as all BMPs pour speculative fire into the bush. Mortars and small arms fire still coming in. It's excellent to see our own

EO infantry on the ground and advancing into the enemy fire. 1215. Valodia in sight. Heavy mortar and small arms fire. One of my guys picks up some shrapnel, but the wound isn't serious. Closing on the town, engaging with 30 mms and AGS-17s. Just ahead, Mundoreal takes the left flank. We draw fire from our two o'clock position, return it and see the enemy running north west. We drive through the town, firing all the way. I try to get comms with the MiGs but no luck. Spot houses some 800 metres farther ahead, Jos giving excellent fire orders. Brief stop at 1320, make comms with Saurimo and hear Ricardo say that Colonel Gino cancelled the MiGs and hijacked the PC-7 for another mission. Another mission? What are they thinking?

"It seemed almost miraculous when we came out the other side of Valodia with only one minor wound and no one killed. Not only had we been receiving intensive enemy fire, but the rear FAA infantry had been firing rifle grenades that were landing between our vehicles and among our infantry. It was this fire, not the enemy's, that wounded one of our men. Inside Valodia we find numerous one-man foxholes that we guess had been dug for protection against air strikes. There is also evidence of a major Unita resupply, with empty ammo boxes scattered everywhere.

"At 1410 we stop for a quick bite and to coordinate our movements with Nevis, who has been behind Mundoreal as a tactical reserve and is now ready to link up with him. Inasmuch as Mundoreal's combat team is already on the left, we decide Nevis should stay on that flank and I'll remain on the right. We start moving in a two-up formation — two platoons of three BMPs leading, with each group maintaining a small tactical reserve for reinforcements or tactical encirclement.

"At 1535 we're approaching the town of Fernandes. Contact in front! Because the bush is very thick to the right, we decide to make a mounted attack with infantry firing from the gunports and main coaxial guns and AGS-17s giving speculative fire. We pass a well-constructed bunker but the enemy have abandoned it. By 1600 we reach the next town of Alberto, just seven kilometres from Cafunfo. We stop to make a TB while Pine orbits in the PC-7 to provide reconnaissance and air support should we need it. He disappears in the direction of Cafunfo, then passes over us just after last light, reporting that he attacked two vehicles moving north out of Cafunfo, destroying one.

"The guys were exhausted after another hard day under fire, but daily maintenance and replenishment of ammunition still had to be done before settling down for the night. Being so close to the final objective, we dug shallow slit trenches in case of a mortar attack. As I had predicted, the enemy was using every single village and town to delay our advance, falling back from one to the next, setting up their heavy weapons and waiting for us to reach a known point before opening fire. Wherever they had high ground, they'd engage us with towed anti-aircraft guns as soon as we came into sight. Because we invariably had to stay on the watershed, we were almost always on the skyline, always on the high ground, meaning the forward elements were always exposed. And there was nothing we could do to change that.

"Had we more helicopters, I might have been able to deploy some of my Special Forces troops behind the enemy lines to lay ambushes for their retreating vehicles and support weapons. That we didn't suffer more casualties was amazing. Unita's mining of the road had not proved all that successful either, due to our driving through the bush. In fact, there hadn't been a vehicle lost to a mine in over a week.

"That evening I sent back a detailed situation report to Ricardo and said that we should be in Cafunfo by 1300 hours the next day. I requested that a PC-7 and MiG-23 be overhead, the first to look for targets along the western side of the Cuango River where Unita was sure to position their indirect weapons and bring down fire as we advanced into Cafunfo. Being so close to our final objective that a Unita attack was very likely, I decided that we'd remain on high alert all night. The guys would have to get what sleep they could between pulling sentry duty.

"While others tried to sleep, I sat up for a long time with the two Unita prisoners, questioning them in detail about the layout of Cafunfo and the defensive positions. What was of particular concern to me was the possibility of mine fields, but they stated that during their time there they'd seen no evidence of either anti-tank or anti-personnel mines. Instead, Unita had established their in-depth defences at the town of Cuango, which lay on the road they had expected to be our main axis of attack. I finally sent them away and crawled into my sleeping bag, mind racing as I went over every detail of the plan and our preparations, looking for any flaw, anything I'd forgotten. It was a long time before I fell asleep."

★ ★ ★

Cafunfo Captured

"It was still dark at 0500 hours when Rolf advised me that de Castro wanted a final co-ordinating conference at 0730. I had to shake my head in bewilderment. We had our plan, we were ready to advance. If he wanted a conference it should have been done the night before so that the crews could have been briefed well ahead of time on any changes. I rogered and then called Ricardo, who confirmed that my request for close air support had been approved and the aircraft and pilots were on standby. As I replaced the mike I realized how lucky we were in having Ricardo as our tactical commander back at Saurimo. A very experienced Special Forces officer, he was always there, always positive, regardless of the time of day or night and gave his entire attention to supporting my every request.

"Dawn was just breaking an hour later. We completed our stand-to and were making final preparations for the last leg into Cafunfo. At 0630 I walked over to Nevis's headquarters to organize our ride back to de Castro's position. Returning about fifteen minutes later, I stopped at the rear of my vehicle for a roll of toilet paper, but Harry said that Paul had already taken it and gone into the bush. About ten metres outside the perimeter I met him coming back, took the roll and continued forward, looking for a suitable spot. It struck me that I was violating everything I'd told my people over the last couple of weeks – such as informing everyone that you're moving outside the TB, such as always having a weapon, such as taking a buddy to stand guard while you're doing your business.

"At that moment I heard rustling in the bushes slightly to my left but thought it had to be one of our chaps looking for his own spot. I heard the rustling again and stopped. Something wasn't right. The next moment a soldier appeared from around a bush. I immediately recognized the distinctive Unita bush cap and the equally distinctive olive-green uniform. I was alone and unarmed and only Paul knew where I'd gone. We stared at each other for a fraction of a second and then, as though in slow motion, he brought up his AK.

"I ducked, spun around and sprinted for my BMP as he opened fire. It was the longest ten or twelve metres of my life, made even longer by the fact that my own chaps were already returning fire from inside the laager area. More small arms fire exploded from behind me and I dashed up to the nose of my vehicle to take cover, then slipped down the far side to the rear where a very distressed Paul, who had last seen me heading into the bush, was screaming, *'The colonel is dead! The colonel is dead!'*

"Jos was already pumping grenades from his AGS-17 as Harry jumped behind his gun and opened up with the cannon. The rest of our guys manned weapons and the bush to our one o'clock position exploded into a cloud of thick dust from the suppressive fire. Adding to the roar on the left was Nevis's group doing the same in case there was an attack on their side. The fire fight broke off after approximately five minutes and the infantry cautiously moved forward to sweep the area. They picked up a quite a few RPG-7 launchers, as well as rucksacks full of RPG rockets, one AK-47, a large number of white phosphorus hand grenades and more rucksacks full of personal kit. Though a number of blood trails were discovered, they found no bodies. Given all the launchers, rockets and WP grenades that the enemy had dropped, it was obvious that their primary targets were the BMPs.

"I checked the front of my vehicle and there virtually wasn't a square inch unmarked by small arms fire, while the ground all around was ploughed up by bullets. It was absolutely incredible that I hadn't been hit. I was called over to the centre of our TB, where a number of people were clustered. Lying on the ground was Colonel André, who had taken a bad flesh wound through the upper part of his right arm. He was in great pain and Charles, my ops medic, started working on him. I decided that he had to be casevacked as soon as possible. He was almost in tears, begging me to take him with us when we returned to South Africa. I promised I would do everything in my power, but I knew it would be virtually impossible to send him to South Africa. He was loaded on a vehicle and carried to the rear.

"I was still shaking from my close escape when I walked over to the BMP waiting to take me to Brigadier de Castro's conference. As I crossed in front of it the driver's foot slipped off the clutch. The vehicle lunged forward, knocking me off me feet and rolling another ten feet before bucking to a stop. I opened my eyes to see the BMP's belly above me, the heat of the fifteen-litre engine burning my face and hands. Had I been walking slower or faster by maybe two seconds, I'd have been crushed under one of the tracks. I crawled from underneath as the terrified driver jumped out to see if I was alive and to apologize over and over. My arm, which had taken the impact of the BMP's narrow nose, was already beginning to swell from heavy bruising. To have already escaped death twice on the morning of what we hoped to be the last and deciding day of the operation made me wonder what was coming next.

"Leaving Jos in charge, I climbed in and headed for the conference. Brigadier de Castro opened the meeting by saying we'd made good progress the day before, then added, 'Except that Colonel Blaauw delayed my advance by two hours'. I couldn't believe my ears. The delay had been caused by de Castro insisting I put Nick, a Priority 1 casevac, in a vehicle and transport him over rough terrain to the rear element. I lost my temper and told him I was *not* happy with his comments and would pass them on to General Marques.

"But this was not the time to get into a shouting match. There were far more important things to work out. With only his staff and senior commanders present, we co-ordinated the plan, which called for my group to take the right and Nevis's group the left on our approach to Cafunfo. We split the town into sectors, with me taking the northern half. As soon as possible, I would circle around to the south-west to capture and secure the airstrip. Mundoreal would take the southern half and then clear the road that led south towards the town of Cuango.

"When I got back the crews were ready, the weapons charged. This was it. Just before we started moving I contacted Ricardo to confirm again that my air support was ready to scramble. He said the pilots were suited up and waiting for my command.

"I have the map open. Another eight kilometres. I trace the road zigzagging along the high ground. From where we are it swings to the north and then gradually bends back to a south-westerly direction for the last two kilometres. We're on the point of moving out when de Castro arrives. A report has come in that Unita is evacuating Cafunfo. He urges us to get going as soon as possible and drive forward to the objective at our best speed. Just after 0900 my group and Mundoreal's move out. The bush here is very dense. Closely-spaced trees either side force us to stay fairly close to maintain visual contact.

"About an hour later Louwrens is overhead in a PC-7 and reporting that he can see well-prepared defensive positions and many troops in the town of Mona-Cafunfo. I check my maps again. It's near the town of Cuango, about ten kilometres south of Cafunfo where the road crosses a small tributary of the Cuango River. Louwrens says that given the probability of numerous anti-aircraft weapons there, he'll refrain from a rocket attack. If he's hit and has to head for Saurimo we'll be without aerial reconnaissance at this critical moment. I concur and pass on the information about Unita evacuating Cafunfo, and that the obvious direction of their withdrawal has to be north towards the next small village of Porne.

"We crest a small hill at about 1200 hours and for the first time see Cafunfo. It lies across a shallow valley with more high ground behind it. From Point 883 on the map, de Castro deploys his battery of D-30 guns, which begin registering on the town. If we start receiving Unita artillery fire during the final dash, they'll give us covering fire.

"Louwrens is circling north of the objective when he reports a Land Rover racing along the road towards Porne. In it are soldiers wearing the red berets of Unita Special Forces. They see him rolling in and the vehicle swerves off the road into a clump of trees. While he can't confirm he's hit it, Louwrens says his rockets went into the hiding place. He is confident that he's taken it out.

"At 1400 hours we're less than three kilometres from the objective and following the curving road towards the south-west. The bush thins and the terrain opens to grassy, rolling hills, making us easy targets. We spread out in attack formation. Pine is calling me from the MiG-23.

"'Moby Dick, Moby Dick, this is Woodpecker, do you copy?'

"'Woodpecker from Moby Dick, read you loud and clear.'

"'Moby Dick, this is Woodpecker, I'm airborne out of my position and will be over your position in figures one-five minutes.'

"I check my watch and map again and realize that we'll arrive at the objective at the same time.

"'Woodpecker, this is Moby Dick. Roger, I'll give you a race for your money.'

"'Roger, Moby Dick.'

Papa Whiskey is also orbiting over Cafunfo. In the back Juba is watching for any sign of Unita. Anything that looks slightly suspicious is centred on the television screen and examined more closely. "It was very tense," Juba remembered. "I could see our forces to the east of the town starting to spread out, expecting a full battle at any moment. I'm searching in all directions with the camera, looking for the enemy and their anti-aircraft positions. So far, nothing."

"We break into the open east of Cafunfo," says Hennie, "spread out into attack formation and start giving speculative fire. A quick glance shows Mundoreal nicely deployed to my left. It's a great feeling to see all the BMPs moving together and racing forward with the 30 mm guns firing short bursts into the objective. Puffing Willy is still with us, its broken piston ring sending a thick cloud of black smoke billowing from the engine compartment. We're about one minute out when Pine comes on the VHF radio to say *he* is one minute away. As we enter the town, he confirms he's overhead and has us visual from the dust trails of the BMPs."

"As Hennie was entering Cafunfo," Pine remembered, "I could hear the tension in his voice. 'Are you ready?' he asked me and I told him, 'Yes, I'm ready with the close air support.'"

"This was the most coincidental co-ordination of ground and air movement I'd ever experienced, and real morale booster," Hennie said. "It gave everyone a great feeling of confidence that our own people were overhead, ready to give us help if we needed it. We slowed and moved cautiously up the main street. Not having received any fire, I kept the infantry inside the BMPs, everyone alert and looking around while the 30 mms and machine guns fired short bursts into alleyways that we passed. We came around a corner to see an armoured car dug into a fixed position between two buildings. Harry gave it about a five-second burst from the 30 mm. Had anyone been inside or around it, that would have permanently discouraged them from trying anything silly. Then, right in the middle of town, Puffing Willy ground to a halt and died.

"Leaving it, we took a side road on the south-westerly edge of the town and came out the other side without encountering any enemy action. I continued along this road and followed it all the way up to the airstrip.

We rolled down the northern side because of the possibility of mines and linked up with Mundoreal, who'd also come through his part of the objective with no problems.

"Pine was still orbiting overhead. By now low on fuel, he congratulated us with a beautiful low pass over the combat group, pulled the MiG-23 up and headed for Saurimo. Louwrens was still maintaining station on the western side of the Cuango River and reporting that everything seemed quiet.

"The southern airstrip at Cafunfo had a hard gravel surface, but Unita had cut trenches across it with heavy road equipment, making it impossible for fixed wing aircraft to land. While looking for a suitable TB location we detonated an anti-personnel mine with no injuries or damage to the vehicle. Setting up where we had a good view across the river should the enemy appear, we immediately started with maintenance, replenishment of ammunition and refuelling to get the vehicles battle-ready as quickly as possible.

"The threat of a counter-attack was great, and if not an infantry attack then definitely an artillery bombardment. Those not working on the vehicles began digging defensive trenches either side of the runway. I made comms with Rolf, who confirmed that they had reached their sector two kilometres to the northeast and were complete with HQ, protection element and logistical elements. I drafted a complete sitrep to Ricardo, confirming the capture of the final objective of Cafunfo on 15 July at 1315 hours. I then asked him if he'd like to be the new mayor, but he said he'd leave that honour to me.

"I sent a small team back to see if they could recover Puffing Willy; they returned, shaking their heads. It was impossible; they couldn't start or even tow it. The good news, however, was that FAA had discovered three huge shipping containers completely full of Belgian beer. I climbed out of my command vehicle to see my guys' three BMPs stacked with crates of Stella Artois. These were distributed around the perimeter of the TB and everyone had a few warm but very welcomed and deserved beers.

"At approximately 1700 hours the sun was sinking into the haze, when we started receiving sporadic D-30 artillery fire from the direction of Porne. It wasn't a heavy bombardment, just occasional shells coming in, but enough to send the FAA troops scurrying out of town and saving the rest of the houses and shops from being completely looted. Although the shelling would become a major problem within a few days, it ceased at sunset and the rest of the night was uneventful."

★ ★ ★

Digging in and Consolidating

"The next morning was a Sunday and I sent half the group down to the river. With a BMP escort covering the far bank, they plunged in for a long-needed wash. I hardly recognized them when they came back.

"Our two prisoners were still with us and after two weeks were reasonably relaxed with us and pleased that they were no longer in the bush. They showed us around Cafunfo, giving us a tour of the main positions. The first place I wanted to see was the hospital. I was particularly interested in checking the register for any mention of our four missing guys at Camaxillo or the three-man recce team that went missing near Cafunfo. Disappointingly, none of their names or any reference was found.

"I still maintain today that if it hadn't been for the information we got from these two little Unita fellows, Mickey and our guys at Cacolo would have sustained serious losses. They had also given us background on the defences at Cafunfo that was invaluable in planning the attack. I would have liked to keep them with us longer, but a request from the governor of Lunda Norte Province to question them himself could not be ignored.

"Two choppers came in and as soon as the supplies had been unloaded the two prisoners and Colonel André climbed on board. As I said goodbye to this fine man I was really sad that, having led his men so well, he couldn't have been with us for the final assault. He certainly deserved the honour. He was flown back to Saurimo and although I couldn't get authorization to have him sent back to South Africa, I made sure he was treated in our sick bay by EO's doctor.

"The resupply included fresh meat and the guys made a *potjiekos,* a traditional South African stew, for lunch. With clean bodies, a few beers and a bowl of *potjiekos* in hand, we felt almost civilized. The rest of the day was devoted to maintenance and further consolidation of our defensive positions. Over the next few days all the supplies from the Unita cache at Muvuca – sufficient to maintain the entire EO/FAA force for at least six months – was transferred to Cafunfo and placed in new bunkers. Brigadier de Castro said that a search of the area around the supply dump had revealed a number of fresh graves that were probably the result of Pine's air strike."

★

"On the 17th of July Ricardo said that he'd be coming out the next day with a number of guys who'd just returned from leave," Hennie said. "He wanted me and Jos to brief them on arrival, introduce them to the equipment and hand over to Rolf. Rolf and I went over all the intelligence reports and it was obvious that Unita had not given up the fight. Not only were we still receiving sporadic shelling, but there appeared to be substantial enemy concentrations still at Cuango and another build-up at Luremo. A message from Ricardo stated that the air wing would be paying the latter a visit that night."

"Carlos had picked up indications that there was a strong Unita presence at Luremo," Pine said. "This was cause for concern not just because of its proximity to Hennie, but also because it was another rich diamond area with easy access to Zaire and fresh military supplies. It lay about thirty kilometres north-west of Cafunfo, and we planned a night sortie. Papa Whiskey took off first with Goose handling the FLIR camera. I gave him about an hour's lead and then launched, with everyone standing outside to watch. Night take-offs were quite impressive, with flame the length of the aircraft when I went to full afterburner.

"As I climbed towards 25,000 feet I adjusted the night vision goggles, which were never used during take off or landing because of their lack of depth perception. Less than half an hour later I picked up the lights of Cafunfo about thirty miles away. The King Air was at 15,000 feet somewhere out there in the dark, looking for the target. I pressed the mike button.

"'Goose, Pine, I'm in the area.'

"'Roger, Pine, I have a target for you – vehicles close to some buildings and a lot of people.'

Excellent. "'Okay, go ahead.'

"'Okay, from Cafunfo take the main road heading north until it makes a sharp bend to the left,' Goose said, watching his television screen.

"I eased to the west and brought the power back to idle, starting a descent and watching Cafunfo slip past on my right. I picked up the road in the NVGs and followed it to the bend. 'Got it,' I confirmed.

"'From the bend continue another five klicks to a fork in the road.'

"A couple of seconds went by. There it was. I keyed the mike button. 'Visual.' A glance under the NVGs at the instrument panel: altimeter slowly winding through 20,000 feet, still enough fuel to see me home, exhaust temperature fine.

"Goose's voice crackles in the earphones. 'Take the left-hand leg of the fork and follow the road until you see a bridge.'

"Another pause and then, 'I see the bridge.'

"'Continue another three klicks and you should see the target next to the road on the left. Lots of vehicles and people walking around.'

"'Okay, I see it,' automatically beginning to calculate where I'll start my roll in. 'I'll be attacking along the road from the north,' I advise, ensuring that Goose knows to stay well clear to the east. An approach from the north will also have me coming out of the attack on a course back towards Saurimo. No point in wasting fuel by going the other way and then having to turn around. You can never have too much fuel in the MiG-23.

"Turning right, mentally computing where I should roll in and flipping the arming switch on the panel as part of the mental checklist. From this point on, squeezing the trigger on the control stick will open the retaining shackles and release the 500-kilogram cluster bomb under each wing. Three primary factors will determine the accuracy of my attack: dive angle, air speed and release altitude. Screw up any one of those, and the bombs will land short or long.

"Everything now is happening on automatic mode, mind balancing my three primary concerns, tiny adjustments with stick and rudder, checking air speed and altimeter, concentrating on the general target picture below. Down through 10,000 feet and I'm getting more details in the NVGs – vehicle lights, buildings, terrain, vegetation. At the same time my peripheral vision is tuned for the flash of a SAM launch or tracers. Passing 8,000 feet, airspeed 400 knots. Everything looking good. It's only fifteen seconds since rolling in, when 6,000 feet goes by and – and – okay – *now* – I squeeze the trigger. There's a strong buck to the MiG as 1,000 kilos of steel and explosives separate from the wings. For the first fraction of a second I wonder if both bombs have gone. Then, yeah, I'm clean, and I haul back on the stick.

"From thirty degrees nose down to thirty degrees nose up in a four-G pull-out, throttle forward through the first and second clips, pressed solidly into the seat by 28,000 pounds of thrust driving me skyward. Watching air speed and altitude. Stick over to seventy degrees of bank, still pulling about three Gs, and looking back for a SAM launch. Wings back to level, then to the other side, and still no sign of anything chasing me. Under the NVGs to scan the panel for rate of air speed decay, back over the shoulder to look for detonation just as white flashes start going off against the green background of the NVGs. *Yeah* – they're on target and I've got my own rough battle damage assessment. Levelling off, I pull the throttle back to normal cruise power, advising Goose that I'm clear of the area and heading direct to Saurimo. He acknowledges and hands me a present.

"'Pine, Goose, you've got burning trucks and secondaries. Nice one. Oom Hennie will be happy. See you back in the pub.'

"'Thanks for the business, Goose. I'll have a cold one waiting for you.'

"My next major worry is getting on the ground. Ten to fifteen minutes out I call Saurimo and they run to light the paraffin tins along the runway. Still on NVGs because of the horrendous visibility, I pick up Saurimo's lights from thirty miles out and lift the goggles to begin recovering my normal night vision. The transition is like going from a brightly lit room and then walking outside into the dark and trying to spot the glow of a cigarette at fifty metres. The airfield lights immediately disappear. I flip back and forth between NVGs and eyes to lock on the airfield and runway lights. Lower landing gear and first notch of flaps before turning crosswind. I'm on a three-mile final, full flaps, quick look through NVGs to check runway aspect.

"At a hundred feet I flick on the landing light, waiting for it to pick up the runway. There's no centre line, just the orange glow of the paraffin flames to line up between. Come over the threshold at 150 knots, mains hit with a loud chirp, let the nose wheel down and hit the button above the throttle to deploy the chute. If it doesn't deploy or if it separates, then I'll have to go to afterburner and go around for another shot. But then there's the deceleration of the drag chute throwing me against the harness. Flames from the paraffin lamps start passing more slowly and I get on the brakes.

Turning off the runway, I taxi to the apron and shut down. There's the whine of the engine winding down as I open the canopy and smell Africa again."

★

"I visited Cafunfo several times after Hennie and his guys had taken it," said Ricardo. "But today was the handover to Rolf and I wanted to make sure that everything was done correctly and smoothly, after which I'd accompany Hennie and his team back to Saurimo. When we landed, I went straight across to see Rolf and Carlos, who had set up their HQ near Brigadier de Castro. They assured me everything was fine, but that Rolf had stepped into Hennie's shoes a day earlier than scheduled. I took a vehicle over to Hennie and his crowd, who were waiting next to the runway.

"As soon as I saw them I understood why Rolf had assumed command a day early. Hennie's people were already in vacation mode. They'd worked hard, done the job and now it was time to unwind. For me to get cross with such a good bunch of people after all they had done wouldn't be right. We had a couple of beers while everyone finished packing. When we got to the helicopters, I noticed that they were carrying three non-military-looking wooden crates. I started to ask about them, but at that moment we were rushed by dozens of FAA troops trying to claw their way in. We were already loaded to capacity and blocked them getting on board, but they were so determined to get out of Cafunfo that some were clinging to the outside as we lifted off. One chap was hanging on the strut next to me, shouting to be let on. There being no room inside, the only thing I could do was to hit him across the knuckles with the butt of my AK-47. Fortunately, it was only about forty feet to the ground."

"As we lifted off," Hennie said, "I looked back and couldn't help feeling proud of our accomplishment. We'd covered over 1,000 kilometres of very difficult and dusty terrain, crossed numerous rivers, bashed through heavy bush, and for the last 150 kilometres had been under almost constant enemy fire. Against the odds, our combat group had arrived without suffering any dead,[40] only two wounded, and with all of our equipment intact. Even

---

[40] Sadly, Nick, who had been wounded on 13 July, contracted pneumonia and died ten days after Cafunfo was taken.

Puffing Willy had refused to quit until we'd taken the objective. It was an incredibly successful operation. Especially so when one considers that most of my guys were from Koevoet – police counter-insurgency operators – with no pukka conventional army training. Yet they had adapted to new terrain, new tactics and new equipment and done a magnificent job. It was a privilege to have led them.

"I had to give enormous credit to my crew commanders, and the greatest respect to my small infantry element for never hesitating to debus under indirect and direct enemy fire to join up with the FAA infantry elements during the final contact drills. No less impressive was the fantastic and courageous job done by the company of Katangese infantry. The rôle played by the EO air wing was crucial, flying day and night missions where, had they gone down, the best they could have hoped for from Unita was a quick execution. On the fixed-wing side, aerial reconnaissance and close air support at critical moments helped tremendously, while the regular and extremely hazardous supply flights and casevac missions by the chopper pilots kept us moving forward.

"As we turned towards Saurimo and Cafunfo fell behind, I was relieved to be heading back, but there was also a sadness that it was over. Only those who were there would ever understand our triumph."

"Unita were still targeting the town and runway," Ricardo said, "so getting airborne safely and heading away at low level was a relief. Riek asked Hennie if he could open one of the mysterious boxes. On Hennie's nod, the top was levered up to reveal a dozen bottles of Mateus rosé. In a few minutes everybody on board save the gunners and crew had his own bottle of wine. By the end of the flight all three cases were empty and some of the blokes had drunk far more than others. When we landed at Saurimo, Chief of the Army General Luís Faceira was there to meet and congratulate them. Riek, feeling no pain, threw an arm over his shoulder and said, *'Ons het die vyand lekker opgefok, hê Genl?'* Taking Riek's exuberance in good humour, even if it was somewhat lacking in military courtesy, he looked at me questioningly for the translation. I cleared my throat. 'Riek said, "We fucked up the enemy nicely, hey, General?"' Faceira laughed and said that, yes, they had fucked up the enemy very nicely, indeed."

★ ★ ★

"I've been hit and the aircraft is burning"

"For the first three days there was little enemy action around Cafunfo," Juba said, "but Unita were busy reorganizing and planning their response. Their first priorities were to begin wearing down our guys and FAA with artillery, and to halt the chopper re-resupply by killing us. Their early warning system was quite effective: as soon as we'd get airborne from Saurimo and cross the Luachimo River their recces were on the radio, telling the batteries that we were en route. Unita had already plotted our low-level routes and positioned 14.5 and 23 mm anti-aircraft weapons to take us out. As a result, our options kept getting narrower and narrower. If they hadn't done so already, it was only a matter of time before they shifted most of their SAMs from other parts of Angola to deal with us.

"After getting through the AAA belt, we were faced with artillery fire on the Cafunfo LZs. We constantly shifted our landing points, but as soon as we were close enough to get comms with our guys the artillery would start. Initially, the shells would be far off their target, but as we turned for the LZ they'd begin exploding under us. Seeing them from the air isn't too bothersome, but it gets annoying when you realize the shells are passing through the same airspace as you. It's even worse when you're on the ground and watching them coming closer and closer and finally exploding around you.

"It was somewhere around 21 July when we took off from Saurimo with lots of rations and FAA replacements. Approaching Cafunfo, there was no shelling until just before touch down, at which point everything opened up and shells started whistling in. I decided to land close to the trenches to speed the off-loading and minimise our time on the ground, but in the process of manoeuvring around some big trees, I ended up directly above a trench. To avoid putting the nose wheel into it, I kicked left rudder to swing the nose away, when Sonny shouted, *'The tree!'*

"'Fuck the tree!' I told him, far more worried about getting these FAAs and freight out before something landed on us. As soon as we touched down – practically in the shade of that tree – the flight engineer was out the door to supervise the off-loading. The FAAs waiting to offload the supplies wanted to jump on board and go home, while those inside refused to get out when they saw the explosions. Everyone else decided it was safer in the trenches and weren't going anywhere. Some of our people came running up to start chucking out the FAAs whose stop this was. As soon as they hit the ground, they ducked for the trenches, leaving our guys and the rest of the crew to pull the supplies off.

"I was holding the controls, when out of the corner of my eye I saw Rolf running towards us. He ran up to the door, threw four cases of beer on board and shouted at the fight engineer that it was for the chopper crews, donated from the cache that Unita had left behind. I pulled collective and we were out of there, just missing the tree and climbing away from the explosions. When we landed back at Saurimo, it didn't take long to start cracking a few beers to calm our nerves."

*

"On 25 July General McKenzie asked us to do another trip to Cafunfo to take across more troops and landmines," Alberts said. "Rolf still had D-30 rounds hitting around his position, which made the idea of landing there with a ton of explosives distinctly unattractive. Suspecting that Unita were monitoring our Russian radios, we decided we'd announce that we were landing next to Rolf, then split up, with me and Arthur setting down at one end of the runway and JC and Juba at the other. If the D-30 did open up, Louwrens was overhead to call in counter-battery fire."

Five minutes out, they contacted Rolf and asked if the expected bombardment had begun. Rolf came back to joke that it was probably still too early in the morning. The two helicopters made a dummy run on his position, then sneaked away towards the airfield, two kilometres to the south. No sooner had they flown over Rolf than shells started falling around him.

Clouds of dust rose as they settled either end of the runway and waited for the FAA troops to off-load the mines, shouting at them to fucking hurry up. The shelling stopped at Rolf's position, which meant that the Unita gun crew were cranking in adjustments to shift to the airfield. Then the last of the cargo was off and they immediately pulled collective to get airborne. A few kilometres to the north Louwrens was trying to spot the D-30, but smoke from the peasants' slash-and-burning made visibility extremely bad from the air. He saw a vehicle, fired a salvo of rockets and immediately reported that he was drawing 23 mm fire, adding that Skeeries was in his back seat and having an exciting first ride. He swung a little farther north in search of the anti-aircraft gun.

"Arthur and I were circling at 500 feet over the town," Alberts said, "when I suddenly heard Louwrens snap, 'Carl, I've been hit bad and the aircraft is burning.'

Oh, Christ.

"Unita were swarming under him. I wrenched the helicopter hard to the north and started climbing in the hope of getting him visual. I called him. 'Louwrens, Carl, just head south. Fly south.'

"'Carl, Louwrens, the engine's burning. There's too much smoke. I can't see. I'm going to have to put it down!'

"All my transmissions were being monitored by Rolf on the ground, as well as Sonny and Juba in the second helicopter. To keep everyone in the picture, I 'double triggered' Arthur so my intercom chatter would be transmitted as well.

"'Louwrens, *please* head south. We're coming to fetch you,' I urged. 'Keep talking, just keep transmitting!'

"But he had gone off the air. For the next few minutes Arthur and I called repeatedly, our eyes scanning the horizon, straining to catch sight of the Pilatus. If there were any way to get back to a safe area, Louwrens would do it. But burning aircraft wait for no one before exploding or incinerating the crew. Another minute went by. Still no sight of him and nothing on the radio.

"If he had managed to belly in the aircraft, then Unita forces were already closing in. To be captured was our most terrifying nightmare. We had to go after him. I thought about Skeeries in his back seat. He was always asking to fly with us, but with the type of sorties we were doing, we'd always left him at Saurimo. It was sheer fate that with Ricardo away in Cabo Ledo, Louwrens had given in to Skeeries' pleas and taken him along. He was due to go home on leave tomorrow!

"Lances of 23 mm tracers ripped past us, accompanied by RPG air bursts. I swung back towards Cafunfo and descended as fast as possible to escape the huge shells. Suddenly, a breathless Louwrens came up on his hand-held VHF radio. He had gotten it down in one piece!

"'*Carl, we're on a tarred road running south.*'"

"Behind his voice was the sound of small arms fire. The only tar road was to the north and we turned around again, descending to fifty feet to see better. No sooner had we taken our new heading than tracers seemed to be coming from every direction. We tried to tell Rolf to send a BMP force out, but he later said all he could hear over his radio was the sound of gunfire. Then Louwrens came over the air again. He was in control and giving me directions.

"'*Carl, fly north along the road.*'

"The road was impossible. That was where the gunfire was the heaviest. I ducked off to the west and flew with the road on our right. Every second that we continued deeper into the shit, the more I was convinced that we would never make it out alive. We frantically searched for anything to indicate where Louwrens was, subconsciously waiting for the one big bang that would end it all. It felt like eternity.

"'*I can hear you. They are shooting at you,*' Louwrens warned.

"Louwrens had just crash-landed, gotten his passenger out and was escaping and evading an enemy determined to capture them, yet he was advising *me* of the dangers. 'Fuck this,' I said to Arthur, 'let's turn further west.' I was flying about 500 metres left of the road, when Louwrens shouted over his portable radio again.

"'*Carl, I can see you! Turn right.*'

"Heart pounding, I brought the controls over. The road loomed ahead and I saw two figures under a tree next to it. We were drawing fire from behind as I raised the nose to slow the helicopter, still not sure if the two under the tree were our boys or Unita.

"'Louwrens, confirm that's you at my twelve o'clock,' I said. But there was so much noise that my call went unanswered. I swung the helicopter parallel with the road and descended rapidly into the tight landing zone. To my right I saw Louwrens and Skeeries run from under the tree towards the helicopter. Louwrens was in front, still clutching his flying helmet, with Skeeries immediately behind him in his blue windbreaker jacket. Through the clouds of dust blowing up I saw a tree looming in front and raised the nose more to avoid hitting it. Just before touchdown, I heard and felt a bang, and the entire helicopter, especially the cyclic and rudder pedals, immediately started shaking violently. The aircraft dropped into the landing zone and skewed around a bit before I managed to keep it on an even keel.

"My first thoughts were that I had put the tail in. That did it, we were now truly fucked. Even sitting on the ground, the aircraft was barely controllable, with the nose yawing randomly left and right. Tracers were snapping past us from behind, and to our horror we saw a group of Unita running down the road from the north. The speed at which we descended must have made it look like we'd been shot down. Agonising seconds dragged by with the chopper trying to shake itself apart. Where the fuck were Louwrens and Skeeries?

"I screamed at Tino Nuñes, who sat mesmerised in the engineer's seat, to get out and look for them. I began to fear the worst – that the tail rotor had hit them. Tino ran to the side door, while I hung out of the window peering back.

"'They've disappeared,' Tino shouted.

"The Unitas running towards us opened fire. If we did not get the crippled helicopter airborne, we were dead. I pulled power and immediately ran out of right rudder. The aircraft swung and started rolling to the left, the main rotor blades barely clearing the ground on the low side. I looked down and saw the torn remains of Louwrens below my side window.

"'*Louwrens is down! Fuck, Louwrens is down!*' I screamed over the radio. Tracers snapped past us. With the right rudder pedal fully in, the aircraft slowly started to hang to the left until we were flying sideways. Barely clearing the trees, we crabbed away, the shaking so violent that I couldn't read the instruments.

"'I'm going to put her down,' I said to Arthur.

"'No, no. Just keep going, for fuck's sake. Keep flying.'

"Lowering the collective straightened the aircraft somewhat, but sent us towards the trees. With no right rudder travel and unable to maintain altitude, I called Sonny and Juba, who were orbiting Cafunfo town, and told them we were going down. Juba immediately answered that we must head south, giving him a constant update on our position so he didn't miss us in the bad visibility.

"Vibrating madly, the aircraft managed to take us five kilometres before I saw the second chopper racing in and heard Juba say he had us visual.

I put her down next to the tar road a kilometre north of the town and Arthur and I leapt from the cockpit. A quick look at the tail rotor showed the blades bent and twisted, with a portion of one missing. Seconds later, Sonny and Juba did an assault landing alongside. We dived through the door and the helicopter leapt off the ground, did a half turn and headed for Cafunfo. Juba was on the radio, asking Rolf that he try to recover the body and find Skeeries.

"Racing north, Rolf and his BMPs fought through one contact after another until they reached the downed PC-7, then back-tracked to where we had landed. They saw a pool of blood and marks where the body had been dragged onto the road and loaded into a vehicle. They came under intense fire and had to withdraw before finding Skeeries.

"The tragedy was that Louwrens, who had been absolutely fearless with both the MiG-23 and the PC-7, had gone down in flames, survived the crash and managed to find a landing zone and talk me in while under fire, only to be killed by the very aircraft that seconds later would have flown him home to safety. Later, Pine and his wife Marina, plus Padre Thinus and Nico had the dreadful task of breaking the tragic news to Louwrens's wife and parents. A few months later I also visited them. The only comfort to his family was that he was killed instantly. Of that I had no doubt. As for Skeeries, I could only hope that his fate was as painless.

"I'm sure that the dust blinded them as they sprinted for helicopter and Louwrens either ran through the tail rotor, or was shot and fell into it. Skeeries had broken his Coke bottle spectacles the night before, and was virtually blind without them. That and the fact that he was not a combatant of any kind, made the chance of him making it back through hundreds of searching Unita troops very remote.

"Unita issued a press statement that they had shot down a PC-7 and a helicopter, and that a second helicopter 'was lucky' to have escaped. The BBC Africa Service, quoting another press statement, said that Unita recovered two bodies, yet the rebels' own Radio Vorgan broadcasting out of Jamba stated that one body was recovered and that one person holding a University of Natal student card was captured. Eight years later, we still don't know what happened behind us that day."

★ ★ ★

"Get down Juba, they're shooting SAMs at us!"

Despite the artillery and anti-aircraft fire, the choppers were still working hard to keep Rolf and Brigadier de Castro supplied. Before lifting off from Saurimo on 28 July, aircraft commanders Juba and Arthur were assured by FAA that not only had they cleared the area of Unita for a ten-kilometres radius around the town, but that there was no missile threat.

Each loaded with two-and-a-half tonnes of supplies, the two Mi-17s took off and climbed above 23 mm range, Juba and co-pilot John Vierra taking the Vic Two position on Arthur and Carl Alberts. Visibility and the handling of the heavily-loaded helicopter deteriorated steadily as they climbed into the overcast, until Juba was instrument-formation flying to maintain position. In the cabin behind him, Carlos tried to catnap. Two kilometres from Cafunfo they made a steep, spiralling descent to the runway west of the town. Carlos hopped out as the cargo was unloaded and replaced with a dozen FAA casevacs. Because of the threat of artillery, Arthur and Alberts were quickly airborne again. Seconds later, Juba lifted off behind them.

"I had come in to make an intelligence assessment of the ground situation," said Carlos. "Rolf was there to meet me and I had just shaken hands with him, when I saw what looked like a flare being shot off north of us. I don't remember what I said, but Rolf looked and shouted, 'It's a SAM!' All we could do was watch helplessly as it streaked towards Juba."

"There was a ravine about 300 metres ahead with high ground to the north and I turned left to be closer to the town," Juba said. "As I climbed through two hundred metres and 180 degrees I increased the bank to forty-five degrees to stay with Carl, who was at my twelve o'clock. The next moment there was a tremendous flash and smoke of an explosion above my head, followed by the sound of metal clanging and screeching.

I shot a look out the window and saw the same missile that had hit us carry on a bit unstable towards Carl and Arthur and pass just underneath them."

"Juba was behind and below us somewhere," Alberts said, "when I distinctly heard a sudden bang and saw the unmistakable white smoke trail of a SAM-7 pass under us. I hit my mike switch.

"*'SAM-7! SAM-7! Get down, Juba, they're fucking shooting SAMs at us!'*

"My helicopter started to gallop viciously," Juba said. "I dumped collective to see if we were still flying and to get down as quickly as possible in the event they fired a second missile. Carl was yelling that a SAM had just been launched and we'd better get out of Dodge. I told him I'd already been hit and was going down. As soon as I realised the aircraft was controllable I increased speed to lose height faster, heading for a spot just south of where I'd picked up Carl and Arthur three days earlier."

"Thinking it was going to be a repeat of what happened when Louwrens was shot down," Alberts said, "I swung the aircraft around and watched Juba slam down in a cloud of dust. It hadn't settled, when a familiar and calm voice came through my earphones. 'Carl, please come and fetch us.'"

"I told Carl we were okay, then shut down and climbed out to assess the damage," Juba said. "The tail pipe was gone on the number two engine and a third of the pockets on one main rotor blade were gone. The missile had actually entered the tail pipe and detonated on its way through the top of the engine cowling and then hit a main rotor blade, missing the main spar by one millimetre. What saved us was the forty-five degree bank. It deflected the heat source and caused the missile to enter the tail pipe higher than it would have otherwise, missing the engine output drive shaft to the gearbox.

"Carlos later told me that the missile had been launched from the high ground on the far side of the ravine. The distinctive white trail he described confirmed to me that it was a SAM-7. Back at Saurimo, the FAA chopper pilots said that I'd been very lucky. Fifteen of their helicopters were shot down before me with SAMs, all with no survivors. In the next five months, three more FAA-crewed Mi-17s would be hit by SAMs, killing everyone on board."

★

With Unita's deployment of surface-to-air missiles, it was clear that they were determined to halt helicopter resupply and casevac flights into

Cafunfo. The few that arrived used randomly selected landing zones and stayed on the ground for only seconds before departing again at low level. The steep, spiralling approaches and low-level departures minimized the SAM threat, but left them vulnerable to small arms and anti-aircraft fire. Unita had also positioned a B-10 recoilless weapon in an attempt to hit them while they were on the ground and feverishly unloading supplies and replacements and loading casevacs. Each landing was "a noisy affair".

"We were subjected to artillery and mortar bombardments every morning at dawn," Carlos said. "We dug in next to Brigadier de Castro's HQ on a ridge north-east of the town and spent a lot of effort increasing the depth of our personal bunkers. We weren't too worried about the shell with our name on it, but rather about the one that said, 'To whom it may concern'. In the midst of all our digging, we regularly joked about how many diamonds we were shovelling away. Fortunately, while the bombardments were pretty damn frightening, we never suffered any casualties from them.

"Brigadier de Castro soon had a bunker that Hitler would have envied. Using the earth-moving equipment abandoned by Unita, he had a large hole dug, then placed a shipping container in it and covered it up, leaving only a narrow entrance at one end. His combat accommodation soon had an air-conditioner as well as a television and VCR. We could only shake our heads. Surprisingly, he was in no hurry to leave Cafunfo, and it soon became apparent why. Short queues of FAA troops would be seen outside the bunker, each chap patiently waiting to be called inside. Whenever we had a chopper re-supply, we noticed the same chaps waiting to board it. It didn't take a genius to work out that they were buying their way back to Saurimo with diamonds. One night when well oiled, the good brigadier showed us a Johnny Walker bottle full of rough stones. The spoils of war! Rolf and I regularly turned down offers of diamonds in exchange for food. Lafras was merciless when it came to the issue of illegal diamonds and more than one EO employee was fired on just the suspicion of dealing in them.

"During my inspection of Cafunfo it was obvious that everything revolved around diamonds. There were a couple of houses across from the clinic where sorting and dealing was done. Despite being looted by FAA, it was easy to see that they'd been very nicely appointed and included their own bomb shelters alongside. In one I found a broken fax machine with a satellite phone still connected. Next to it lay a document signed by

Kongolo Mobutu, the favourite son of Zaire's president. He had been in Cafunfo to collect diamonds as payment for his father's support of Savimbi. I later learned that just a few days before Hennie had entered Cafunfo, Kongolo had departed in a black Mercedes Benz convertible in the company of his French mistress and the Unita area commander.

"To the bewilderment of FAA, we used the quiet part of the day to get the town working again. Water pumps were repaired, roads were graded with the heavy equipment abandoned by Unita and the mining companies before them, and a clinic established. The bush telegraph was working well, and many of the *povos* who had fled from Unita almost two years previously started trickling in. Many were in very poor physical condition, having preferred the hardships of the bush to living under Unita. Within weeks the market had started up and houses were being cleared of rubble.

"A question that had not yet been answered was the fate of our MIAs. I interviewing scores of those who had remained in Cafunfo, but there were so many conflicting accounts, most of them based on third- and fourth-hand information that I could find nothing solid. I was taken to a number of locations where someone had heard that someone else had seen a white man – the clinic, the jail, a water tower. It was time-consuming and frustrating but I had to persevere. Each new version contradicted everything else I'd heard. The main problem was that Unita was wary of the *povos* in this area and had restricted them from areas where anything relevant was going on.

"What I thought was a breakthrough came when interviewing a Portuguese-trained medic who had stayed in Cafunfo during the occupation. He mentioned a white male he had treated for gunshot wounds. But my excitement was dashed when it turned out he was talking about an Israeli mining engineer who had been hurt in a drunken brawl before Unita had taken the town. Eventually, all that could be concluded was that our KIAs had been brought to Cafunfo at some stage and that the MIAs had been flown by Savimbi's personal Fokker F-27 to Unita's southern headquarters at Jamba."

*

Pine Pienaar was still in action and a mission near Saurimo on 6 September remains the most memorable of his flying career. "It was one of my last sorties in the MiG-23," he recalled. "We knew where a large number of Unitas were concentrating in two areas about forty kilometres apart, both roughly the same distance from Saurimo. It was about a 15-minute flight and I was leading, with 'John', a former student from my instructor days in the SAAF as my No 2.

"We found the target and I rolled in, dropped my bombs and pulled off to wait for him. At that point I started getting a fuel warning light that's designed to come on when you're down to 600 litres. A quick look at the fuel gauge told me there was still plenty. I checked the fuel tally with John. His reading tallied with mine, so everything seemed okay. About two seconds later it came on again and stayed on. The hell with it. Systems went down so regularly that I decided it was malfunctioning. We climbed to 20,000 feet and were heading for the second target, when the engine flamed out. I tried to relight the fire, but nothing happened. I was out of fuel.

"Very, very frightened, I thought about ejecting, but immediately discarded the idea. Because of the poor maintenance I didn't trust the seat to work properly or the parachute to open. Even if it did work, we were over Indian country and I had no wish to end up in Unita's hands. Though I'd read nothing in the flight manual about the gliding characteristics of the MiG-23, I decided it was my only option. I immediately brought the sweep lever forward, jettisoned the two remaining bombs and turned for home, which was forty kilometres away.

"My GPS had gone out and when I checked with John, his was out as well. *Shit.* There was one more option. The Angolans had mounted a really cheap GPS on the metal ring between the windscreen and canopy and I punched in the numbers direct to Saurimo. My eyes went to the altimeter and then back to the GPS. It was working!

"The engine was still wind-milling, which gave me enough hydraulic pressure for the controls. John stayed right with me the whole time, talking me through it, reading off airspeed and altitude, which was a tremendous help. As I approached the Saurimo airfield I can tell you my heart was pounding. By the time I passed through 10,000 feet I was ten to twelve kilometres out – still too high. I glided over the airfield at around 6,000 feet, then turned on a right downwind, turned crosswind and set up my final approach a mile and a half out at 1,500 feet. I hit the gear lever and watched the three green lights on the panel come on to say the landing gear was down. Easy, easy, coming over the threshold, ease the stick back.

The mains touched and then there was a *big* thump as the nose wheel made contact with the tarmac.

"My first impression was that the nose wheel strut had collapsed. What I didn't know was that all three had collapsed. With a grinding shriek, the aircraft went sliding down the middle of the runway on its belly, John calmly informing me that I was leaving one hell of a trail of sparks. Almost 5,000 feet after setting down, I ground to a stop, with John's voice in my earphones saying, 'You've got a lot of smoke, you better get out of there.' It wasn't until I raised the canopy and jumped out that I realized that there was no rubber between the MiG and the runway. Without enough hydraulic pressure to lock the undercarriage down, they'd folded as soon I'd touched down. I ran like hell off the runway, but she just sat there and the smoke finally dissipated.

"It's a real tribute to the strength of the aircraft that it suffered only superficial skin damage. Unfortunately, the Angolans had nothing to lift it with – no crane, no jacks, nothing – so it was just written off. A T-54 tank hooked a cable to it and dragged the MiG-23 off the runway. It's still sitting there today. It turned out that the fuel tanks had never been topped off. The fuel gauge itself is designed to be set by hand to what's been put in the tanks. Someone had set it to Full."

★ ★ ★

Cacolo (again)

"My wife and I were taking a relaxing holiday in the Far East," said Hennie, "when I picked up a copy of the Bangkok morning paper and read that early in August Unita had retaken Cacolo. Fortunately, Mickey and his team had already gone, leaving the town in the hands of the local administrator and the Home Guard commander. In the absence of a professional defence, Unita overwhelmed and slaughtered the Home Guard, along with the civilians they accused of collaborating with the enemy.

"Sitting on the hotel veranda with my morning coffee, I couldn't help being angry that all the effort to capture it had been wasted by FAA's typical lack of planning, intelligence gathering and foresight. How could anyone not realize that Unita would begin to launch counter-offensives as soon as the conditions favoured them? I sighed and motioned for the hovering waiter to refill my cup. This could mean only one thing: we were going to have to mount another operation to retake the town."

*

"On my return from leave two weeks later I stopped in Cabo Ledo for a couple of days. I was enjoying a *braai* with the instructors, when a message came through from Saurimo. A reported Unita presence east of Saurimo had seen Ricardo take my combat group to investigate. They had reached the Luachimo River about ten kilometres east of Saurimo, crossed the make-shift bridge that had been built by FAA after Unita had destroyed it back in April and completed a recce that found nothing. On their return, Paul was crossing the bridge when suddenly the supports collapsed. The BMP slid sideways off the steel tracks and landed upside down in the flooding river. Despite frantic efforts by the rest of the group to right it, they were too late and Paul drowned. Stunned, I read the message again and walked away from the *braai*. I'd known Paul since I was commander of 5 Reconnaissance Regiment, where he had been one of my signals officers. On the way to Cafunfo he had not only been my driver, a fairly lowly position, but also an excellent signals officer who ensured that I had comms at any time day or night. His death sent me into a deep depression."

"Ricardo had led this particular reconnaissance," Carlos remembered. "I was manning the radio at Saurimo, when the group came back and Ricardo brushed straight past me without a word. This was totally out of character. We had been to school together and friends for a long time. Before I could ask anyone what was wrong Paul's body was carried into the sick bay and I heard the whole story. Ricardo, who had known Paul and his family for years, had had to witness the entire incident, helpless to change the outcome."

"When I stepped off the aircraft at Saurimo, more bad news awaited me," Hennie said. "A week after I'd left Cafunfo, Colonel Nevis led a small combat element north towards the town of Porne. Riding in a DAF lorry, he was on his way back when the vehicle went over an anti-tank mine and he was killed. Of all the Angolan officers I met, he was by far the most impressive, a cheerful and courageous man who would certainly have reached general rank. His death was a great loss for FAA and a personal loss for me.

"Ricardo was flown back to Luanda to take command of another project and I was appointed the EO base commander at Saurimo and, in effect, the operations group commander. General Marques, who had been the theatre commander during the Cafunfo operation, was replaced by General Mendez and he and I went to work on a plan for retaking Cacolo. All of my BMPs were still in Cafunfo, so a few were flown from Luanda to Saurimo by the Russian Il-76s and we began forming a new combat group. Our guys set about modifying them with new radios and additional machine gun and grenade launcher mounts, before going over them to check that they were in good mechanical order. Rolf was transferred back to Saurimo as my 2iC."

On the night of 17 October Unita attacked the FAA base at Lugia, just twelve kilometres west of Saurimo, killing nine of the defenders for eight of their own. At midnight, General Mendez asked Hennie to deploy an operations group and by 0500 EO had reached the Lugia base. Flanked by the BMPs, the ex-Koevoet trackers began the follow-up. With years of experience tracking Swapo insurgents in Namibia, they were masters of the game. As the Namibians and South Africans closed on them, Unita first abandoned a wounded comrade on his stretcher. EO hit the contact in early afternoon and captured two Unita soldiers, but in the middle of it Tetius Haasbrooke was struck by an overhanging branch as he was ducking into his turret and suffered two fractured cervical vertebrae. He was soon on board a helicopter back to Saurimo, then flown directly to Lanseria, but would never walk again.

On 1 November the EO combat group set off from Lugia for Cacolo, followed by FAA's 39th Battalion. On the first day of the advance one of the black ex-Koevoet operators spotted an anti-personnel mine and called over a FAA sapper to lift it. It had been booby-trapped with an anti-tank mine and the resulting explosion killed the sapper, blowing him into the air, and seriously wounded the EO operator. He was fortunate that the AK magazines in his chest webbing took most of the force, but his eyes were badly lacerated by sand.

"That afternoon saw us scramble for the first of many casevacs," said Alberts. "Our new doctor accompanied us and started working on our guy as soon as we landed. The casevac went off pretty smoothly and after he was cleaned up at Saurimo, he was flown down to Olivedale in the King Air. He survived, but lost both eyes.

"Tango Romeo had just taken off with the first casevac, when we got another call. A BMP had hit a mine and one crew member had injured his neck badly. Charlie and Juba orbited while we loaded him and lifted off before the B-12 could zero in on us. When our King Air pilot returned that night after twelve hours in the air, he had to set off again for Lanseria."

When the choppers landed after the second casevac, it was discovered that the fuel bowser had been flown back to Luanda in an Il-76. Air and ground crews frantically turned to hand-pumping fuel from the underground bunkers into drums, then hand pumping from the drums into the choppers. Without filters or electrical earthing, it was a dangerous and exhausting four-hour process for each aircraft. The Angolans' lack of foresight was staggering.

"On 3 November General Mendez told me that he wanted to send the helos to Luena, a two-hour flight," Hennie said. "I didn't even bother counting to ten, before informing him that I would halt our advance for the duration of his proposed mission, as I refused to be without a casevac facility. Mendez backed down and cancelled the mission. Then Jos went down with malaria and had to be flown out, a serious loss, as he was my most capable ops controller. The following morning, without consulting me, Mendez sent the helicopters to Luena. I was livid."

Rolf's combat group were driving determinedly towards Cacolo. Having lost their BMP in the mine explosion the day before, Jan Kellerman, Callie and Andre were riding in a Ural truck with the logistics element, when they drove into an ambush. Gunfire exploded around them. Jan suddenly slumped and collapsed over the FAA driver. The others opened up with the AGS-17 and PKMs as mortar fire started raining down.

"Rolf's urgent request for a casevac came into the ops room, but the helicopters weren't back from Luena," Hennie said furiously, "and Mendez was nowhere to be found. He was finally tracked down in Saurimo town and called back to the base. The choppers didn't return from Luena until 1600, at which point Juba and JC jumped in and headed west. When Mendez saw them take off, he stormed in and threw a tantrum, shouting that I had tasked them without his permission. We were in each other's face and it was the closest I've ever come to hitting a general officer."

"The combat group had been under stand-off attack just prior to our arrival," said Juba, "and on our way in we identified enemy infiltration routes that told us there were plenty of Unita still in the area. Jan was still breathing when we landed. While the other chopper orbited we loaded him, two FAA wounded and one FAA dead into the chopper. The doctor worked on Jan all the way, got him stabilized and into our sick bay. The King Air didn't get back from Lanseria until 2230. Jan was still alive on the flight to South Africa, but was certified dead on arrival."

"From our advance the previous June, Unita knew exactly which route we had to take," Hennie said, "and were determined to halt us with delaying actions west of the Alto Cuilo bridge. Rolf stopped for a helicopter resupply and to brief everyone, then set off again at 1100 hours, coming under accurate B-12 and 106 mm recoilless fire when they reached the river. Spotting enemy infantry on high ground west of the bridge, he hit them with the Tattra's rockets."

Rolf was effectively halted by the ferocious Unita defences. Close air support was needed, but in the quiet weeks before Cacolo had been overrun, EO's fixed wing pilots had resigned from the company and moved on to other flying jobs. Deeply concerned for his men, Hennie turned to the Angolans. "I persuaded Colonel Gino and Mendez that we needed an airstrike, then sat in on the briefing Gino gave a fresh-faced SU-22 pilot. This young fellow took off and to my great relief saved the day with an accurate, low-level attack, which routed the enemy. Soon after, Rolf found a crossing point farther up the river and managed to get the combat group across. As they were climbing the deeply cut road, one of the ex-Koevoet trackers riding on the lead BMP screamed to stop. The driver slammed on the brakes just short of a trip wire strung across the road. If he hadn't spotted it, the anti-tank mines buried on either side of the cut would have destroyed the BMP and cleaned off everyone riding on top. It was a close shave."

For the next three days the ops group doggedly advanced under long-range B-12 and mortar fire. "At 0700, 9 November, General Mendez criticized me for the slow progress towards Cacolo, saying we should simply drive forward and occupy the town," Hennie said. "I had to remind him that they were on ground controlled by Unita and that there was still the Tchicunda River to cross, after which they still had another ten kilometres to the objective. Mendez sneered that, 'The South Africans are frightened of Unita.' When I heard that I exploded and told him to leave my HQ. He later returned and apologized to me and my staff for the remark."

"It was the afternoon of the ninth day when Rolf reported that they were on the outskirts of Cacolo and awaiting a re-supply before moving in," Alberts said. "Our two tired helicopters were loaded with ammunition and two weeks of rations, plus a generator and a cooler filled with beer, which we thought they might like. After cramming fifteen guys in each helicopter, we left on a dog-leg route that would take us through areas of least enemy concentrations. We briefed our PKM gunners that on the last two-minute run in, they were to shoot at anything that looked remotely suspicious."

"My chopper was still so heavy when I arrived at the LZ," Juba said, "that I had to do an assault landing on the open patch of field. As I went through transition my chopper decided it didn't want to fly anymore and I put her down with thirty kilometres per hour still on the clock and went bundu-bashing through some small trees with the nose."

"Nine days after setting off from Saurimo, the combat group reached Cacolo," Hennie said, "sending Unita retreating just as we had done back in June. A much appreciated signal came in from Eeben Barlow in Pretoria, congratulating us on the success of the operation. Rolf consolidated and worked hard to stabilize the area, setting up strong defensive positions with mortars and the Tattra to respond to any Unita bombardment. The administrator, who had escaped into the bush just ahead of Unita's attack in August, came back and gradually the locals began to trickle in. Although the town was hit repeatedly with B-12s and 82 mm mortar fire up until our withdrawal at the end of 1995, Unita never attempted an infantry assault.

"Angola's Independence Day was 11 November, and we had a victory parade at Saurimo, with all the local dignitaries present and some of our guys passing in review with BMPs. At my insistence, a special citation was read by the governor of the Lunda Sul Province, praising the SU-22 pilot who had done so well in assisting the ops group. Credit should be given where it's due, and I really wished that young man could have been decorated for an outstanding performance under very difficult operational conditions. Four days later, Eeben asked me to fly down to Cape Town for Jan Kellerman's funeral. I knew his father, a retired colonel in the SADF and it was my sad duty to brief him and Jan's mother on what had happened."

★ ★ ★

United Nations and Blue Berets

"The next month Unita agreed to talks on ending the war and United Nations monitors began arriving in Saurimo," Hennie said. "We developed quite a positive relationship with these UN guys, especially the Russians, giving them intelligence briefings and helping them out where we could. A Bulgarian major and Russian NCO were sent to Cacolo, where they insisted on staying with EO, knowing that in the event of a Unita attack, our guys would stand and fight. They would not move anywhere without a South African escort. We even delivered their UN-supplied rations when we made our regular chopper flights to Cacolo."

"The most memorable of the UN Blue Berets was Yuri," Carlos said, "a very fit Russian Spetsnaz major who could have been my twin brother in appearance. We immediately hit it off with him – and he with us, joining us on our early morning runs and PT and dropping into *Gang Goggas* Corner in the evenings for a few beers. A veteran of Afghanistan, he pointedly refused to discuss his time there, which, as Special Forces operators ourselves, we respected. Maybe it was our common background of Special Forces, but we soon took him into our confidence, something that didn't go down especially well with a number of the other UN monitors, particularly the few Yanks and New Zealanders. He flew out to Cacolo and stayed with our guys, sending back to Luanda reports based on the briefings we gave him. He showed us congratulatory messages for the fine work he was doing, laughing that the UN would have a collective coronary if they knew it was all based on our intelligence assessments. He occasionally showed us UN assessments, which were utterly valueless. Whoever their senior intelligence officer was, it was clear he didn't know Africa, had lousy sources and an extremely incompetent staff.

"When our people were withdrawn from Cacolo, Yuri came out with them and refused to return, describing those who took our place as complete military amateurs. We treated him to a trip to South Africa, where he stayed with Hennie, whose family fell in love with him. Had anyone told us ten years previously that we'd become close friends with a serving Russian Special Forces officer, we'd have said he was smoking some bad shit. But Yuri did become a close friend and we were sorry when his six month UN posting was finished and he returned home. Some time later, the Russian colonel who had taken over from him told us that Yuri was dead. He'd gone into hospital soon after getting back to Russia, but by the time cerebral malaria was diagnosed, it was too late."

★

"As negotiations were going on in Lusaka, Unita was still conducting operations," Carlos said. "Based on this and Savimbi's renunciation of the 1992 election results few of us believed he was genuine about bringing the war to an end. He lobbied the US and United Nations to force the MPLA to get rid of EO, painting us as a cause of the war, rather than a tool that brought him to the negotiating table. Because we were South African soldiers for hire, he received a sympathetic hearing from various members of the international community. What none of them questioned or seemed to understand, was that if he was serious about a peaceful settlement, our presence should have made no difference one way or the other.

"Neither did they question continued Unita activity outside areas supervised by a very thinly stretched UN monitoring force. General Ben-Ben, Unita's chief of staff, claimed that there was disagreement within the movement about whether to end the war and that he did not have complete control over some elements. Alternatively, the attacks were blamed by Unita on banditry. In actual fact, the so-called 'dissident' or 'bandit' attacks were a carefully organized resumption of low-level guerrilla activity to remind the *povos* – should they be thinking of supporting the MPLA – that Unita was still a force to be reckoned with.

"In high-level meetings in Luanda and Lusaka, General de Matos repeatedly told Alouine Blondine-Beye, the UN secretary-general's representative in Angola, that the presence of Executive Outcomes was not negotiable. We were an integral part of his defence force and likely to remain so for a long time."

212

"During this period we worked very well and very closely with the governor of Lunda Sul province and the interim government," Hennie said. "The co-operation between myself and General Mendez improved, with daily conferences to review the security situation, which remained calm in our area. For the first time in more than two years mining companies were flying in and driving into the bush, while the locals could move freely. We established a clinic in Saurimo town, which was about four kilometres from the airfield, and the general population viewed us as heroes.

"The general feeling was that the Cafunfo operation had given Unita such a blow that, especially after FAA retook Huambo and Soyo, they had to sue for peace. What no one knew was that, as Savimbi negotiated an end to the war he was establishing new routes for arms as his forces regrouped and rested and waited patiently for us to leave.[41] And here he was helped by various members of the international community who knew little about Savimbi and nothing about the war.

"Soldiers-for-hire were evil people, they all decided, and none more evil than South African soldiers-for-hire. So international pressure – particularly from the Clinton Administration, which was offering a massive aid package – was placed on the MPLA government not to renew our contract. In early December my entire combat group was airlifted back to Cabo Ledo, where we waited for a couple of weeks before being flown back to South Africa for Christmas leave."

*

"On our return to Cabo Ledo in early January 1996, we went through the process of handing all our equipment back to FAA under the gaze of United Nation monitors, whose attitude and demeanour towards us was in marked contrast to the likes of Major Yuri. The Boeing arrived from South Africa, and as we loaded our personal and company kit the starchy Blue Berets made careful notes. It was all slightly ridiculous. When the time came for us to board, our Angolan friends, some of them weeping openly, pushed the UN people aside to shake hands and embrace us. Among them

---

[41] Six months after Executive Outcomes left Angola, Unita launched a major attack against Negage in Uige province. The airfield from which Savimbi had made his escape after the 1992 elections was captured, but the town held.

were those who had been so distrustful and hostile when we'd arrived over two years earlier. As the last of our blokes was heading up the stairs, they broke into spontaneous applause, shouting, '*Viva, Africa du Sul!*'

"We settled into our seats and two officious UN monitors stalked the aisle doing a head count. General Luís Faceira brushed past them to the cockpit, asked for the microphone and turned to face us. He thanked us for our courage and for our sacrifices, promising that when the war was over, we would always be welcome in Angola. We were friends for life, he said, his voice catching, brothers of Africa. He came back down the aisle, gripping shoulders, shaking black hands and white hands. He waved one last time, and the door closed. As the Boeing lifted off everyone strained for a last look at where the adventure had started, many of them blinking back tears. Our Angolan contract was over.

"But a contract for Sierra Leone was being finalized, for which the best of our guys were recruited. Those who declined the offer returned home, where they disappeared into civilian life. As for me, I'd had enough of fighting for a while and accompanied them."[42]

*

One of the questions often asked of Executive Outcomes, was how they could have so easily turned around and fought people they had supported for so long. When the author asked Oom Hennie the question, he answered with this:

"I had worked with Unita from 1976 and was for a time Savimbi's personal SADF liaison officer. I knew him well. I believed in him as the great hope for Africa. I had saved his life. He had my absolute loyalty.

"As was explained earlier in this book, in 1992 there was a general election in Angola in which Savimbi came a very close second. In the lead up to elections an official residence had been constructed in Luanda to accommodate whichever man – Dos Santos or Savimbi – came second and Savimbi was offered this and the position of deputy president.

"For whatever reasons, and despite all his previous rhetoric about

---

[42] "Later, one journalist known for his sensationalist and inaccurate reporting used photos taken of me in Angola and wrote articles naming me as EO's ground commander in Sierra Leone, when in fact I never set foot in the country," Hennie said.

accepting the will of the people, Savimbi claimed that the elections had been fixed and headed back to the bush to continue the war. Many rank and file Unita soldiers, as well as senior Unita generals who had dedicated their lives to his struggle, were abandoned, sacrificed to ensure his escape, and died in the subsequent mini-war that exploded in Luanda. (General McKenzie survived, but was so disillusioned with his former leader that he joined FAA. Others stayed to join small opposition parties.)

"Between Savimbi's resumption of the war and EO's retaking of Cacolo, tens of thousands of Angolans, mainly civilians, were killed or displaced as the result of his megalomania and refusal to work within the democratic system he had claimed was his goal. As I said, I knew him well and had believed in him. I had given many years helping to plan and execute military operations that would eventually force the MPLA to allow elections. When they finally came, his refusal to abide by the results – flawed though they may have been – was a betrayal of everyone who had supported him, to include the many young South Africans who had died helping him from 1976 to 1988. He had betrayed me, too. The reader may find this a specious rationalization. That is, of course, your prerogative – just as it was mine to turn my professional skills against him.

"When it became known that Executive Outcomes was fighting in Angola, Savimbi was scathing about the MPLA hiring mercenaries, ignoring the fact that he himself had done so over the years. EO had in fact killed one at Soyo, and we had killed more on the way to Cafunfo. Former SADF colleagues in South Africa who maintained links with Savimbi passed on a personal message from him to me. The first part of the message was that he was aware that I was in Angola with Executive Outcomes and was deeply disappointed by my involvement there. The second part was that should I or any other Executive Outcomes employee be captured, we would immediately be executed. That, of course, was his prerogative.

"I invite you to draw your own conclusions."

★ ★ ★

Appendix: Sierra Leone

It's amazing the number of wars I've covered in Africa where there just happen to be diamonds. Of course, the side that's dressed in rags and running around with guns invariably has someone telling those gullible enough that his side is only fighting for democracy and human rights. What he doesn't mention is that his side would really like to get their hands on those diamonds. And the gold deposits. And the ... well, you get the picture.

And speaking of pictures, if there's ever one made about Sierra Leone, it'll be a cracker. Imagine the opening scene as a 4X4 filled with black and white mercenaries and one journalist (that's me, played by Robert Redford for the gravitas) enters the village. Cut to: sweaty close-up of narrowed eyes following its progress. Above the buzz of flies whispers of 'South Africans'. The 4X4 bumps into the market square and the gathered throng freezes.

One woman suddenly shrieks, "South A-fri-ca!" – and the words become a mantra for everyone. "South A-fri-ca! South A-fri-ca!" Children dart in to touch their heroes, racing away in giggling triumph. A woman grabs my arm. "They saved us! They are saints!" These veterans of the Namibian and Angolan wars, case hardened tools of the old apartheid regime, cast shy looks at the dancers. "This happens every time we come here," one mumbles, ducking his head in embarrassment as the ululations gather strength. "They really like us."

But I'm getting ahead of myself.

★

With no great leap of imagination, Sierra Leone might serve as an African cliché. Everything political correctness forbids mentioning is there: indolence, poverty, natural wealth, voodoo, corruption, cannibalism and cruelty beyond measure. It is Kurtz's "The horror! The horror!" in a modern *Heart of Darkness*.

Established for freed slaves in 1787[43], its 27,000 square miles contain the richest alluvial diamond fields in the world. There's bauxite, gold, platinum, suspected oil deposits and a quarter of the world's titanium oxide. At Independence in 1961, the country exported rice, cocoa, a fifth of the world's ginger and the currency was on par with the US dollar. Today, it's right up there with Afghanistan as one of the most impoverished nations on earth.

The greed of Sierra Leone's post-Independence leaders differed only by degrees of magnitude. By the time President Joseph Momoh took power in 1987, the capital of Freetown, once a jewel in the British crown, was an embarrassing eyesore: streets a succession of potholes, electricity and water that worked only sporadically, and civil servants going unpaid. Even more short-sightedly, Momoh's thievery left little for the army, foolish in a continent where *coups d'etat* can be the *plats du jour.*

So when he heard that a group of junior officers was on its way to discuss back pay, he decided there was enough under the mattress to see him to a comfortable old age and hopped a helicopter for Conakry. When the Boyz from the Barracks realized they had just overthrown the government, it was a race for the radio station: the first to seize the microphone was Captain Valentine Strasser, who breathlessly announced that he was now Chairman of the National Provisional Ruling Council. The less fleet-of-foot elevated themselves to Secretaries of State (SOS) and Permanent Liaison Officers (PLO), then flipped coins to see who got SOS for Mines, SOS for Treasury, for Defence, for Tourism, Fisheries, Trade and Industry, before divvy-ing up all the PLO positions. It was tough, but as patriots they knew where their duty lay.

Things were not so simple in the hinterland, where the Revolutionary United Front under Alfred Foday Sankoh was butchering illiterate peasants wholesale. Former Corporal Sankoh, imprisoned for a 1971 coup attempt and amnestied in 1980, had gone on to receive guerrilla training in Libya, where he met Charles Taylor of neighbouring Liberia. The two connoisseurs of *filet du paysan* became fast friends,

---

[43] The British bought land from local chiefs in what is now Freetown for the express purpose of resettling former slaves from Jamaica and Nova Scotia. In a cruel irony, many of the initial group of 400 freedmen were killed and eaten by the same tribes who sold the land for their settlement. Of those who escaped the massacres, most died of disease. Subsequent resettlements laid the foundation for an educated, English-speaking elite who would dominate the government and army after Independence.

spending hours in their desert training camp dreaming of their UN vote.

Almost twenty years later, Taylor and his chum 'Prince' Johnson (native-born, with a catchy first name and educated in the US) toppled Liberian president Samuel Doe. The capital of Monrovia, itself founded by freed African-American slaves, fell in 1990 amid scenes of armed, drugged-out adolescents in blonde wigs, feather boas and necklaces of human fingers. Doe, who had allegedly eviscerated his predecessor alive and eaten his liver, was killed by Johnson, who was himself tortured to death on video by good friend Taylor. Cannibalism a long and honoured West African tradition, the last voice on the tape is one of Taylor's cronies saying, "Switch it off, it's time to eat."

Once settled into the presidential palace and his UN vote secure, Taylor began providing arms to Sankoh in exchange for diamonds. Momoh's overthrow by Strasser, et al, in April 1992 was marked by an increase in RUF atrocities against the rural population, attacks against military convoys for guns and ammunition and mission clinics for medical supplies.

By January 1995 the RUF had overrun the Swiss-owned Sierra Ore and Metal Company (Sierromco) bauxite mine at Mokanji, and the US/Australian-owned Sierra Rutile titanium oxide mine at Gbangbatok. They were also promising to execute 17 Western hostages, among them half a dozen Italian nuns. The murder of an Irish priest gave force to the threat.

As the rebel attacks moved closer to Freetown a stressed-out Strasser & Co began grabbing kids off the streets, giving them a gun, a uniform and a few words on their sacred duty to Sierra Leone, then shoving them into the jungle. Their sometimes salaries of $20 and two bags of rice a month, coupled with the prospect of the RUF pouncing on them, convinced a fair number to do a bit of looting, murdering and amputeeing themselves, and gaining the sobriquet of 'sobel'. (Soldier by day, rebel by night.)

The moribund 12,000-strong Republic of Sierra Leone Military Force (RSLMF) was incapable of halting the 500 or so rebels, who were now threatening Freetown itself. Worried about further destabilization of the region, the Economic Community of West African States Military Operations Group (ECOMOG) had deployed some 3,500 Nigerian, Ghanaian and Guinean troops against the RUF, but low morale and cultures more attuned to siestas than combat made them unconvincing warriors. (They'd tried a spot of peacekeeping during Liberia's civil war, where they were less known for keeping the peace than enthusiastically stripping the capital of everything that wasn't red hot or nailed down.)

The loss of the Kono diamond fields to Sankoh's neanderthals shut the last of Sierra Leone's foreign revenue earners; suddenly there were no millions flowing into the ... uh, treasury. Almost as bad was that the diamond smugglers, who paid good money not to have their bags examined too closely at the airport, suddenly had nothing to pay anyone not to look for anymore. And to top it off, the pesky rebels were threatening Freetown itself. It was a vexatious moment. Were the boys to do a Momoh and high tail it for the tall and uncut, or bring in some muscle?

Muscle it was, and Jersey Island-based Gurkha Security Guards agreed to train the RSLMF under the command of the legendary American mercenary Robert McKenzie. However, on 24 February, while scouting the Malal Hills for a suitable training site, McKenzie was killed in a surprise encounter with the RUF after being deserted by accompanying Sierra Leone troops.[44]

At an Organization of African Unity mini-summit, the dejected Sierra Leone delegation listened wistfully to the Angolans, who described in detail their satisfaction with Executive Outcomes. It was, they insisted, the only practical solution.

Eo Deploys

Before EO had pulled the last of its personnel out of Angola, an advance party was already in Freetown. By May, 56 black and white former Special Forces, 32 Battalion and Koevoet operators were quartered in Cockerell Military Headquarters in Freetown, where their introductory briefing painted a bleak picture. Despite untold natural wealth, institutionalised corruption had turned Sierra Leone into a beggar country, made worse by the predations of Foday Sankoh, whose only claim to military expertise was never losing a fight against unarmed civilians. Other than demanding that the youthful junta step down and the country cleansed of all Western influence – to include embassies, aid organizations and investors – Sankoh

---

[44] Badly wounded as a paratrooper with the 101st Airborne in Vietnam, McKenzie was retired with 100% disability. After a year of university, he went to Rhodesia, completed the gruelling SAS selection course and rose to the rank of captain, becoming one of the most decorated soldiers of that war. He subsequently fought in conflicts around the world.

had no known political agenda. Until the RUF was neutralized and the mines restarted, the World Bank, IMF and donor countries had cut off all funding. EO's objectives were clear: engage and destroy the RUF, while denying them their sources of funding. The parallel with Angola was unmistakable.

From RSLMF stores they were allocated a brace each of long-wheel-base Land Rovers, Bedford lorries and BMP-1 armoured fighting infantry vehicles. The South Africans removed the Land Rovers' soft tops and doors and mounted a 12.7mm heavy machine gun in place of the back seats. A roll bar with AGS-17 was added to each Bedford, the lorries' sides replaced with sandbags, and a 14.5mm HMG fitted to one of the BMPs. Air support would initially consist of an Mi-17 gunship and an Mi-24V, both flown by a Belarussian crew, grizzled veterans of Afghanistan who spoke no English.

EO's first task was retraining selected units of the RSLMF at the Mile 91 base (91 miles from Freetown) near the town of Yonibana. Under command of PP, a former Special Forces lieutenant colonel, they set off from Cockerell, the drive through Freetown slowed by thousands of cheering civilians.

"I felt like a WWII general driving through a liberated French town," PP sheepishly admitted. "It was great." The feeling of euphoria evaporated 25 miles later. On the outskirts of the small town of Newton charred and mutilated bodies surrounded half a dozen burning vehicles, the result of an RUF ambush just minutes earlier.

The appearance of the modest convoy saw cars and vans tagging on until PP estimated they had a tail of almost 120 vehicles. His Sierra Leone driver – dubbed "One-mile" for answering any question about distance to the next town with "One mile" – kept a steel helmet next to him and, at seemingly random moments, settled it on his head. "I watched this ritual a few times and realized that he donned it shortly before passing areas littered with destroyed vehicles. Some had been there for months, others were quite fresh. One-mile became my early warning system. When the helmet went on, I warned everyone to be ready for a possible ambush."

Arriving at Mile-91 without incident, they were shown their new charges. It would be a challenge. Aside from having no battle-training, the Sierra Leone soldiers were high on marijuana or gin most of the day. Sighing philosophically, EO concentrated on the basics, settling into a routine of morning PT (much loathed by the Sierra Leoneans), marksmanship and field craft.

The schedule was interrupted one morning by the base commander, Major Samura, who reported that rebels had been harassing the locals and promising to attack nearby Yonibana. When EO patrols sent the rebels scurrying out of the area, a grateful village chief presented the training team with a goat and two enormous pineapples. On slaughtering the goat they found a live kid, to which PP gave his son's nickname of Bee-Bap. Bee-Bap followed him everywhere.

★

Because of the limited infrastructure and vast areas of double- and triple-canopy jungle, EO's pre-contractual analysis stipulated the movement of men and equipment by air. Aside from fulfilling their own requirements, resupplying remote RSLMF bases by air would prevent a ready source of munitions from falling into RUF hands. To provide the needed lift capability EO initially leased,[45] and then purchased two Mi-17s at a cost of approximately \$500,000 each.[46] A requirement for emergency casualty evacuation was satisfied by the acquisition of two Hawker Siddeley Andovers, one of which was placed on permanent standby at Lungi Airport near Freetown.

Whilst awaiting delivery of their helicopters, the pilots were given a conversion course in the gunships, which the Belarussians refused to relinquish for actual operations, seeing the South Africans as a threat to their own contracts. When the Mi-17 gunship, flown by an EO crew, was downed after ingesting a flock of birds, the relationship became distinctly prickly. The biggest problem with using the Belarussians for close air support was that they spoke no English. The interim solution was to place Alfred, a Moscow-trained RSLMF officer, on board as an interpreter.

When their own Mi-17s arrived, EO's pilots volunteered to provide top cover for the immediate extraction of the Mi-24 crew in the event they were downed on their reconnaissance flights. This went some way in

---

[45] The lessor was Soruss, an air charter company that operated Mi-8MTV-1s and provided the Belarussian gunship pilots.

[46] "We soon dubbed them 'Daisy' and 'Bokkie,'" chief pilot Charlie Tait said, "the former because she behaved a bit like a cow, and the latter due to being as fleet-footed as a young springbok."

healing the rift, which was soon festering again when EO convinced the junta that the Mi-24's potential was not being realised due to the risk of blue-on-blue incidents. As a result, two South Africans were soon at the controls of the Russian gunship for EO operations.

"It's a formidable machine," Tait said, "and we grew quite fond of *Renoster*, so nicknamed because that 12.7-mm gatling gun gives it a certain resemblance to a rhinoceros. As is immediately apparent to anyone who has flown both types, a lot more thought went into the design of the Mi-24 cockpit than the Mi-17. At sea level there's bags of power. Straight and level with full pods at 300kph, she is exceptionally agile for an aircraft of 13 tonnes, and with both cockpits and other vital areas protected by titanium armour, one feels quite secure. The sense of security is bolstered by the weapons systems, which include 57mm rocket pods, 30mm grenade launchers, 7.62-mm minigun packs and the 12.7-mm gatling gun."

★

As soon as the RSLMF company had absorbed what they could in three weeks of training, PP led them back to Freetown, where planning was underway for an attack on the rebels threatening the capital. Under operational command of Rolf, it was a combined air-ground operation, with the Mi-24 and two M1-17s in support of the mechanized ground force. EO reconnaissance commandos located the base at Moyamba, some twenty miles from Freetown, before the mechanized force swept through it. Subsequent radio intercepts revealed that over 30 rebels had been killed and many more wounded. On EO's side, "Pan," a former Koevoet operator, lost an eye to RPG shrapnel, while three Sierra Leonean troops received minor shrapnel wounds. The RUF survivors retreated to the Malal hills, where they would be dealt with later. Freetown was secure.

★

"Though our employers were overjoyed and keen to be identified with EO," Carlos smiled, "they invariably reminded us of adolescents playing at being grown-ups. Getting them to buckle down to their responsibilities was like trying to convince exuberant teenagers to eat their spinach and do their homework before going out to play. Strasser himself, 'The Chairman,' was a tall, round-faced 27-year-old who, behind ever-present Ray-bans, appeared to be stoned out of his head most of the time. He had no interest in matters of state, preferring to remain undisturbed at his official residence – except for late night disco crawls, Ray-bans still firmly in place.

"Captain Kenneth Mondeh, the very personable Chief of the Army, was another twentysomething whose grasp of military affairs was almost non-existent. He invariably fell asleep during planning sessions, waking at the end with something along the lines of, 'Congrats, men, on a bloody good show!' Mondeh loved to swing his weight around and we learned how to push his button when we needed something done in the same decade.

"The third unforgettable character was Tom Nyuma, a great fan of Rambo and *Soldier of Fortune* magazine. If the badges and patches he wore were believed, Tom was the only soldier in the world who served simultaneously in the US Rangers, SEALs, Special Forces and Airborne. Nonetheless, he was enormously enthusiastic and the only junta member to occasionally deploy with EO on the ground. All of them had bodyguards, but Tom's were the most feared for their bullying and license to steal.

"On the periphery of these youngsters, but far superior in terms of leadership, was Brigadier Julius Maada-Bio. Part of the unintentional *coup-d'etat* and now Chief of Defence Staff, he was reasonable, unexcitable and always open to advice. His priority, however, was to fill the void left by the reclusive Strasser, leaving the military effort to the others under EO's guidance."

If their employers were pleased with the outcome of EO's first action, it was nothing compared to the man and woman in the street. When word of EO's success in pushing back the rebels was broadcast on the local radio station, Freetown's inhabitants went wild with impromptu street celebrations. The South Africans could go nowhere in public without being crushed by grateful admirers. However personally satisfying it was, they knew it had been a fairly minor operation designed as much to safeguard the capital as to assess the RUF's tactics and abilities. There was still much work to be done.

Taking the Initiative

The plan for retaking the Kono diamond fields had taken shape as a three-week campaign. Because of the RUF's history of ambushing civilian and army convoys, the advance would necessarily be slow and cautious. Once the South Africans reached Kono, they'd have to clear it house-by-house and then conduct time-consuming area patrols before declaring the area safe.

Practically on the eve of setting off, there were mutinous mutterings in the ranks: under no circumstances could they begin the operation before watching the 1995 Rugby World Cup Final. Afterwards, with morale sky high at the Springboks' victory over the New Zealand All Blacks, 46 South Africans and Attie, their monkey mascot found in Freetown, climbed into their vehicles and headed east. Trailed by an RSLMF company under Tom Nyuma, the first day saw them cover the 130 km to Masingbi, where the BMPs were driven off their transporters and carefully checked, everyone aware that the next 50 km stretch was effectively controlled by the RUF.

"The next morning everyone was pumped up at the prospect of heading into unfamiliar terrain and the certainty of combat," PP said. "Only little Attie was unfazed, scampering from one shoulder to another and chattering and scolding incessantly until someone handed him a biscuit."

Weapons were checked, the 12.7 and AGS-17 mounts given a spray of lubricant and riflemen picked their positions behind the sandbags. To bolster their firepower, a few EO-trained Sierra Leones were included on the Bedfords, an arrangement that didn't please everyone. Nyuma's daily distribution of Pegga Packs, "moral booster" sachets of gin, were already being consumed in quantity by the nervous troops. PP's radio crackled. The Mi-24 was wheels-up out of Lungi, twenty minutes away with a South African crew. Show time.

"We said our farewells and set off, my Land Rover followed by 'Fearless Fred' Marafano, a former British SAS sergeant major in the second Land Rover, backed by a Bedford, then a BMP trailed by the second Bedford and BMP."

They hit the first ambush ten minutes later.

"The gunship crew spotted movement, radioed a warning and came in with the 12.7mm," PP said. "The ambush had been laid in and around a school alongside the road and what I remember most clearly about the first minute or so was the number of RPG-7s flying around. (Both the rebels and RSLMF loved them because of the noise they made.) Out of the vehicles, we brought down accurate small arms and mortar fire, then advanced to find eight bodies and numerous blood trails leading into the jungle.

"Fred and I headed after them, followed by about 30 of Tom Nyuma's reluctant warriors. Some 100m into the bush I glanced behind and suddenly felt very lonely – the only two people following the spoor were Fred and myself. We looked at each other, decided discretion and common sense were the order of the day and about-faced rather smartly. Back on the road, I brought in 81mm mortar fire on possible escape routes. While this was going on, the lot who'd abandoned us were posing victoriously around the bodies for Tom's video camera.

"From that point the circus began, with one ambush after another. The rebels favoured high ground and defiles, so as soon as I identified a suspect area we'd advance on foot until making contact, with the Land Rovers' 12.7s in support, leaving the less manoeuvrable BMPs behind, then mortaring probable escape routes and positions. The rebels started leaving warning messages in each small village we came to – the heads of innocent locals on stakes. The grizzly evidence badly unnerved the Sierra Leonies, but only hardened our determination to kill more of the fuckers."

They stopped to reload magazines, get some water down their throats and check the maps. The road climbed gently for the next 250m and disappeared to the right. With the gunship scouting ahead, there was a whispered conference and Fred, PP and six others proceeded quietly up the hill on foot.

"As we rounded the corner we surprised something like 25 rebels sitting along the right side of the road," PP vividly recalled. "Because they could hear our vehicles at the bottom of the hill, they'd assumed that's where we all were and were laughing about how they were going to fuck us up. They managed to get off a couple of RPGs and some AK fire, all very inaccurate, because we were already shooting the shit out of them. When the smoke cleared, twelve more were dead. From the heavy blood trails, at least half those who escaped were wounded. Again, we mortared areas they'd run towards. We fought our way through eleven ambushes over those 50km and reached a tiny village called Bumpe just before dusk."

They were now only a few kilometres from Kono and almost within sight of the town's Yengema airstrip, when someone realised that comms back to Freetown had been forgotten in all the excitement. Signaller Johan quickly assembled the radio and PP told Freetown where they were stopping for the night. The Cockerell ops room sounded puzzled. This was only the second day of a projected three-week operation.

Freetown: "Say again your current loc stat?" [Location status]

PP: "Yengema."

Freetown: "Uh, confirm Yengema?"

PP: "Affirm."

Freetown: *"Bliksem!"* [Damn!]

Tom Nyuma's company occupied the middle of the village, while EO consolidated on the outskirts where the road ran through tall elephant grass and disappeared around a gradual turn towards the airport. As night fell the BMPs were driven into the grass and hidden and the Land Rovers positioned to cover their rear. As soon as the two 120mm mortars were set up and ammunition made ready, PP went over the next day's plan, which would start with a bombardment on the airfield, followed by a quick advance into Kono.

"Talking over the day's events, we learned that Johan's birthday was tomorrow," PP said, "and as sort of a pre-celebration, we each had a couple of Tom's Pegga Packs. I can tell you, after almost a dozen contacts and most of the last 50 km on foot, we were exhausted. We unrolled sleeping bags in a few burnt-out houses lining the road. Jos and I stretched out on a scorched veranda, with Attie, a seasoned combat veteran now, falling asleep in the rafters above us."

*

"At dawn I was snatched awake by the sound of RPGs, followed immediately by a terrified Attie leaping from the rafters onto me and burrowing deep into my sleeping bag. Needless to say, I nearly shat myself when this fucking monkey landed on my head."

After an anxious minute or two, they realized that the rebels were attacking Tom's company from the opposite side of town. Thinking to outflank him, the rebels disengaged and shifted around to attack from the direction of the airport. As Tom's boys were loosing off RPGs and long bursts of machine gun fire at nothing, Jos and his crews were waiting patiently in the BMPs.

"We saw them appear around the bend in the road and move silently towards us, totally unaware of our presence," PP said. "They were about 100 feet away when the BMPs opened fire, blasting ten of them off their feet. The shocked survivors turned and fled towards the airport followed by me and two of my black EO soldiers. The rebels had never experienced hot pursuit and I don't know who was the most amazed when we came around that bend, us at seeing them walking along the side of the road in single file, or the rebels when we opened up."

PP waved a Land Rover forward. "Much to my surprise, Johan was driving, peering between the steering wheel and the dashboard with a very worried look on his face; this was not his scene, he was a radio man. I ran across the road to give orders to the gunner, then grinned at our signaller. 'Happy birthday, Johan, I hope you're having a nice day!'

"You're fucking mad!" he shouted over the roar of the 12.7.

"As we advanced I began calling in fire from our two 120mm mortars. We took the airport at 10h00, consolidated and got our first resupply when Juba came in with the Mi-24 and delivered six cans of Black Label beer to Johan for his birthday."

*

Two hours later, PP led the force into Kono, everyone poised for the first shot. But they were entering a ghost town where nothing moved. The first sight that really captured their attention was a wall on a roundabout. Stacked along the top were almost twenty heads, more messages from Foday Sankoh's freedom fighters.

EO occupied an old casino atop a volcanic outcropping that offered an all-round view of the area. When the badly shaken Sierra Leone company arrived PP positioned them in and around town. By last light on the third day Kono was declared secure.

"That night we were sitting around a fire, when Tom Nyuma produced a bottle of Johnny Walker Black Label," PP said. "I nearly fainted when he poured about a quarter of it on the ground, explaining that it was a Sierra Leonie custom to give some to their ancestors and slain warriors. I decided there and then that I would keep a bottle of cheap whisky with me at all times for the ancestors, to spare the expensive stuff for ourselves."

*

Though vastly outnumbered by the enemy, EO had killed more than 100 rebels and wounded many who would eventually die from lack of basic medical care. The South Africans suffered not a scratch; basic infantry skills, experience and common sense had given them the edge. As soon as they were settled, patrols went out, widening daily to a radius of about 20 km. It was an enormous area for only 46 men, but their presence saw most of the 30,000 inhabitants returning within a week to re-establish Kono as a booming diamond centre.

The Wordu Massacre and Reprisal

A few days after settling into their new headquarters, they heard small arms fire coming from the outskirts of town. "Eight of us dived into a Land Rover and headed for the airport, meeting over 100 of Tom's troops legging it towards us," PP said. "We tried to turn them around, but they didn't want to know, shouting, 'The rebels are coming! The rebels are coming!' We moved forward until a couple of RPG-7s shrieked past. Piling out of the vehicle, we responded with our AKs and very accurate fire from the 12.7 that sent them fleeing south at speed. Afterwards we learned that there had been no more than thirty of them. That they had routed almost 120 Sierra Leone troops, and that only eight of us had seen them off, told the whole story."

"Aside from their poor training and lack of motivation, what struck us about the Sierra Leone army was their enormous consumption of marijuana from morning till night," Carlos remembered. "Supplemented by Pegga packs, our client's troops moved in a cloud of smoke ahead of a trail discarded empties. Between the marijuana and the gin they were in a constant haze."

*

The subject of atrocities in Sierra Leone has been widely reported, but no newspaper article or official United Nations report can truly describe the horror they saw.

"The RUF killed and mutilated in the most horrific ways imaginable," Carlos said. "Amputations of arms, legs, lips, noses and ears by machete were commonplace. Other things were far worse. We never hardened ourselves to the sight of women who'd been gang-raped and then had burning stakes rammed into their vaginas. Or of men who, after the tendons in the backs of their hands had been severed to prevent them grasping anything, had the same ad hoc torture instruments driven into their anuses and left to die a slow and excruciatingly painful death.

"We found victims whose vaginas and anuses had been sewn shut with fishing line, others whose stomachs had been sliced open, filled with half-inch-long honey ants then crudely stitched closed." Not one of EO's soldiers was unaffected by what they witnessed, but it was the scale of the massacre at Wordu that truly stunned them.

Wordu lay about twelve miles south of Kono, a typical Sierra Leone farming village whose inhabitants had probably never seen Freetown or even cared who occupied State House. EO patrols had regularly passed through it, gathering information and dispensing basic medical care. In retribution, a group of rebels spent a night gang raping many of the young women and girls and subjecting others to agonizing tortures, before the survivors were forced into their huts, which were then set on fire; those who tried to escape the final atrocity were chopped down with machetes.

The South Africans heard distant shots and raced for the village. "We leapt out of the Land Rover prepared for a fight, but the rebels were gone," PP said. "Then we just stopped and stared at a scene straight from Hell. Huts were still blazing and the smell of burnt flesh hung in the morning air. As the huts collapsed into embers, it was clear that those inside had been burnt alive. By our count, at least 265 men, women and children had died. The only survivors were two babies, not more than a few months old, found under their mothers' bodies. It appeared that the young mothers had died protecting their infants.

"We immediately launched a follow-up operation, killed six and captured our first prisoners, who revealed they had come from an RUF camp near the village of Gandorhun, about 25 kilometres to the south. By that night we were already planning an attack."

Aerial reconnaissance found the camp some seven kilometres west of Gandorhun, its location confirmed by intercepted radio messages that a helicopter was flying over the area. Additional damning information came from a kidnapped teenager who'd escaped the camp soon after the attack on Wordu. He said that when the raiding party returned, they were laughing and boasting about of their success. His description of the camp's lay-out was icing on the cake.

"The day before the attack, Jim Hooper, whom some of our blokes had met when he was covering the Namibian war some years earlier, arrived on one of the choppers. To keep him out of our hair while we worked on the plan, we put him in one of the Land Rovers making a routine area patrol.

"By the time the patrol returned we had everything set. Daisy and Bokkie would insert blocker groups on the most obvious escape routes around Gandorhun and the camp. As soon as they were in position we'd open up with mortar fire, followed by the Mi-24 to send the survivors running like hell and right into them. It was no place for a journalist, but after some special pleading on his part, I relented and allocated a place for him on the insertion. He was waiting for the briefing to begin, when Tom Nyuma arrived. As Jim wrote of it later:

I leapt aside as a shiny 4X4 skidded to a stop. Bodyguards in mirrored sunglasses staggered out under the weight of chromed pistols, shotguns, Bowie knives and hand grenades. One, with a set of fetching ear protectors perched atop his head, also carried a machine gun and about fifty yards of ammunition belt wrapped around him. The mere weight of it all had him pop-eyed.

They were followed by their boss, Colonel Tom Nyuma, one of the five *coup d'etat*-ers back in '92. To the everlasting joy of all Sierra Leoneans, he was recently promoted from captain to colonel, skipping the tiresome ranks in between, and added S.O.S. of Defence of the NPRC of Sierra Leone to his other S.O.S.s. He held on to all his P.L.O.s for old time's sake. It's rumoured that the main requirement for holding the high-octane titles is being able to say them all without a crib sheet or taking a breath. You probably think I'm joking.

Colonel Tom strutted past his bodyguards, the patches on his vest proclaiming him 'Ranger,' 'Airborne,' 'SEAL' and 'Special Forces.' His clear favourite was a skull and crossbones with the warning, 'Mess With the Best, Die with the Rest.' Tom, who went from being an impecunious captain with an attitude to a senior government minister, purchased the patches through *Soldier of Fortune* magazine. Tom is 26 years old. The reader will sleep better knowing he was also in charge of the war. Sort of. Technically speaking.

Inside, PP is briefing the Belarussian gunship pilots and Colonel Tom. Next to Tom is a major whose men have been guarding the diamond fields since the South Africans chased out the rebels. Of course, his keeping a *very* close eye on the fields had nothing to do with him being close to Tom's sister, or that Tom had one or two ideas about what to do with those diamonds. And you should be ashamed of having such a suspicious mind.

PP taps the map: This infantry company will advance to this point, our fire force will be inserted here, mortar teams landed there, the gunship will orbit over here until ... . The Russkies listen intently, making notes on their own maps. The major is content with the plan; so content he's been snoring gently since the briefing began. A blinding flash fills the room. *Duck!* It's Tom's official photographer. Tom bebops up to the map to explain how the attack should be conducted. Volodya and Valerii's eyebrows lift and meet in bewilderment. The South Africans smile fixedly. Two more flashes for the Freetown newspapers and Tom takes his seat. PP carries on as if nothing has happened.

"The next morning we received a radio message from Freetown that one of the choppers was grounded because of fuel contamination," PP recalled, "forcing a quick revision of the plan. Fred would now lead a ground force towards Gandorhun while a mortar and protection team would land atop a high outcropping within range of it and the camp. As soon as Fred was in position we would mortar the town with the two 81mms, while the 120mm would hit the RUF camp some five kilometres to the west. Fred loaded his Sierra Leone troops on the Bedfords and left immediately, at the age of 59 still eager for a fight. We then did our final planning and preparation, took off and were inserted by mid-afternoon.

"Gazing down from our 120-metre-high vantage point, I quickly identified targets in and around Gandorhun. As soon as Fred radioed he was ready, we started dropping rounds. When night fell, I swept the area west of us with NVGs. And there the camp was, a crude circle of white heat sources under the double-canopy jungle. Campfires. Right where Carlos had said it would be. I gave my mortar man the range and distance and the first 120mm round dropped down the tube. I waited until the flash of impact, gave him a slight adjustment and we stonked the shit out of them with a combination of white phosphorous and HE. Many of them detonated in the trees, acting like air bursts.

"The heavens then opened with a tropical downpour and we spent a very cold, wet and sleepless night wrapped in our ponchos. We were supposed to be uplifted at first light but word came that *both* choppers were now grounded because of fuel contamination. We'd have to sit tight until they sorted out the problem.

"I still had plenty of ammunition and kept up sporadic fire on and around the rebel base throughout the day. That night we were better prepared for the rain but not for the ants. I woke around 4 a.m. and almost choked with laughter at seeing Jim dancing about, slinging clothes left and right and brushing inch-long army ants from his skin. A few hours later we were sipping black coffee in the morning sun when word came that the choppers were on their way.

"Fred and his troops were sitting in Gandorhun just a couple of kilometres away, but his radio wasn't working so we decided to land and see that everything was okay. As soon as we set down, Jim, unnoticed by the pilot, hopped out the opposite side and began snapping pictures. We had a quick word with Fred and climbed aboard for take off. Jim heard the change in pitch and realised that we were on our way. He ran to the chopper just as it was lifting off and grabbed the door, hanging by his fingertips. Fortunately, Carlos was sitting behind the gunner. As Jim remembers it:

> Dripping with cameras, I was out the door and looking for snaps, when I saw the wheel struts lengthening on Bokkie. Deafened by the whop-shriek of blades and turbines, I next saw the gunner frantically motioning me to return. *Are the bad guys coming? Is someone shooting at us?* When the wheels actually left the ground, the prospect of being left to the tender mercies of the RUF prompted a mad dash and leap that left me clinging cat-like to the bottom of Bokkie's door. Hands grabbed my wrists and hauled me inside 100 feet above the jungle. 'That'll teach you to get out of my helicopter without telling me,' the pilot said over a few beers that night. 'If you'd just stayed there, you silly twit, I'd have come back for you.'

Radio intercepts later revealed they had killed 36 of the rebels, wounded numerous others and convinced them to abandon the camp. PP could only hope that among the dead were those who'd wiped out the little farming village of Wordu. It was another feather in EO's cap.

Intelligence Ops and the Kamajors

"The intelligence side of things was most intriguing," said Carlos. "The junta had no idea of its value, even less about how to conduct intelligence operations. They weren't interested in how the material was collected, analysed or its benefit to operational commanders."

Carlos had started by talking to employees of Sierra Rutile and Sierromco. After years in the country, they possessed volumes of information and their observations on the culture, tribal customs, affiliations and personalities were invaluable. Sources that had to be approached more diplomatically and delicately were missionaries and NGOs. While many refused to speak to him, others had seen RUF atrocities and were willing to help, provided neither they nor their organizations were publicly acknowledged.

"Part of that willingness was the result of our helping Children Affected by War," he said. "The interior of the country was awash with kids orphaned by Sankoh's thugs. With no one to care for them, they were either going to gravitate to the RUF for food, turn to prostitution or die. Because our helicopters often returned empty from up-country, we offered to fly them back to Freetown. The poorly funded Catholic organization gratefully accepted our offer and were always there to meet our armed Mi-17s loaded with orphans. Before we finally left Sierra Leone, CAW bestowed a rare official commendation on EO for its help. It was probably just as rare to see a group of tough mercs get a little misty-eyed by the thanks for saving so many innocent lives."

*

As commander of the Kono Diamond Fields Area, Rolf worked hard to build trust with the local population. Among his first priorities was removing the anti-personnel mines that Tom Nyuma's troops had placed as a disincentive to illegal diamond mining. Humanitarian concerns, plus his establishment of a clinic and combined local council to administer the region's daily affairs, so endeared him to the tribal leaders that he was made an honorary chief, a rare honour for a white man. It also saw more and more intelligence on the RUF volunteered by the locals.

Considerable emphasis was placed on intercepting RUF radio transmissions. Even the best trained armies can sometimes be indiscreet; to EO's delight, the RUF were always indiscreet, the example set by Sankoh himself. A radio operator during his short military career in the British West African Forces, he would "cackle for hours on the air. Their childish word codes were easily unravelled, and they helped us by maintaining a punctual radio schedule, coming on the air at 0700, 1300 and 1600. Despite numerous hidings resulting from their poor comsec [communications security], they never learned and persisted in their daily sessions of verbal diarrhoea."

As in Angola, aerial surveillance was also a cornerstone of EO's intelligence gathering. When other sources identified a possible RUF base, night sorties were flown over the area, EO personnel hanging out the ramp looking for heat sources under the jungle canopy. If their night vision goggles revealed campfires arranged in a circle they knew it was an RUF base (civilian campfires were random and widely spaced). The location was pinpointed by GPS and transferred to a map as soon as they returned to Cockerell.

An event that wove together the effectiveness of aerial reconnaissance and signals intelligence was one they christened the 'Red Helicopter Gunship' incident. With PP in the right seat of the newly-purchased Cessna 337, Paddy McKay was circling over the Mano River bridge, a suspected point of entry for weapons and medical supplies from Liberia. Unable to spot any activity from altitude, he asked Paddy for a low pass. Carlos was monitoring RUF frequencies back at Cockerell when the radio speaker crackled excitedly.

Mano River Bridge: "Call the leader! Call the leader!"

Sankoh: "Yes, brother?"

MRB: "Sir, we are under attack by the Red Helicopter Gunship and are taking deep cover because the attack is very strong and they know where we are."

Sankoh: "What is wrong with the five-oh?" [12.7mm heavy machine gun.]

MRB: "It is not with us because we are taking deep cover in the bush."

The first thing Carlos noted was that the RUF needed to brush up on their aircraft identification. The second, given that their few radios were allocated only to important areas and units, his suspicions had been confirmed. He waited until PP returned to mention the 12.7.

"Monitoring of RUF transmissions was done under the supervision of our own signals intelligence chaps, who became so familiar with individual voices, that even without the associated call signs, they could walk directly to the relevant spot on the map to do updates. Collation was done by us and the junta intel staff before the product was disseminated. We did have an initial problem. The last thing you want is for the enemy to know you're listening to him. To our astonishment and fury, however, when the RUF came on the air a Sierra Leone would grab a mike and begin screaming insults. We eventually broke them of the habit, but it was a struggle.

"Prisoner interrogations can be gold dust in terms of tactical and strategic intelligence. The problem, particularly in the early stages, was our hosts' summary executions of them. Once we convinced them of the intelligence potential and began getting the occasional prisoner to interrogate, it was never necessary to apply any sophisticated interrogation techniques. Simply being in the presence of a 'white wizard' was normally enough to frighten them into revealing everything they knew. Their infantile grasp of military matters, however, meant that terms of reference had to be on a kindergarten level. It was frustrating and time-consuming, but worth it.

"Of immense value was the support we received from Chief Sam Hinga Norma, a traditional leader from the Bo area. A former officer in the colonial British West African Forces, he had attended Sandhurst and done a posting with the British Army on the Rhine in the 1950s. His quick grasp of military matters made him one of the few Sierra Leone personalities we talked to on an equal level and he became an enormously valuable ally."

More crucially, Chief Norma commanded the allegiance of the Kamajors, traditional hunters, providers for their clans, guardians of traditions and avowed enemies of the RUF. West Africa is the birthplace of voodoo, and the Kamajors were dedicated practitioners of this traditional magic. For them, the torture and massacres of innocents was proof of the RUF's evil; they were equally incensed by the rebels' claim to magical power through Sankoh's wife. This was not only beneath contempt, but a direct threat to their own role in society. Fiercely independent, the Kamajors were intimately familiar with the dark rain forests and on close terms with the animals and spirits who lived there. Armed only with ancient shotguns and razor sharp machetes, they moved ghost-like through the deep shadows.

"The RUF feared our helicopters," Carlos said, "but those could be seen, they were tangible; the Kamajors, however, existed on a different plane altogether. In a land of pervasive superstition, they were the rebels' worst nightmare. They were aloof, as befitted their status, faintly amused by the black and white men from South Africa who had come to help, but our allies, for which we were immensely grateful. Of course, one of their regular requests that we could not honour was that young RUF prisoners be returned after interrogation. These, they explained, were particularly tasty in 'rebel stew'.

"Chief Norma was an enigma for the junta, who not only suspected him of political aspirations, but also feared the magic of the Kamajors. I was discouraged from dealing with him, but his contribution was too important to be ignored and I persisted in consulting him, albeit very discreetly. He soon established a network that ensured a daily flow of information from the Kamajors. The fact that the local people supported the Kamajors rather than the RSLMF meant that their input also reached me via the Kamajor channel. We maintained a most rewarding relationship with Chief Hinga Norma. He not only greatly increased our military effectiveness, but enhanced our understanding of a complex society."

At Cockerell Carlos installed the first classic operations centre ever seen in West Africa, a showpiece the junta couldn't resist showing to every passing fireman, especially their ECOMOG allies from Nigeria, Ghana and Guinea. It was here that joint planning between the junta, ECOMOG and EO was conducted. When Carlos wasn't travelling to collect information or conduct interrogations, he settled into a daily routine of preparing intelligence analyses that were radioed to the various field commanders. He also provided the Chief of Defence staff with a daily briefing and had the freedom to interrupt them at any time with urgent information.

International concern about EO's presence made it politically expedient to share intelligence and strategic appreciations with selected members of the diplomatic community. This had to be done quietly, for no Western country was willing to be associated with EO, and it was worth a diplomat's career to be found in their company.

"Ours was a unique situation and we felt it appropriate to keep important players in the picture," Carlos said, "if for no other reason than to allay suspicion that we were planning to take over the country for ourselves: once we'd tidied up the mess they were unwilling to tackle, we'd be heading home for a well earned rest."

Because of Sierra Leone's historical connection to the United Kingdom and it's Commonwealth membership, the British High Commission served as EO's primary conduit for out-going information. "We were fortunate in having Peter Penfold, an urbane, professional and pragmatic high commissioner with a sound understanding of Africa in general and Sierra Leone in particular," Carlos said. "If the West wasn't prepared to step in to stop the slaughter, then perhaps we were the next best alternative. I'm not ascribing words or thoughts to him that weren't there, but I hope that was Penfold's perception of us. Certainly his support was based to a large extent on our professionalism and discipline, and the fact that we had done more than anyone to halt as vile a group of monsters as ever swung a machete. At his request we regularly briefed visiting Foreign Office officials, who let drop that his reports, which were unstinting in praise of our efforts to stabilize the country, went right to the top of the British government."

The Americans under the Clinton Administration were a different story. Carlos learned that the ambassador had received an unambiguous directive from Washington to have absolutely nothing to do with EO. The political incorrectness of being briefed by South African mercenaries far outweighed gathering solid intelligence. He did, however, maintain a cordial, albeit very distant, relationship with the CIA Head of Station, who, unlike the Brits, had a poor handle on the situation. "I shudder to think what he sent to his masters back at Langley," Carlos said.

When the latest fighting in the Liberian capital of Monrovia erupted in late 1996, the US Marines established a task force HQ at Lungi for the evacuation of Western nationals. Returning from the interior one day, Bokkie landed at Lungi to refuel. With Carlos was an American working for an international firm that specialized in hostage negotiation. A former special forces officer, "Larry could speak the Marine lingo fluently and we silently followed him to the task force HQ, where he soon had his fellow Yanks eating out of his hand.

"They gave us a tour of a C-17 transport aircraft, then we were invited by the task force commander to a briefing. He was cheerfully chatting away, when an agitated major entered and indicated something disastrous was happening. The colonel excused himself and the two huddled close, the major whispering urgently and casting sidelong glances at us. We heard '*Executive Outcomes!*' above the whispers. The briefing came to a screeching halt as the embarrassed colonel saw his career going down in flames. Grinning but sympathetic, we acceded to his request and promised *never* to mention the incident."

Sankoh's Voodoo Priestess

The most significant intelligence break came from a businessman who'd just returned from neighbouring Guinea. Over lunch, Carlos learned that Sankoh's wife and three others had been arrested in Conakry for trying to sell unregistered diamonds. Carlos rushed back to Cockerell for an immediate meeting with the Chief of Defence Staff. Inasmuch as an extradition treaty existed between the two countries, it was imperative that they had the opportunity to interrogate her. But no mention of EO – it must go through normal diplomatic channels.

Accompanied by most of the junta, he departed from Lungi for the thirty-minute flight. Not long after take-off a bearing in one of the helicopter's engines disintegrated and they turned back, the terrified junta members and hangers-on praying fervently to whichever god or spirit looked after them. Transferring to one of the Andovers, they were soon on the ground in Conakry, where the Sierra Leone contingent screamed into town in an ambassadorial motorcade, much to the amusement of the more relaxed Guineans.

"The rest of us occupied the airport VIP lounge, where we made a serious dent in the supply of Skol beer," Carlos said, "before the motorcade came screaming back with Mamma Sankoh and her three underlings. As they were led up the boarding stairs I was not impressed. Here was an accessory to mass murder being fawned over by her nervously smiling captors. As soon as the Andover lifted off, I handcuffed and blindfolded all four, explaining to the junta's shocked staff that these were prisoners, and would be treated as such. On landing, I put them in isolation cells in the military police building and denied access to anyone but us."

A grossly overweight and cunning harridan, Mamma Sankoh underwent her first interrogation the next morning. Aside from being

Sankoh's official consort, she was also his chief voodoo priestess, foretelling the future (though she'd rather slipped up in this case), casting spells and assuring Sankoh's followers that bullets would run off them like water. Even the junta, almost all of whom ascribed to those beliefs to some extent, treated her with caution. Her smirking self-confidence was boundless.

"I knew that we had to penetrate that arrogance, but I wasn't familiar enough with the culture, customs or mentality to find the chink I needed. Fortunately, I had Jonathan (not his real name), a young and well educated Sierra Leone officer who had done military training in the UK. Not only could he simultaneously translate between English and Krio, the local pidgin, but could sense the slightest nuances of what I was looking for during an interrogation.

"When I turned to him for advice, Jonathan smiled and said, 'Simple. Until now she's always gone where she wants to go, eats enough for five people and likes to read the newspapers. So we put her in solitary confinement, cut her rations to normal proportions and deny her reading material.' Within a couple of days, Mamma Sankoh's gluttony prevailed and she was ready to start singing. Had I been Jonathan's boss, I'd have promoted him on the spot."[47]

It soon became clear that Mamma exerted enormous influence on Sankoh and possessed extremely detailed knowledge on the RUF as a whole. The interrogation of her and her three companions provided the first detailed database on the RUF, allowing Carlos to compile the entire Order of Battle almost down to the lowest murderer, as well as diagrammatic sketches of every RUF base. She also revealed how they moved 'blood' diamonds onto the world market, the names of the middle men, and where and from whom the RUF bought weapons. It was priceless information. The RUF would suffer terribly for her love of food.

Ruf on the Run

Modifying their tactics to suit the new war, the Air Wing was as busy as it had been in Angola. "The Kamajors knew the bush and could provide good intelligence," Juba said, "but they didn't understand radios or how a GPS worked so it was up to us to back up their information with aerial

---

[47] Jonathan was later recognized by the British High Commission as an exceptional officer and given a twelve-month military course in the UK.

reconnaissance. The camps were well camouflaged and in order to confirm the presence of rebels, orbit heights as low as 100 feet above the trees were necessary, which brought us well within the range of small arms fire."

Though the RUF's motley collection of German and Eastern bloc weapons was certainly capable of bringing down the Cessna, the one weapon that concerned the pilots far more was at least one 12.7mm the rebels were known to possess.

"When the camps were positively identified as being active," Juba continued, "an accurate plot was made and detailed planning took place with the involvement of all the players. The Alpha Jet pilots of the Nigerian Air Force, for example, gave their input on dropping 250 kg bombs, while the Mi-24 crew decided which close air support packages they'd carry. Primary and alternate LZs were selected for the insertion of mortar teams. The Mi-17 pilots planned their approach and departure routes, as well as search and rescue procedures for downed aircrew and missing ground troops. In the event of a casevac, the recovery procedure was discussed and where the wounded would be flown before evacuation to a better-equipped hospital than the one in Freetown. If additional fuel was anticipated, 200-litre drums would be pre-positioned in secure areas closest to the target.

"On the day of the attack, the Mi-17s were loaded with mortar teams and protection elements, troops briefed and SOPs reviewed. Radios were checked and frequencies allocated. The aircraft took off at planned times, to ensure that the mortar teams were set up before the attack was initiated by the Alpha Jets. As soon as the Alpha Jets pulled off, the mortar barrage began, with the ground forces commander in the 337 providing fire control corrections as the Mi-17s orbited a short distance away. Once the target had been saturated, the Mi-24 hosed down the area with its 12.7 to discourage anyone waiting to engage the Mi-17s during the landing phase. Sometimes the LZs were so tight the jungle was only a few metres from the rotor disk, making us sitting ducks for an RPG. At moments like these – with experiences from Angola still fresh in our minds – we got slightly edgy when the troops took too long disembarking.

"The Cessna remained overhead to control the sweep lines, which can be difficult as the tree canopy was often too thick to maintain visual contact. If they encountered rebel fire that prevented forward movement the Mi-24 was called in to neutralise the pocket of resistance with, depending on the terrain, the 12.7, mini-guns, rockets or grenades. Once all resistance had ended, the troops gathered documents, weapons and equipment and moved to a designated LZ. Prisoners were immediately uplifted and taken to the nearest base for tactical interrogation, while the rest of the attack force was flown back to base before nightfall."

★

The Kamajors enthusiastically took to their new rôle as people hunters and soon found a large RUF logistics base at Koindu on the Guinean border. Aloft in the Cessna, PP and Paddy identified a dirt airstrip under construction just outside the town. A helipad showed evidence of recent use, leading Carlos to conclude that arms and diamond dealers had been landing there. PP moved his assets to Kenema and launched the attack.

"Using the Cessna for command and control, I inserted a mortar team on the north-eastern side of Koindu and under its covering fire had the second Mi-17 insert the fire force to the north. As soon as they were established, I shifted the mortar fire to targets to the south and west and ordered the fire force team into the town. They encountered little resistance and quickly secured it. I uplifted the mortar team, shifted it to the fire force and the two groups swept southward towards Buedu, conducting area patrols during the day and ambushes at night. Three days later we returned to Kenema for a debrief, then back to Freetown."

With the RUF on the run, PP and Carlos escorted a few of Sierra Rutile's directors and engineers to Gbangbatok for a survey of the facilities. The Mi-17 settled inside the large complex of abandoned equipment and burnt-out buildings, where the company had built a very nice golf course. It was clear from abandoned golfing clothes, shoes and clubs in the clubhouse that the employees had left in a hurry the year before. A keen golfer, Carlos scored a fine set of clubs for his off-duty moments in Freetown.

Though the rebels had abandoned the site at the first hint of EO's interest, a mobile security force was needed to allow Sierra Rutile to restart mining operations. Monitored by PP in the Cessna, a combined Sierra Leone/EO convoy left Benguema for Mile-91, then down to Moyamba before the final stretch to Gbangbatok. Area operations commenced immediately to ensure that the area was safe, after which they settled down to a daily patrols. When word of this reached Freetown, personnel from the various NGO's began trickling back, many cadging rides in EO's helicopters.

Minicoup, Kailahun and Kangari Hills

A conspiracy was bubbling in Freetown. Chairman Strasser's reclusiveness, alleged devotion to marijuana and disinterest in at least keeping up the appearance of a head of state was becoming acutely embarrassing. There was nothing for it but to remove him and a plot was hatched by Maada-Bio, Mondeh and Tom Nyuma, who waited until the last minute before advising EO's senior officers not to be overly concerned by what would happen that morning at Cockerell. Nothing violent, just your basic eviction was planned. Whereupon the plotters marched into Strasser's office and told him he was through.

A protesting Chairman was thrown unceremoniously over Mondeh's shoulder and carried to a Soruss helicopter. En route to Conakry, it was explained that he could keep the millions he'd stolen from the country so long as he didn't make waves about the change of government. Maada-Bio was sworn in as head of state and immediately announced his intention to hold elections.

*

After that spot of low comedy, fresh radio intercepts indicated a new RUF base at Kailahun near the Guinean border. This made sense, given its distance from areas controlled by EO or the RSLMF and the fact that it offered a quick escape route in the event of an attack. The Kamajors and aerial surveillance soon confirmed its location.

Drawing from the Kono detachment and newly-arrived EO personnel, PP assembled a company-size force at Kenema, where the town's mayor found him and Carlos living under canvas. Clucking disapprovingly at the standard of accommodation, he moved them to a luxurious guesthouse owned by a Lebanese diamond dealer. The closed Lebanese society in Sierra Leone wasn't known for welcoming outsiders (much less South African mercenaries) into their homes; it was a clear sign that their efforts were appreciated. It was also, they admitted happily, better than their tent at the airfield.

Aerial surveillance was stepped up. Carlos found himself on the Mi-24 during an armed reconnaissance when a small group of armed rebels were spotted crossing open ground. The normally phlegmatic Belarussian pilot brought the Mi-24 around and triggered a beehive of flechette rockets that put an end to them. Carlos gave him credit for a nice bit of shooting.

By now a desperate Sankoh was offering $250,000, paid in diamonds, to anyone who could shoot down one of the helicopters. "It was an attractive figure," Carlos observed dryly, "which we figured might eventually tempt someone to give it a try. Then one day our heads snapped up at the sound of French on one of the RUF radio nets. Two names, 'Michel' and 'Henri,' were noted. It was a Belgian accent, said someone. There were a couple more transmissions the same day, and then nothing. Chinese whispers about three white men with the RUF filtered up from the interior. We never identified them, but the same whispers said that they were so appalled by the conditions and the sad state of the 12.7mm they were expected to use, that they quickly decamped to more salubrious surroundings."

Satisfied that he knew the layout of the Kailahun base and the surrounding terrain, PP put the final touches to the operational plan. A 200-man RSLMF force acting as beaters would advance from Daru to send the rebels running into EO fighting patrols waiting in the "Elbow" loop of the Moa River. The beaters would then secure the town and establish a permanent base.

"Fighting patrols usually consisted of two sections," PP said, "but where the threat was a bit greater, I'd deploy a platoon, dropping two fighting patrols from each chopper in different spots to establish a presence in three areas. This left the RUF guessing where we were and many literally walked into the patrols. Their losses to our daytime 'Seek and Kill' patrols and night-time ambushes made them extremely cautious about moving through their former areas of control. Accustomed to butchering defenceless civilians, finding themselves on the receiving end was extremely demoralizing."

This tactic was built into the Kailahun plan, ensuring that the rebels would not only be trapped between RSLMF beaters and the guns of EO, but that many who slipped away would inevitably be killed along the narrow jungle trails. But at the final co-ordinating conference, the nervous Sierra Leone commander said that his 3:1 superiority in men, plus heavy machine guns and gunship support wasn't adequate. In that case, PP said resignedly, you stay here and we'll improvise.

The attack was launched with the insertion of two-section fighting patrols in three different locations east of Kailahun. Instead of being trapped, however, the rebels fled across the border. When this was confirmed, the relieved Sierra Leone commander allowed EO's choppers to ferry his men to Kailahun, where their continuing reluctance to engage the enemy saw only one confirmed RUF kill. One EO patrol almost died of laughter, however, when a rebel stumbled into their position the first night. Luck was with him and he escaped, screaming, "South Africans! South Africans!" until his voice faded into the jungle.

*

By the beginning of 1996 EO's initial objectives had been achieved. The immediate threat to Freetown had been neutralized, the diamond fields were back in government hands, and the Sierra Rutile complex was starting up again. As a result, elections had been scheduled and candidates were out pressing the flesh and making promises in their determination to be the next president. The country was more stable than it had been in years and the economy slowly but surely picking up. But there were still incidents of RUF atrocities and areas of instability that EO needed to address.

With much of their original manpower permanently established at Kono and Gbangbatok, an airmobile strike force dedicated to hitting RUF bases was formed at Sumbuya. Of particular interest was the Kangari Hills area, just south of the Matotoka-Masingbi main highway. Recent ambushes convinced PP that there was a base within easy walking distance.

A week went by with nothing seen from the air. They *had* to be in there. On the evening of the seventh day, PP and Johnny Maass, his 2iC, were thudding up and down a grid block. Eyes teared in the wind stream and began to ache from the flickering green in the NVGs. The chopper pilot finally announced that fuel was getting low and they'd have to head back in a few minutes. They were on their last north-to-south leg, when Johnny nudged him and pointed. Hidden under the trees, a crude circle of rebel campfires stood out in the NVGs. They took a GPS plot and flew happily back to Freetown.

"It was a well concealed and defendable position," PP admitted, "consisting of shacks built of corrugated iron looted from nearby villages, with three narrow jungle trails radiating from it. A number of nearby small rivers and streams offered additional escape or approach paths."

Detail planning and preparation started for the biggest operation EO would conduct in Sierra Leone. Choosing Magburaka as his launch pad, he assembled his 50-man airmobile force, EO's two Mi-17s, two BM-21 multiple rocket launchers, and an RSLMF company. Two Nigerian Alpha Jets, the Belarussian-crewed Mi-24[48] and the Cessna were placed on standby at Lungi airport. The day before the attack PP positioned RSLMF platoons on roads to the north, south and west of the target to cover the enemy's most likely escape routes, then waited until last light to move the BM-21s and a protection element to Makali, between Matotoka and Masingbi.

In the air before dawn to check comms and see that everyone was in position, PP ordered Johnny Maass to lift off with the mortar and fire force teams. As the Mi-17s orbited a mile away, the little Alpha Jets passed over the target, then came around to place their 250kg bombs on the preselected co-ordinates.

"The Mi-24 was supposed to be next," PP said, "but the pilot kept asking in Russian, 'Where's the base? Where's the base?' Alfred the interpreter was having problems understanding me. Time and patience were running out and I asked Paddy if we could lead them onto target. Paddy 'rogered' and I told Alfred as simply as possible to follow us; the moment the Cessna was over the base we would pull up and they could come in with their rockets." Skimming the tree-tops at full throttle, Paddy hauled back on the yoke and they shot upwards. Behind them the Mi-24's pods were already trailing smoke as swarms of flechette rockets streaked towards the RUF base.

PP switched frequencies and directed the first chopper to drop the mortar team on high ground just north of the base, then immediately ordered the BM-21s to open fire to cover their insertion. As soon as the last 122mm rocket had impacted PP had the second chopper insert its fire force team just north-west of the target. As they touched down, he brought in 81mm mortar fire on and around the base to cover their advance. The fire force pushed forward, but the dense jungle and possibility of a rebel ambush slowed their advance.

---

[48] "Fearing they were losing out on the action, the Russkies had lobbied hard for inclusion in the operation, over my loud objections," PP said.

"It was late afternoon, after our second refuelling of the day. Paddy was holding a tight orbit when I saw a group of about twelve rebels running down one of the jungle trails towards Johnny. Neither was aware of the other and I immediately told him to lay an ambush. When the rebels burst into view, his two PKM gunners shot them to pieces. A few in the back spun around and headed back to the base. Johnny immediately set up his two 60mm mortars and I directed their fire from above, killing and wounding more. Johnny started moving into the base but encountered fairly stiff resistance. With light fading quickly, he prudently decided to withdraw slightly and put out small ambush groups. That night another six or eight rebels were killed as they tried to sneak away under cover of darkness.

"I was overhead again at the crack of dawn. Checking that everyone had comms, I brought in mortar fire to cover Johnny's group as they made the final push. The surviving rebels attempted to defend the position, but yesterday's pounding and the sounds of South African ambushes during the night had left them exhausted and terrified and they were quickly dealt with. Johnny's team destroyed food stores, burnt down the base and then carried on with area operations for the rest of the day, chasing the rebels towards the Sierra Leone stopper groups, where more of them died. Badly battered and confused, the survivors squeezed themselves into the jungle and hid.

"I decided to withdraw my teams the following morning. They were waiting for the Mi-17s, when an RPG-7 was fired from the jungle. One of our blokes was turning when it sliced across his back, the tail fins cutting his webbing strap and leaving a fist-sized hole. Johnny dealt with the hidden rebel and brought in a chopper to casevac our man to Freetown, while the rest of the force was withdrawn to Magburaka.

"With only one wounded on our side and upwards of eighty rebels killed and many more wounded, Kangari was one more in a string of very successful operations. As a postscript, my forty-some hours in the Cessna over those three days saw me becoming quite an accomplished pilot, but I had a helluva sore bum for a few days."

Elections and 'Joi-Koi'

With the RUF on the run and EO's presence in Freetown and other important population centres minimising rebel intimidation, the country began to prepare for UN-supervised elections. EO's greatest concern was that Maada-Bio might not relinquish power if the vote went against him. If that happened, the company's policy of working only for recognized governments meant they'd have no choice but to withdraw from Sierra Leone. But to their quiet satisfaction and the surprise of many, Maada-Bio stated that he was content in his position and had no political aspirations.

Just prior to the elections, which Sankoh boycotted – "for no other reason than the overwhelming mood of the people was that he should be hung, drawn and quartered," Carlos said – an excited report came in from Lunsar that a group of RUF was heading towards Freetown. A mobile team immediately departed by vehicle. The report had placed the enemy force on the main road east of Lunsar, when, in fact, it was already west of the town. The mobile team hit them unexpectedly and one of EO's most popular operators, a former 5 Recce member, was killed.

★

The elections went forward as planned and newly-elected President Ahmed Tejan Kabbah summoned PP and Carlos to State House. A former United Nations official, Kabbah was, in Carlos's view, "an easy-going, sometimes rather naïve, head of state more interested in compromise than being assertive". A concerned Kabbah revealed that there was foreign pressure to terminate EO's contract. If he gave into that pressure, however, there was a strong possibility that certain people in the former junta, along with their army supporters, would attempt to seize power. "We emphasized to President Kabbah that, as the legitimately-elected head of state, he was our boss. Until he decided that we should go, we would ensure his personal security as best we could."

At the South Africans' suggestion the new president implemented a weekly war council that met every Friday afternoon at State House and included himself, his military high command, EO and senior commanders from the three ECOMOG contingents. Supported by the Nigerian general, PP stressed that Sankoh wasn't finished until his headquarters and senior people were neutralised. They made such a nuisance of themselves in presenting the case, that President Kabbah finally gave his authorization to proceed with the operation.

"So I was back to my 'sky office', flying long reconnaissance missions over the area where Carlos placed Sankoh's HQ," PP said. "It took me five days to locate it in the Kambui hills just south west of Kenema. From morning to dusk, Carlos and I went over maps and int reports and worked out the details of the plan. The Nigerians gave me three 105mm howitzers and crews, and I got four Sierra Leone companies to augment about forty of my South Africans. I was also allocated our two Mi-17s and the Cessna for reconnaissance and Command and Control.

"I assembled the entire force at Kenema and set up a tent city. After our final briefings and preparation I moved my three artillery pieces to a point between Pendabu and Penama under Neels Brits, a very capable artillery officer. Using the Sierra Leone companies as stopper groups again, I deployed them to the north on a Blama-Kenema line, west on the Blama-Sendumei line, east on the Penama-Kenema line, and south on the Sendumei-Penama line. When the artillery reached its selected position between Penama and Pendahu-Gofor they were followed by my fire force group. When everyone was in place, I flew over Neels's position, turned towards the rebel HQ and called for one spotting round. The shell impacted, spraying tendrils of white phosphorous and sending up a cloud of brilliant white smoke. I gave one correction and the next one was on target. I then ordered battery fire for effect with HE, and kept them going for ten minutes. It looked quite spectacular from the air.

"After the first bombardment I started playing a psychological game: four rounds at 1500 hours, then eight at 2215, followed by ten more at 0300 and another six at 1100. Varying the times, I continued like this for three days. By the end of the third day the rebels started surrendering en mass. One dishevelled and shell-shocked group of about twenty arrived in Blama and said they'd had enough. Another group of eighty gave themselves up in Potoru and 140 more pitched up in Kenema."

Interrogations revealed that the first salvo had wiped out an entire command group as it was presenting a briefing around a sand model. Many more were subsequently killed when they ran into the Sierra Leone blocker groups. Some 120 rebels had been killed, with an unknown number wounded or MIA. EO's one disappointment was that Sankoh had been elsewhere. On the fifth day they withdrew to Kenema for a debriefing and afterwards returned to Sumbuya. When PP arrived the following day in Freetown to brief President Kabbah and the war council, he was told that

Sankoh had requested a ceasefire so that negotiations with the government could begin.

★

In the two weeks before the ceasefire went into effect Carlos learned that the RUF were concentrating in the Moyamba hills just south east of Rotirunk. With a request from the Sierra Leone high command for a pre-emptive strike, PP was back in the air, long days spent scanning the jungle. It was a Sunday morning when an ill-disciplined rebel sent a stream of 12.7 mm bullets *thump-thump-thump*ing past the Cessna. PP smiled grimly. He'd found the base.

When PP returned, 'Eric,' who was overseeing site security at the Gbangbatok rutile mine, asked EO's HQ if his team could have the operation. It was unfair that PP and his fire force had all the action, while they just did normal security work. PP agreed to stand down.

Eric split the EO force into small teams, each in vehicles with an element of the RSLMF, and advanced on the rebel base from different directions. Orbiting overhead in the Cessna, he moved the teams into position and, when everyone was ready, sent them rolling towards the objective. One team ran into trouble on the second day when it hit a large RUF force. Unable to determine just how large, the commander withdrew his team, established a laager with his Sierra Leone element manning perimeter defence, and asked to be uplifted.

The request for extraction was relayed from HQ to Charlie Tait in his Mi-17. PP cautioned against it: there was room only for the EO element and the Sierra Leones would not want to be left behind. HQ nonetheless approved the extraction. As PP predicted, when the Sierra Leones saw EO climbing on board, they abandoned their positions and clawed their way in. With almost 60 people, some clinging to the outriggers and external fuel tanks and those inside standing on the wounded, the Mi-17 was dangerously overloaded. But with no ground protection, they had to get airborne. Attempting a running take off, the wheels hit an abandoned vehicle and the helicopter was down. Overhead in the second chopper, Juba settled into a marshy clearing nearby. This time the Sierra Leones decided they'd stay on the ground, but crew and fire force sprinted across and Juba lifted off.

The Sierra Leones remained with the damaged helicopter until last light and then withdrew to a position farther south. Under cover of darkness, the rebels slipped in to torch the Mi-17, an unfortunate and expensive loss.

Negotiations and Violations

Despite the uneasy calm that had settled over the country, PP and the Nigerian general continued to caution President Kabbah against trusting Sankoh. From their interrogations of Mamma Sankoh and others, they were convinced that the RUF leader would not honour the ceasefire.

PP had just returned from a war council meeting at State House, when a report came in that a civilian convoy had been ambushed on the Mile-91 road. Pulling a camo shirt over smart civilian trousers, he grabbed his AK and webbing and followed Johnny Maass to the waiting Mi-17. With Juba flying and Steve as the flight tech, they lifted away from Cockerell. Twenty minutes later, they found six burning vehicles surrounded by bodies and a trail of loot leading towards the small village of Magbosi. They were circling over it when the rebels opened fire. Juba hit his mike button and noted tracers passing behind them. "fuck the tracers behind us," the co-pilot shouted, "check out the ones in front of us!"

Steve opened up with the 12.7. The mud and thatch huts exploded, terrified rebels spilling through the gaps in search of healthier surroundings. PP, sitting on the auxiliary fuel tank, was firing through the starboard window, when Juba horsed the Mi-17 around so steeply that he slid off.

"Johnny saw me pinned to the floor by the G force and started laughing so hard he stopped firing. Juba was shouting furiously to keep up the rate of fire. I shouted back that if they'd let me off the fucking floor, I'd be happy to. He looked over his shoulder, saw what was happening and rolled level long enough to free a third of his fire force team, and the circus began again. Though we saw a number of the rebels go down, we couldn't determine how many we'd killed or wounded."

On their return to Cockerell, they were called in by the Sierra Leone high command who demanded to know why they'd violated the ceasefire. PP explained that the RUF already violated it by an ambush against civilians, and that when they started firing at the chopper, he, Johnny and Steve had responded in kind. Call it self defence. His explanation was accepted and President Kabbah lodged an official complaint with the RUF, who denied any involvement.

"Our EO boss was also the *'moer in'* [pissed off] with us," PP said, "but Juba put it to him nicely that the rebels were running away aggressively and that is why we fired on them. Although that quieted him somewhat, he knew his customers too well and wasn't entirely convinced. That night Johnny and I went over to the air wing's house for our usual debrief, which meant reliving the day's highlights over a few beers. We were greeted by grinning chopper crews and *Nowhere to Run, Nowhere to Hide* from the soundtrack of *Good Morning, America* playing at full volume."

★

With the peace process back on track, the fire force base at Sambuya was designated as the transit point for EO personnel waiting to be flown back to South Africa. Having seen discipline slip in other wars when soldiers prepared to go home, PP restricted everyone to base after sunset. Shebeens – local drinking parlours – and the ever-present ladies of the night (dubbed 'Night Fighters') were a combination that too often led to trouble.

Turning in after an evening of barbeque and beer, one such group were awakened at midnight by bursts of automatic fire. PP and Johnny cautiously slipped outside to find a mob of angry soldiers on the perimeter. They learned that an EO employee had sneaked out and gotten into a drunken argument with a Sierra Leone soldier over the favours of a Night Fighter. The dispute escalated into a gunfight and the local troop had been shot dead. His comrades, emboldened by marijuana and Pegga Packs, were now firing over the base and baying for South African blood.

When morning came, some 200 soldiers had gathered in front of the base, the situation aggravated by the sight of the body still lying where it had fallen. He was suddenly everyone's brother and they wanted revenge. By now seriously annoyed by the shots cracking overhead, PP deployed an all-round defence, with the Land Rovers facing the main gate. He raised Freetown, let HQ listen to the firing and gave them a quick sitrep.

"I was fired up and told them I'd kill the fucking lot of them if they kept shooting towards me and my men. But HQ asked me to try negotiating to save the day. 'No problem,' I told him, 'over and out.' I put the mike down and ordered the 12.7 gunners to cock their weapons. The sound of those bolts slamming forward got their full attention and the shouting died to a whisper. I turned to my sergeant major and said, 'Piet, I'm going over there and talk to the officer in charge. If they shoot me, you have my full blessing to kill the lot of them.'

"I can tell you I felt very lonely as I walked towards that smoked-up, drunken mob. I singled out a Sierra Leone captain and told him to remove the body. It was wrapped in a tarpaulin and placed on a pick-up truck. As it headed off for Freetown, this captain started mouthing off at me very aggressively. I interrupted even more aggressively. 'If you want war,' I told him furiously, 'I'll give you fucking war! Now get your people back to base or suffer the consequences.'"

The Sierra Leone officer looked over PP's shoulder into the muzzle of a 12.7 and suddenly decided maybe things had gotten a little out of hand after all. Just a little. And yes, it might be a good thing if his troops did go back to their base. In fact, now that the subject had come up, he was just about to suggest that very thing. And led a very subdued mob away.

"I'd already learned that there'd been four or five witnesses to the shooting and ordered the military police to do an identification parade. The culprit was quickly picked out and handed over to the civil authorities in Freetown. When I got back, Maada-Bio, and his staff, were so pleased with the way I'd handled the situation that they organized a disco in our honour. It was another episode for my diary. Never a dull moment in Africa."

★

Nineteen months after EO's arrival in Sierra Leone, the six-year low intensity conflict came to an end. On November 30 1996, Alfred Foday Sankoh signed a peace accord with Ahmad Tejan Kabbah, the democratically elected president of Sierra Leone, in Abidjan, the capital of Ivory Coast. EO's contribution in bringing the rebels to heel in Angola had been repeated in Sierra Leone, but in a replay of the first contract, the Clinton administration began pressuring Kabbah to send them packing. The success of the elections and the RUF's destruction, they insisted, was ample proof that the South Africans were no longer needed.

"And so our contract was terminated," Carlos said. "However, in a final and highly confidential report to Kabbah and selected members of the international community, we predicted that within months of our

departure, two events would happen. The first would be a coup atte...
from within his own military, where there were a number of aspirants to
the country's leadership and the wealth that would come from it. The
second was that Sankoh's thugs were still lurking in the jungle and had no
intention of handing over their guns. It was inevitable that the war would
start again. But no amount of reasoned argument could sway Clinton's
advisors, who, holding out the lure of loans and aid, held the tiny nation and
its people to ransom.

"So we bowed to the inevitable and began packing up. That our
departure was premature was amply demonstrated five months later when,
on 25 May 1997 Major Johnny Paul Koroma, in league with Foday Sankoh
and supported by Sorussair, the Russian helicopter charter service
operating out of Freetown, overthrew Kabbah, who fled to Conakry. The
fact that Kabbah's own military would collaborate with their enemies to
take power confirmed our worst expectations. But there was nothing more
we could do."

★ ★ ★

Postscript

In October 1997 the United Nations passed Security Council Resolution 1132 condemning the coup, imposing an arms embargo on the new junta and supporting ECOWAS[49] in its efforts to restore President Kabbah to power. Under considerable international pressure, Koroma's Armed Forces Military Council signed an agreement that included the re-establishment of Kabbah's government. But the newest looters of Sierra Leone had no intention of abiding by their word. ECOMOG returned and, with the planning and support of Sandline International, a relative newcomer to the ranks of private military companies, chased Koroma's and Sankoh's forces from Freetown and restored Kabbah to power in March 1998. In January, the RUF attacked again, capturing much of the capital, before being driven out by ECOMOG once more. Up to 5,000 people, mostly civilians, died in the fighting.

Ignoring Foday Sankoh's rap sheet, the United Nations pressed Kabbah to re-open negotiations. When assured of ministerial positions in the government, the RUF signed yet another cease-fire agreement, this one to be supervised by UN peacekeepers. The United Nations Mission in Sierra Leone – UNAMSIL – built to over 11,000 (it was eventually mandated to and reached 17,500). In a bid to force more concessions from Kabbah and the UN, RUF gangs operating in defiance of the ceasefire, attacked and captured almost 500 Indian peacekeepers. Inexplicably, despite keeping their weapons and being in radio contact with the UN commander, Indian Army Major-General Vijay Jetley, the peacekeepers-turned-prisoners were ordered not to resist.

---

[49] Economic Community of West Africa States, from which ECOMOG was drawn.

The usual liberals, to include President Clinton's special envoy to the Reverend Jesse Jackson, rallied in support of 'meaningful' negotiations. Previewing his position on Saddam Hussein three years later, Jackson said that Foday Sankoh could play a "positive role" in bringing about a peaceful settlement. *The Washington Post* described Jackson's statement as "grotesque," adding, "The RUF is a criminal gang, soaked in the blood of thousands of civilians…. The U.S.-U.N. effort to restore the peace agreement that [Sankoh] has shredded would leave Sierra Leoneans at his mercy indefinitely." But to the delight of those who decried the use of force except by "freedom fighters," UN negotiators secured the Indian prisoners' release with payments of food, medical supplies and radios.

(Back in South Africa, Carlos and PP could only shake their heads.)

The rebels launched yet another attack on Freetown, prompting a British deployment of 800 paratroops to secure Lungi Airport for the evacuation of foreign nationals. In a display of criminal naiveté, the United Nations still recognized the RUF as a legitimate political party. This was at odds with Sierra Leonean refugees who, bare-handed, stormed Sankoh's party headquarters in Freetown and handed him over to the British, demanding he be tried for war crimes.[50]

In order not to annoy RUF gangs controlling parts of the interior, diffident UN forces were forced to ask permission of the thugs before crossing their lines. One such group, 'The West Side Boys,' led by an illiterate, self-styled 'brigadier,' already had a chilling history of atrocities and brazenly established roadblocks in the Okra Hills region, where they continued their favourite pastimes of mutilation, rape and murder. Emboldened by UNAMSIL's determination not to violate their civil rights, this group abducted eleven British soldiers and threatened to kill them if Foday Sankoh and others were not released in Freetown.

In an interview with CNN, a Sierra Leonean journalist who saw a colleague die at their hands says, "These people are dangerous and unpredictable. They kill without thinking about it."[51] But Major-General Jetley, who affects eyeliner and a hairnet, refuses to take action, and instead pays more ransom for the release of five. Farce has been elevated to insanity in the theatre of the absurd.

---

[50] Sankoh would eventually be tried and convicted of mass murder. He is currently serving a life sentence in Freetown.

[51] CNN.com.world> August 28, 2000

...mused and deploy an SAS squadron to ...ligence-gathering techniques similar to those ...by Executive Outcomes (some former EO employees may even have provided briefings), a dawn helicopter assault is launched. Twenty minutes after the first shot is fired, the freed hostages are lifting away in a Chinook helicopter. When the fight is over, 25 rebel bodies sprawl across the squalid camp, another 18 in custody. Like Executive Outcomes before them, the British had spoken a language the RUF and its various factions understand, a message so clear that the remaining rebels begin surrendering *en mass*. The war was over.

Until the next Foday Sankoh crawls from under a rock in Sierra Leone.

*

Tragically, SAS Trooper Brad Tinnion, one of the British rescuers, died in the assault. His death, like so many others in that country, must be laid at the feet of naïve bureaucrats and well-meaning liberals who refused to recognize evil; who were unwilling to make cogent, life-saving decisions; for whom logic was inadmissible and moral absolutism the greater evil.

These are the people who, under the flag of human rights, railed against the few millions paid to EO to destroy those whose only path was terror, then ignored the billions spent on deploying and paying UN soldiers to avert their eyes as thousands of innocents died. Died, one must remember, at the hands of murderers already defeated by Executive Outcomes.

Indeed, they are the same people who deplore the very existence of private military companies, who believe that psychopaths and megalomaniacs can be persuaded through rational discussion. They have been demonstrably wrong every time – as untold graves bear silent witness.

* * *